THE TRUSTEE'S GUIDE

An Essential Handbook for Trustees, Beneficiaries and Their Advisors

Howard I. Gross
Pierre E. Richards

LawFirst Publishing
The Connecticut Bar Association
New Britain, CT

LawFirst Publishing
Connecticut Bar Association

LawFirst Publishing
The Connecticut Bar Association

First published in 2003 by LawFirst Publishing
This edition: 2009
LawFirst Publishing is a division of the Connecticut Bar Association

ISBN 0-9740069-0-4 (previously ISBN 1-881758-64-8)

Printed in the United States of America
15 14 13 12 11 10 09   1 2 3 4 5 6

The Connecticut Bar Association
30 Bank Street
PO Box 350
New Britain, CT 06050-0350

DEDICATION

Howard Gross dedicates this book to his wife, Susan Gross.
Pierre Richards dedicates it to his late wife, Mulan Yang.

Without the patience, encouragement and inspiration of our wives, it would have been a lonely road to the completion of this work.

Howard and Pete

Contents

About the Authors

Howard I. Gross was educated at the University of Connecticut, B.A. and the University of Connecticut School of Law J.D.

Mr. Gross is counsel to the law firm of Levy & Droney, PC, Farmington, Connecticut, where he concentrates primarily on estate and business planning and commercial law. A founding member and past president of the Estate and Business Planning Council of Hartford, he has lectured extensively on estate and business planning before business and professional groups and on television. He is a member of the American Bar Association. He is also a member the Hartford County and Connecticut Bar Associations where he serves as a member of the Sections on Probate and Trust Laws of those associations.

From 1979 to 1997, Mr. Gross was a member of the Professional Ethics Committee of the Connecticut Bar Association. As an officer, he served as Treasurer and Secretary of the Executive Committee and was a member of the Board of Governors and the House of Delegates. He has also been a member of the Lawyer Pilot Association and the Association of Former Intelligence Officers, and he is past Chair of the Board of Directors of the Bradley Air Museum (now the New England Air Museum). Mr. Gross lives in West Hartford, Connecticut.

Pierre E. "Pete" Richards is a graduate of Colgate University, B.A., where he majored in English. He graduated from the Pennsylvania Bankers Association Trust School at Bucknell University. He received a Certified Financial Planner designation from the College for Financial Planning in 1985.

He recently completed his long career as a trust officer and Certified Financial Planner. He has managed various divisions of trust departments for banks in Colorado, Connecticut and Pennsylvania, and prior to his retirement was the manager of Mentor Trust Company, a broker-affiliated trust company that has since been acquired by First Union National Bank. Currently he serves as a consultant to the trust industry on a part-time basis, and specializes in training financial advisors on the responsibilities and uses of trusts. He lives in Wyndmoor, Pennsylvania.

Mr. Richards has published a number of articles in Trusts & Estates and other industry publications. He has been a speaker for professional organizations, including the Bank Marketing Association, the Banking Law Institute and the Investment Management Institute. He has also taught courses at the American Institute of Banking and has conducted several workshops for members of the Institute of Certified Financial Planners. He is a past director of the University of Hartford Tax Institute and the Philadelphia Estate Planning Council.

The two authors are longtime friends and associates. Mr. Richards was a founding member and Mr. Gross was a charter member of the Estate Tax Workshop, a Hartford organization of trust professionals dedicated to the constant improvement of the trust and estate profession.

Acknowledgments

No book of this nature can succeed as the work of only one or two authors. We are indebted to the following for their instructive reviews of the original of our work, and most especially to Marvin H. Lapuk, J.D., C. P. A., and George A. Baker, J.D., former Probate Judge for District of Tolland, Connecticut, whose hours of help on Part Three are sincerely appreciated.

Hon. John A. Berman, Probate Judge (retired)
Probate District 155, West Hartford, Connecticut

Peter G. Carey, CLU, General Agent
Mass Mutual Life Insurance Co., Hartford, Connecticut

Murray A. Gerber, MBA
Private Investor, West Hartford, Connecticut

Roman Herz, President
Herz Financial Group, Farmington, Connecticut

Charles F. Huber II, Managing Director
William D. Witter, Inc. New York, New York

Judith M. Keppelman, Partner
Robinson & Cole, Hartford, Connecticut

Paul Martel, President
YHB Investment Advisors, Inc., West Hartford, Connecticut

James H. McLaughlin, Vice President
Mellon Private Asset Management, New York, New York

Lewis W. Merrow III, MBA, CLU, ChFC, Regional Director of Agencies
Canada Life, Vernon, Connecticut

G. Michael Richwine, Executive Director
Riggs & Co., Washington, DC

Andrew M. Sullivan, Jr., CPA, Partner
KPMG LLP

Introduction

This book concerns itself only with the family trust, or personal trust. We don't deal here with pension trusts, business trusts, trusts for purely charitable purposes or other such trusts. It is the kind of trust that, in its many forms, is established under a will or trust agreement to provide primarily for family members or friends of its creator. It can range from a simple probate-avoidance trust that can be closed out in a few weeks after the death of the individual who created it, to a dynastic trust that can last for generations. In one form, it can provide basic financial management for those who need it, such as minor children, financially unsophisticated or incapacitated adults, or those who are financially astute but apprehensive about potential incapacitation in the future. In others, it can be more elaborate, offering relief from complex tax laws, providing a defense against the claims of creditors, or serving as a vehicle for the management and continuity of a business interest.

It also happens to be the kind of trust for which an individual is frequently appointed as trustee. While there is much information available on how to use trusts, what exists on how to administer them is often quite technical and difficult to access for the layman. We hope this book remedies that.

There is a wide variety of trusts that can be called family trusts. We explain the essence of many of them in the Appendix. Those that we have not covered are either variations on the major types or arcane devices that are better left to the management of professional trustees. Whatever type of trust you are called upon to administer is likely to be based upon one or more of our descriptions.

However, all trusts are customized to fit specific purposes. Motor vehicles have certain common basic components, such as engines, drive trains, chassis and bodies, but they are ordered with options to suit the owner, such as variations in horsepower, and torque, automatic or manual transmissions, differences in ride and handling, and seating capacity and comfort. Similarly, trusts share basic requirements, such as a creator, one or more individuals who benefit from them, someone to administer them, instructions to be followed, and assets. Beyond that, each trust is also fitted with "options", such as beneficiary designations, specific directions concerning investments or the use of money, the number and type of trustees or the term of the trust. And as with the design of a motor vehicle, the expense of construction and operation may also be taken into account.

Our book can help you if you fit any of these three descriptions.

1. You have been, or are likely to be, appointed as a trustee. Perhaps some individual in need of a trust has carefully considered your qualifications for this assignment. Or, as more often happens, you have been named as a trustee chiefly because you are a close relative, a trusted advisor, or just a good friend. You might also be replacing a prior trustee who declined the appointment or who served for a while and then could, or would no longer, act.

In either case, if you accept the appointment, or if you already have, you want to know how to perform your duties in a responsible manner and you desire to protect yourself in the process. This book should help you to understand your responsibilities and perform your duties better. It can't protect you from lawsuits, but it may increase your sensitivity to dangerous situations, so that you can protect yourself. It just might also give you second thoughts about taking on the job at all, as some trusteeships deserve to be declined.

2. You are the beneficiary of a trust, on the receiving end of what a trustee does. If this is the case, you need to know if your trustee is performing according to accepted standards and is treating you fairly. This book can provide insights as to what you should expect from your trustee–and help you keep your expectations within reason. The trustee may be a corporation, such as a bank or trust company, an individual, or some combination of a corporation and individuals. Corporate trustees, despite their highly regulated environment and collective skill, are capable of mismanagement. An individual trustee is even more so. He or she operates without benefit of bank examiners or auditors, may have little in written policies or procedures to follow, and may have no specialized training or experience. An individual trustee is therefore particularly prone to errors, oversights and misguided actions, or just plain neglect.

3. You are an advisor to or agent for either the trustee or a beneficiary. You may be an accountant, an investment manager or a broker, for example. You take your responsibilities seriously, but you may not have had much experience with trusts. You want the advice you give to be informed and practical, and you want your services to be appropriate. You also want to be aware of any potential liabilities you might incur. This book will help you to know what a trustee does, and how he or she should behave.

This book is a guide for non-professionals. If you join a guided tour through a museum, your guide's purpose is to explain, provide insights, educate and make you more appreciative. In the wilderness, your guide may have the more serious purpose of helping you reach your destiny without being consumed by some large predator. In this book, the purposes are similar. One objective is to give you a working knowledge and appreciation of what being a trustee is all about, including a little history where we think it helps. Another, at least as important, is to alert you to dangers in the path and to help you create effective detours around them, or at the very least to prepare for unavoidable confrontations. We want you to complete your tour of duty as a trustee safely and successfully, and derive some satisfaction in the process.

Suggested Reading for the Adventurous

Much of the information in this book is drawn from *Restatement of the Law Second - Trusts*, published in 1959, and *Restatement of the Law, Third* (Prudent Investor Rule) published in 1992. These works were prepared by the prestigious American Law Institute from extensive research of common law, case law and other sources . While they do not constitute law itself, they state legal principles that apply, or should apply, in courts across America having jurisdiction over trusts. Although not written for the layman, the Restatements are for the most part readable. These and other sources are listed with their publishers and other information in the Bibliography.

You can also read state statutes on trusts, often available in annotated volumes. These statutes and commentary can be heavy reading, however. Most individual trustees find it more convenient to obtain the kind of information found in them from their lawyers.

In August of 2000 the Uniform Trust Code was approved and recommended for enactment in all states. This is worth reviewing, as it is intended as a replacement for the cobbling of common law and statutes that serves as trust law in many states currently. A draftsman of trust instruments might want to incorporate some of its provisions.

When to Talk to a Lawyer

As our book is intended not for the high priests of the legal temple, but for ordinary mortals, we have tried to make the material easy to digest where we could. We hope that we have done the right thing by sparing you numerous footnotes referencing inaccessible court cases and the like. We have intentionally glossed over nuances, exceptions and legal theories that might be applicable to situations we describe. Where we have had to use legal terms, they are explained in the text as you encounter them, and in a glossary at the back of the book.

We have included a number of legal forms, but they are not meant to encourage you to draft trust instruments. They are there for you to think about rather than copy. We thought, where we include them, that they would be the best way for you to see information that you might need and then share it with an attorney. They might also be helpful to that attorney, too, if he or she is not a specialist in trusts and may not have easy access to such material.

We encourage you to seek the aid of qualified professionals and not rely totally on a mere guide for initiates to the world of trusts. If you have a specific question about your duties as a trustee (or your rights as a beneficiary or duties as an advisor), you should consult an attorney who can answer your question based upon whatever law that applies. This book should condition you to know when it is time to ask for professional assistance, but don't be afraid to err on the side of caution.

This is a "How To Do It" book , but in resistance to a current trend, we have not named it a trustee's guide for "dummies" or "idiots." If you think you are in either of these categories, you better put the book back on the shelf. Trustees must have reasonable intelligence in order to function (other basic attributes are listed in Part One, Chapter I), and they must have a sense about knowing when and where to find qualified advisors. However if, like the main character of Joseph Conrad's Lord Jim, you have "ability in the abstract," you will succeed, however little you know about trusts now.

Have an interesting, safe and rewarding journey through the term of your trust.

PART ONE

What You Need To Know Before You Agree To Be A Trustee

Chapter 1

Should You Accept The Job?

If you have been selected to act as trustee, consider yourself honored. Someone thinks you are so trustworthy and capable that you should be the one to manage his or her assets for him or herself or people important to him or her. Our congratulations!

Before you bask in the warm rays of pride, however, you should know that most people who create trusts have little understanding of what a trustee needs to be or do. They may know that the basic job is to manage investments and to carry out the terms of the trust, but few have any appreciation of the legal responsibilities or the potential people or asset problems that confront a trustee. It's often a choice made merely on the basis of a family affiliation, a friendship, or faith in what a professional advisor has had to say. Even astute creators of trusts rarely use any kind of systematic process to select the best possible candidate, such as the list of desirable attributes included at the end of this chapter.

You probably won't be given much advance information about your duties, either. By this we mean that, unless you ask, you won't be given this information before the settlor has signed the will or trust agreement. Sometimes, as in the case of the will of someone who has already died, it's too late to make important changes. You may then have to either reluctantly accept or reluctantly decline. On the other hand, if the settlor informs you of his or her intention to name you as a trustee before he or she has put their signature on the will or trust agreement, you have an opportunity. It is to ask to be included in the process of designing those trust provisions that will affect your role as trustee. This is an opportunity you should take advantage of, once you have prepared yourself for this involvement.

Definitions

People who create trusts are commonly called "testators" if they create trusts under their wills. If they create trusts under a trust agreement or a declaration, they are referred to as "settlors," "grantors," "donors" and, more rarely "trustors." To keep matters simple, we'll just call the creator of any type of trust a "settlor," or sometimes "grantor" because of that term's special tax significance.

When we have to refer to wills and trust agreements collectively, we'll use the term "trust instrument" or "governing instrument." A trust agreement, incidentally, is sometimes called a "deed of trust, but as that is also a term used for a mortgage document, we'll avoid it's use.

Trusts created by wills are called "testamentary trusts" and do not become effective until after the death of the testator. Trusts created under a trust agreement become effective at the time they have been funded. Funding is the initial placement of assets in the hands of a trustee who has accepted his or her appointment under an executed trust instrument.

Trusts may be revocable or irrevocable. A testamentary trust is irrevocable. Trusts under an agreement may be either revocable (but may become irrevocable later), or irrevocable at their inception. A "living" trust is a trust created by a settlor typically for his or her own benefit, or perhaps for the joint benefit of testator and his or her spouse, and is normally revocable.

If you have been approached about serving as someone's trustee, there are certain things you need to know about. We list these briefly below, and we enlarge upon some of them in subsequent chapters of Part I. So far as possible, a potential trustee should be included in the process of drafting the trust instrument, and we'll explain why. Here are some questions for you to think about.

A. What Are You Required to Do?

There are certain principles and duties of trusteeship that you should understand at the outset. They are rarely explained in the will or trust agreement, although it probably would be a help to the novice trustee if they were. These have evolved from long, legal tradition and incorporate the following principles:

- As trustee, you are the legal owner of the trust property, but the equitable interests, the benefits, belong to the beneficiaries. You may be able to buy and sell the assets, but the income from them - and eventually the legal ownership itself—must flow to the beneficiaries. This is a separation of the attributes of property that does not apply to you as owner of your own personal assets.
- You are expected to manage trust assets in such a way as to assure that the benefits of a trust flow to the beneficiaries, and to no one else. At all times, you must put the interests of the beneficiaries above your own, as well as above those of others who may be directly or indirectly associated with the trust. This requirement affects, among other things, how you acquire or dispose of investments, how you manage expenses, how you retain advisors, and how you disburse funds and information to the beneficiaries.
- You must administer the trust to carry out its intended purpose. This usually includes a duty to treat all beneficiaries impartially, although the trust instrument may direct or recommend preferential treatment for one beneficiary over another, a surviving spouse over the decedent's children, for example.
- You are personally responsible for failure to properly exercise your responsibilities as a trustee, and the penalties for this can be damage to your prestige and financial loss. Some trustees have even gone to jail because they were convicted of illegal acts (the chief one of which seems to be embezzlement).

The trust instrument, which is an instruction sheet, sets forth more specific duties. It tells you what to do with the trust funds, even if it does not tell you much about how to invest them. It tells you what distributions to make, to whom you are to make them, when to make them, and how much discretion you have in making them. You don't necessarily have to agree with the settlor's instructions, but you must carry them out. Are these instructions clear? Are they legal? Are they possible? Those are the three tests. Of course, your personal beliefs may be in such conflict with the settlor's objectives that you might turn down an appointment even if the trust meets these tests. For example, you might believe that the trust unfairly excludes certain family members, and therefore you don't want to be a party to it.

B. What Kinds of Assets Will You Be Required to Manage?

If the trust is to be funded immediately, you will know what kinds of property you'll be expected to manage. But if the trust is to be funded in the future - for example, when the settlor dies - there may be no telling what the assets will be. A business owner may sell that complex business interest of his or hers and invest the proceeds in marketable securities. On the other hand, a stock and bond investor might someday take a fling at running an ostrich farm, or inherit a partial interest in an Indonesian mattress factory.

Obviously, stocks and bonds are far easier to manage than a farm or a factory. The question is, will you have to become involved with assets that may be difficult to manage, and if so, are you equipped to do so? You should not accept an appointment as trustee until such time as you have a reasonably clear understanding of the asset composition.

The size of the trust is also important. A $50,000 trust intended to provide for ten different beneficiaries will probably generate too little income to help any of them. A small trust could serve a valid purpose, however, if it were used to provide for a terminally ill beneficiary.

For you, a factor to consider is whether the trust will be large enough to give you sufficient flexibility to manage it and generate enough income to run it. Will there be enough assets so that you can diversify them, if that is an investment requirement of the trust instrument or prevailing law? Will beneficiaries be competing to exhaust a trust they know can't last long? Can you be paid sufficiently? There is a certain amount of work and responsibility involved on your part, no matter how small the trust. With a small trust, your fees may be insufficient, or they may be too disproportionate a share of the trust assets and income –a source of potential criticism from beneficiaries who may try to have your fees reduced.

Definitions

The assets of a trust are the "principal" or "corpus" of the trust, or the "trust property." They are what an individual or a business might call "capital," as opposed to the income produced by them. In personal trusts, income is distributed to, used for, or reserved for future distribution to certain beneficiaries, and is treated as separate from principal.

The distinction between principal and income is an important one for trusts. One class of beneficiary may be entitled to the income, while another may be entitled to the principal. Principal and income are different things for fiduciary accounting and tax accounting purposes, too.

C. Who Are the Beneficiaries?

When a trust is established, you may not know who the specific beneficiaries will be. An interest in the trust may someday pass to individuals who are yet to be born, or who will become eligible for trust benefits only if a certain event happens. To the extent possible, however, you should have a reasonable understanding of whom the trust is intended to benefit, and to what degree. Construct a list that shows this information, along with addresses and any other useful information, such as dates of birth, citizenship and relationships to other beneficiaries.

Some beneficiaries can be so remotely located that communication or foreign law is a problem. If you need a signature in a hurry, you could find it exceedingly difficult to get in touch with someone living in a jungle peninsula of Costa Rica. If there are likely to be beneficiaries who are mentally or physically challenged, you'll want to know if you can work with them or their representatives effectively.

The vast majority of beneficiaries are reasonable people who appreciate a conscientious trustee, but occasionally you'll encounter beneficiaries who are difficult to deal with for personal reasons. They may be financially unsophisticated or resentful that "their" money has been "tied up" in a trust. If you are patient, willing to educate them and demonstrate that you are working in their best interests, you can often mollify these individuals. Others can be just plain unreasonable, and once in a while you might encounter one who is abusive or threatening.

A trust littered with beneficiaries who are scoundrels, malcontents and sociopaths is probably best avoided. Trustees and beneficiaries don't have to get along, unless their mutual animosity interferes with carrying out the purpose of the trust. But why look for trouble? Contentious beneficiaries can be time-consuming to deal with, and there is always the possibility that one of them might cause you real financial or physical harm. It helps to know in advance something about the personalities and background of people you will be dealing with.

Definitions

A beneficiary is anyone who benefits from a trust (although you'll find out when we discuss taxes that, for tax purposes, a charity that receives a distribution from a trust is not always considered a beneficiary). A beneficiary can be a current beneficiary who receives benefits now, or a future beneficiary who will be entitled to benefits later. Beneficiaries who are to receive the remaining trust assets when the trust ends are called "remaindermen."

Beneficiaries can also be classified as primary or contingent. A primary beneficiary has an interest (called "vested") in a trust that can be defeated only by his or her death or the exhaustion of the principal, even though the interest might be a future interest, such as the right to succeed to trust benefits upon the death of a parent beneficiary. A contingent beneficiary, on the other hand, might participate in the trust at some future date if certain events fall into place. A child, who will receive income from a trust only if his or her father dies before attaining the age of 45 (because his or her father will receive the interest free of trust upon reaching that age), has a contingent interest in the trust.

Also think about conflicts among beneficiaries and how they might complicate your management of the trust. Trusts are notorious for conflicts between income beneficiaries and remaindermen when they are not the same, because each group has a different interest. Income beneficiaries want all of the income they can get, while remaindermen want the trust assets to grow in value. A trust which benefits both the surviving spouse and the children of the settlor is a good example of a trust with a built-in potential conflict, if the children of the settlor don't participate in income until the spouse dies–especially if the children of the settlor are not also the children of the surviving spouse. Investment policies shaped for one class of beneficiary can hurt the other, leaving the trustee in a potentially deadly crossfire. You'll need to follow the instructions in the trust instrument carefully and be scrupulously even-handed in such situations.

D. How Long Will the Trust Last?

The average life of a trust is supposedly fifteen years, according to some statistics, but some last for decades. Unless you know that your trust will have a short life, you may be entering into a commitment that could last as long as you do. Do you want to be managing a trust in your late retirement years, for richer or poorer, in sickness and in health, till death do you part? There are ways to disassociate yourself from a trust, as we explain in the final chapter of this book. However, a trustee, when he or she accepts the appointment, assumes a moral obligation to the settlor to provide as much continuity as possible. Therefore you should give consideration to the fact that this could be "permanent employment."

E. Will You Be Sharing Responsibilities With Co-Trustees or Others?

There may be co-trustees with whom you are directed to share duties and responsibilities. Co-trustees need to agree upon how they will manage routine duties, such as keeping records and reporting information to beneficiaries, and how assets are to be held in safekeeping or otherwise secured. They also have to participate in more substantive "discretionary " duties, such making investment decisions or deciding how to use principal. If you have to work with co-trustees, will they be acceptable working partners? The answer is important, because, under most circumstances, you can be held accountable for actions (or lack of action) by a co-trustee.

Co-trustees should also measure up to the list of criteria below under Section H, and they should be cooperative, as well. The trust instrument can smooth the way by providing remedies when co-trustees find it difficult to agree. For instance, it can provide that one trustee will prevail over others with respect to certain decisions, or have the exclusive right to make them.

If a bank or trust company is your co-trustee, you can expect that it will insist upon possession of the assets and control over investment management and tax work, and that it will want to perform all ministerial duties, such as record-keeping, making routine remittances and issuing statements. Essentially your duties will be to share in making important decisions and monitoring the actions of your co-trustee, unless the trust instrument provides otherwise. This could actually be a convenient arrangement for you, as it relieves you of all of the more tedious aspects of trust administration and puts them in the hands of a professional organization. And whatever you receive as compensation will have a higher element of profit in it, because your operating costs will be minimal.

Having a corporate co-trustee doesn't relieve you of all responsibility, however. Corporate trustees have demonstrated time and again that they aren't infallible. You should question investment and tax decisions, and you should be particularly careful about policies and actions that appear to be more for the corporate trustee's convenience or profit than in the best interests of the trust. For example, you would want to protest the actions of one actual corporate trustee that routinely charged a 6% fee on all "income" collected for its trusts, including tax refunds due to its own overpayments of estimated taxes!

Other parties, such as an investment counselor or a business valuation expert, may also have to be consulted on a courtesy or mandatory basis. Some might even be given the right to make very important decisions, such as determining when a business interest is to be sold. It is not at all unusual for a settlor to want the trustee to have the assistance of his or her favorite advisors. They might even want you do business with them, such as making trades through a particular broker.

Definitions

A "courtesy" consultant is one who must be consulted but whose advice need not be followed. A "mandatory" consultant's directions must be carried out.

This is something you should be wary of, as it can amount to accountability without control for you. Even if you think you are protected by exoneration clauses in the trust instrument (always dubious), it is generally not a good idea. You should be free to choose your own advisors and do business in a way that benefits the trust rather than a particular side-party. It is rare that a designated outside consultant or businessperson can make a unique contribution to the administration of a trust.

F. Will Your Fees Be Sufficient?

You might want to act as trustee out of a pure sense of duty to a family or a friend, in which case compensation may be of secondary importance. Otherwise, there is little reason to assume responsibilities if you won't be fairly paid to carry them out. Your fees should be payment for your labor and your skills (two separate components), and they should also compensate you for assuming certain kinds of exposure to liability.

Start with what you should be paid for routine clerical work. It is always difficult to estimate in advance how many hours you might spend performing the menial tasks of trust administration in a given year. You should try to do this anyway. Try to divide the job into the different clerical tasks you'll have to perform, and estimate for each the time in hours that you are likely to need in order to perform them. Calculate what the cost would be if you had to pay a clerk, secretary or paralegal to perform this kind of work on an hourly basis. This will give you a rough idea of what you should be paid for just the routine work.

At a higher level, you should determine what you should charge on an hourly basis for your skills and experience when they are called upon. For instance, if you are an investment manager by profession, what would you be paid for managing the trust's assets if they belonged to an individual client? If you aren't a professional, but just "pretty good" at managing investments, adjust your hourly rate downwards to a fair amount. If you have to farm such work out to others, reduce your fees by some reasonable amount, keeping in mind that you still have to monitor and approve the work of outsiders.

Finally there is your exposure to risk, which should figure into your compensation package. We discuss risk management in Part Two, Chapter II, but for now, consider this. The risks that you take as a trustee come in many forms. It might be your fault if trust assets are lost or decline in value. You may mistakenly pay income to the wrong beneficiary. You may have to defend yourself against beneficiaries who accuse you of self-dealing. These are only a few of many possible examples. If you can't protect yourself from such hazards with insurance or exoneration arrangements, you should be compensated for doing so. But how? It is immensely difficult to put a price on potential liabilities that are unknown. If you can't obtain fiduciary liability insurance (which is difficult for an individual trustee to find), we suggest as a rule of thumb, that you increase your combined fee for clerical and skilled work by 10%.

You can calculate the sum of the above elements as a percentage of the trust's assets, to be applied annually. Is it larger than a state statute allows? Will the settlor approve? If it is too late for the settlor's approval, will the beneficiaries or a court approve?

These are just the basics. This topic is important enough for us to have devoted extensive attention to it in Chapter VI.

G. Whom Can You Call Upon for Help?

Unless you are an attorney or a trust officer with much varied experience, you'll have to call on others for help. The likely candidates are an attorney, a tax consultant, an accountant and an investment manager, all of whom should have trust experience. Trust law is a specialty, as are trust taxation and trust accounting, and trust investing is subject to certain principles and rules with which an investment manager should be familiar. You may not need all of these specialists, and you may need some of them only on occasion. But it may take some legwork to assemble your team.

With respect to attorneys, you should retain one to represent you as trustee of the trust, when needed. If you find yourself in a conflict situation where your personal interests are different than those of the trust, you should call upon the services of a separate attorney to represent you as an individual. An attorney representing you as trustee might be called upon to help you with such tasks as interpreting language in the trust instrument or collecting a debt from a trust creditor, while a personal attorney might assist you in defending yourself against charges of self-dealing brought by beneficiaries.

A good source of recommendations for specialists is a bank trust department or trust company, or a law firm that does trust work. Some trust officers, such as those with tax and accounting responsibilities, might even be willing to moonlight themselves, if their company has no policy against it. Be wary of "back scratching," where one professional recommends another more to repay a past favor or encourage new ones than to provide you with the most appropriate helpmate.

If you need an insurance consultant, you could probably begin with your own personal insurance agency, although it may need to refer you outside to specialists in fiduciary liability. Cost and the quality and extent of coverage are dominant factors in insurance policy selections, so you will have to shop around. You might also need the services of a broker, as well as those of a custodian who would be responsible for the holding of assets in safekeeping.

H. Do You Have "The Right Stuff?"

Now it is time to hold up the mirror. Do you have the qualifications to be appointed as a trustee? From a legal stance, they are surprisingly few. In some states, you could be under age eighteen, an alien, a resident of a different state, a beneficiary, or the settlor. Let's disregard the legal requirements and look at the practical ones:

Integrity

You should be honest. Banks and trust companies are regularly audited and examined, but as trustee of an inter-vivos trust, you may be subject only to the inquiries of beneficiaries. You may have many opportunities to enrich yourself or others at the expense of the trust, but you must ignore all of them.

Intelligence

You should be at least of ordinary intelligence. You don't have to be brilliant, but you should be smart enough to perform routine tasks, arrive at decisions in a logical manner, and know when to ask for help. Because you may be dealing with others having less integrity than you, "street smarts" are a plus.

Prudence

You should be prudent. You can't take unseemly risks with other people's money. You'll need to keep good records and document your actions in the event you have to defend them.

Conscientiousness

You should be diligent. Beneficiaries depend on timely remittances and reporting. Accuracy and timeliness are important in dealing with investments, tax authorities and the court.

Availability

You should be reasonably available. Beneficiaries have emergencies, and assets may require sudden attention. This doesn't mean that you have to have the twenty-four hour availability of a tow-truck operator, but you should have reasonable business hours during which you can be reached. If you are a constant traveler or have other pressing responsibilities, think twice about acting as a trustee.

Fairness

You have a duty to deal with the beneficiaries impartially, so you should be fair-minded by nature. This requires the ability to arrive at decisions by carefully weighing different considerations. For instance, you may be faced with a request to pay for improvements to one beneficiary's residence while another beneficiary desperately needs nursing home care. If funds were insufficient for both purposes, you would have to decide whether to cut back or eliminate entirely the request of the former beneficiary in terms of what is fair to both.

Good Health

You should be healthy, with a reasonably long-life expectancy. It may be unreasonable for you to be expected to last as long as the trust might, but continuity is important for trusts, particularly as it relates to carrying out long-term investment programs and building relationships with the beneficiaries over time.

Financial Responsibility

From a beneficiary's point of view, you should also have enough money to make good any losses caused by your negligence or criminal acts. If you find this requirement disturbing, you should at least be capable of being bonded or insured for losses to the trust. One advantage for beneficiaries that corporate trustees have over their individual counterparts is that their pockets are deeper. Can you obtain bonding or other coverage against losses due to your own negligence that will at least restore to the beneficiaries what they have lost?

Special Legal or Financial Skills

Trust administration involves law, accounting, taxation, investing, and general finance. It is a rare individual who is experienced in all of these fields as they relate to trusts, and it is not essential that you have experience in any of them. You can – and should – rely on professional advisors for assistance when you need it. You can also delegate much of your work to professionals. However, it is helpful if you can supervise others, drawing upon your own knowledge and experience. If you are skilled enough to perform much of your own work, you can also justify a larger share of total fees paid out by the trust.

Ability to Communicate Well

Trustees do not have to have degrees in English or journalism, but it helps their cause if they are effective communicators. This overlooked skill, together with the basic requirement of empathy, can go far in promoting good relationships with beneficiaries and others. We address communication at length in Part Three, Chapter I.

Patience and Empathy

Beneficiaries may have difficulty understanding the principles of trust administration and why things can't be done the way they want them or as soon as they want them. They may be very young and inexperienced, mentally frail with age, preoccupied with personal problems, or just not very bright. If you are patient with them and make an effort to understand their situations, your relationships with them will be enhanced.

Sense of Humor

Finally, a sense of humor can help. It might do to retell here a somewhat shopworn story by a master of self-deprecation. Abraham Lincoln, who carried his share of burdens, once said he often felt like the man who had been tarred and feathered, and was being ridden out of town on a rail. When taunted about how he was enjoying the ride, the wretch replied that if it weren't for the honor of the thing, he'd just as soon walk. If at times you feel, as Lincoln did, that you are more abused than honored, a gentle wit may salve if not save. Gently applied, a sense of humor can reduce friction in your dealings with others. It is the oil in the engine of life.

Chapter II
Reviewing The Trust Instrument

We probably don't need to tell you that you should review the trust instrument before accepting an appointment as trustee. It might be helpful for us to tell you how to do it, though. Wills and trust agreements can be imposing documents if you're not a lawyer or a trust officer.

The purpose of a review is to find out:

- what you are asked to do, and for how long
- what freedom and restraints will apply
- what protections you will have against liability
- how you will be compensated
- who else will be involved with the administration of the trust
- how you can resign or be removed

Don't be shy about asking the settlor for a look at the trust instrument before he or she signs it. Your input is an important part of making the trust work, and you should have an opportunity to contribute on such subjects as your responsibilities, authority and compensation. A settlor may be reluctant to share certain details of a trust instrument with you until your services are needed. There may be personal revelations that he or she wishes to keep private. If so, ask for general information about the intent of the trust, and ask to see the pages of the instrument that deal with everything else.

As you read, keep an eye out for anything that seems incomplete, vague or incomprehensible. A trust that loses some tax advantage because of improper drafting is not your problem, but an unclear intention that may have to be interpreted in court is. You should also make sure that the final document is properly executed, and that any schedules (lists) of assets or other documents referred to in it as attached, are, in fact, attached and complete. Lawyers who draft trust agreements sometimes leave the completion and attachment of schedules up to the settlor, insurance agents or others who may have the specific information.

If your review raises questions, they should be addressed to the settlor, if he or she can answer them. Otherwise you would be better off discussing them jointly with the settlor and his or her lawyer, especially if they concern points that may involve legal issues.

The Basics of Proper Execution

- Is the signature that of the settlor?
- If not, is it signed by an attorney-in-fact having the authority to do so under a power of attorney and state law? (No one can sign a will other than the testator.)
- Is the document dated where a date is called for? (Sometimes there is a blank for a date in the body of the trust instrument.)
- Has it been witnessed?
- Has it been notarized? (This is necessary if the trust is to hold real estate.)
- Do the dates for the signatures of witnesses and notaries correspond to the date for the settlor's signature?

If you suspect an improper execution, you should not be a party to the trust until it has either been corrected or until you have been satisfied that it is correct.

A. Dispositive Provisions

Your job, as trustee, is to manage and dispose of the trust assets, according to the terms of the trust instrument. Some trust instruments introduce the provisions concerned with the purpose of the trust with the heading "Dispositive Provisions." Whether or not those provisions are identified in this way, you'll recognize them as the provisions that tell you what to do in such terms as, "pay the income to...," or, "use the principal for the maintenance, support and education of...," or "distribute the remaining trust assets to...."

1. The Trust Purpose

The Trust purpose might be quite straightforward. In the case of a typical revocable living trust, it will state that you are to:

- manage the trust assets for the benefit of the settlor;
- pay him or her all of the net income and so much of the principal, including all of it, as he or she requests from time to time;
- if he or she becomes incapacitated, apply the income and principal for his or her maintenance, support, health and welfare; and
- upon his or her death, pay the remaining trust assets to the estate (or perhaps directly to the beneficiaries, if the intent is to avoid probate).

Other trust documents can be more complex, or even obscure. A trust may have multiple beneficiaries with different interests. For example, there may be a provision directing you to use the income and principal for the maintenance, support, health, welfare and education of the settlor's surviving spouse and children. Here, the economical draftsman has left you with such questions as, whether a fifty-five year old spouse's education should come before that of the teenage children. Or whether the trust should pay for the education at all, if there is only enough money to shelter and feed the spouse.

Try to imagine what kinds of decisions you might have to make, and ask the settlor to clear up any ambiguities. You might want the attorney to use a few more words to create separate provisions for the spouse and the children, leaving out education for the spouse. You might suggest that the settlor indicate preferences, such as putting the welfare of the spouse above the education of the children. You could also ask for a definition of "education." Should it include private schooling, vocational schooling, attendance at unaccredited schools, graduate school, or the occasional course in flower arrangement?

Look over the entire trust instrument for help in interpreting the dispositive provisions. For instance, there may be a separate section explaining that troubling word "education."

Illegal Trusts

Illegal trusts are rare, but we want to mention that trust purposes must be legal ones. A trust can not require the trustee to break a law, such as by defrauding creditors of the settlor. A trust created for an illegal reason, such as one created as a form of bribe, is also invalid, although this may not be apparent in the trust instrument.

A trust is also illegal if it is against public policy. For example, a trust to provide for the training of safecrackers or to pay the fines of rock musicians who damage their hotel rooms, or to make a large distribution to a daughter if "she will divorce that shiftless wastrel she married," would be against public policy.

These are fairly obvious examples, but a trust that withholds benefits from beneficiaries for years on end is also against public policy, as it puts funds out of circulation for too long. A whimsical purpose might also be against public policy, as was determined long ago in British Columbia, Canada, where an attempt was made to create a trust that would provide boys with knickers having a legend on the waistband. This seems like a harmless waste of money, but wasting money is counter to the interests of society.

On the other hand, subtle revenge may not be out of reach. A trust that provides one "good" nephew with all of the annual net income except for one dollar, and gives the "bad" nephew that remaining dollar on his birthday, would probably pass muster (but you might not want to be the trustee). What is and is not against public policy may not always be clear, but generally a trust must have a useful purpose. However, a trust with an illegal or stupid purpose could continue to exist until someone cared enough to challenge it.

Naturally you won't want to become involved with an illegal trust. You should probably avoid trusts that do not make a lot of sense to you, too, even if they have innocent intentions, because you won't have your heart in your work.

2. Tax Minimization

Trusts often include provisions that are concerned with estate or income tax planning on both federal and state levels. These can make for difficult reading. For example, you may have to contend with formulas for allocating assets between a marital deduction share and a non-marital deduction share. The federal tax laws are especially complex. (The late William E. Simon, a former Secretary of the Treasury, supposedly once remarked that it would have been nice if the Internal Revenue Code had been written with an objective in mind.)

Consequently, a trust intended to minimize federal taxes may refer to many sections and subsections of the Code, and use its arcane terms. Examples of trusts with dense tax provisions are those that take advantage of the federal estate tax marital deduction and the federal estate tax credit, charitable trusts, and trusts that minimize the tax on generation-skipping transfers, to name a few (*see* the Appendix for descriptions of these trusts). To a lesser degree, state taxes may also influence the drafting of a trust instrument.

If you don't understand what you are reading when you come to complex tax provisions, it's time to ask for help. The Appendix explains a number of trusts in terms of their tax considerations in the section headed, "A Variety of Trusts," and the Bibliography lists books that will be of help. You may have to consult an attorney if an understanding of a particular provision is essential to your proper administration of the trust.

3. Assets

You don't normally find much information about the assets among the dispositive provisions. Sometimes the inclusion of special provisions in a different part of the trust instrument may hint at this, such as a provision to consult with a particular accountant about an identified business interest. There may be a reference to specific assets or a specific amount in the dispositive provisions of some trusts. More often, the assets aren't closely described in the trust instrument. There may be only a reference, such as "the rest of my estate," which is specific but unrevealing.

To find out what assets are subject to the trust, you'll probably need to look at schedules attached to the trust instrument. A life insurance trust, for example, should have an attached schedule of policies payable to the trust by reason of the settlor's death. A living trust, to be funded during the settlor's life, should have a schedule of the assets with which it is to be funded. Sometimes there is no list of specific property items. Trust assets may be defined merely as what is left over after other assets have been disposed of from the settlor's estate, or as whatever comes into the trustee's hands. Many wills describe trust property as "the residue of my estate," for example.

4. Beneficiaries

Dispositive provisions identify the beneficiaries and state whether they are to receive benefits currently or in the future, whether they have absolute rights to benefits, or whether payments are at the discretion of the trustee or contingent upon something happening.

The beneficiaries do not have to be identified by name, but there are limits on how vague the trust instrument can be. For example, it's fine to leave assets to "my children" or "my grandchildren," but a trust that tries to set up schemes for controlling property over more generations may run into trouble with an ancient and often baffling legal obstacle called the "rule against perpetuities." For example, a trust that runs for the lives of the settlor's spouse, his or her daughter and his or her daughter's children, and then distributes trust property to the daughter's grandchildren could violate this rule. If you think a trust might violate the rule against perpetuities, talk to the lawyer who drafted it, or consult the lawyer you have retained to represent the trust.

The Rule Against Perpetuities

Baffling though it may be, you need to have some understanding of this concept. The common law rule against perpetuities began its development in 1681 when the Earl of Arundel created trusts of long duration to protect his descendants from his firstborn son's insanity. The findings in the resulting Duke of Norfolk's Case developed into the important modern day rule that places limits on how long most trusts can last. In most states, the term limit is measured by the lives of specified individuals who must exist at the time the trust is funded, plus an additional twenty-one years.

The method for recognizing a violation of the rule is:

- identify the future interest that is to pass to someone;
- determine if it is possible that it will vest after twenty-one years beyond the death of the last specified individual living when the trust was funded.

How could a trust that runs for the lives of the settlor's spouse, his or her daughter and the daughter's children and then distributes to his or her daughter's grandchildren violate the rule? If only the wife, the daughter and one child of the daughter were living when the trust was created, the daughter could subsequently have more children, which might extend the term of the trust beyond that allowed.

Some state laws provide remedies for a possible violation with "wait and see" statutes, so that the trust is terminated only if and when a violation occurs. Others have done away with the rule of perpetuities altogether, passing statutes that cancel out or redefine the common law principle. A few states have abolished the rule of perpetuities. Alaska creates an exception to it for certain beneficiaries with respect to non-vested trust interests. These states have left the latchstring hanging over the gate for statute-shopping settlors with dynastic ambitions, and more states may seek to compete for dynastic trusts in the future.

5. Distributions

As trustee, you'll be in charge of making payments to beneficiaries. The trust terms may instruct you to make regular income payments, use principal to meet particular needs when you decide that it's necessary, or make payments triggered by an event such as the beneficiary reaching a certain age or the termination of the trust. But there are other variations. Sometimes income must be accumulated for later distribution, or a beneficiary might have a right to withdraw principal, such as the right to withdraw the larger of (a) $5,000 or (b) 5% of the trust principal annually.

Making required distributions is relatively easy, as long as you follow the instructions in the trust instrument, make sure you have properly identified the beneficiaries and comply with tax reporting requirements. If a distribution is contingent upon a certain event, you'll want to verify that the event has taken place. A beneficiary who is entitled to a share of principal at age twenty-five should furnish you with a birth certificate or other credible proof of his or her having reached that age.

Additionally you might be given the power to pay principal to a beneficiary, or apply it for his or her use, as you determine in your sole discretion. This could be according to an ascertainable standard, such as welfare and support, or you might have unlimited discretion to pay or apply principal for one or more beneficiaries as you see fit. In either case, you'll have to exercise your judgement.

Definition

The Internal Revenue Code uses the term "ascertainable standard" to mean specifically: health, education, maintenance and support. Other terms, such as comfort, happiness, enjoyment, and the like, are considered too subjective to be ascertainable.

In reviewing discretionary powers, you should consider how frequently you may have to use them, how much background investigation will be required on your part if you do, and how difficult it will be for you to reach a decision. Be forewarned that when they uncover a liberal discretionary-use power, beneficiaries can be inclined to make frequent assaults on trust funds, for all kinds of perceived needs. Starting a winery in Maine can be a joyful undertaking for a beneficiary who doesn't have to invest his or her own money in it.

We include a short chapter in Part Three, Chapter II that discusses what you should consider when making required and discretionary distributions.

B. Administrative Provisions

While the dispositive provisions are the entree on the trust instrument menu, the administrative provisions are an important side course. These provisions, also called trustee's powers or grants of authority, determine what you may do, what you must do and what you can't do.

Administrative provisions often merely restate the authority given to trustees by common law or statutes so that the trustee and others have a ready reference, but sometimes they alter this authority. We review here typical provisions included in wills and trust agreements drafted by attorneys with estate planning skills. Some of them are frequently drafted to be more limiting than these represented here. For instance, you might be specifically prohibited from pledging trust property to obtain a loan.

The main purpose of these specific provisions in the trust instrument is to facilitate your dealings with third parties who need the comfort of a specific authorization for the transaction you need to complete to do your job. Settlors sometimes also include administrative provisions that limit your authority. They might feel strongly that you should not do certain things, such as invest in stocks of companies that circumvent United States child labor laws. Restrictive provisions may also be included to thwart a dishonest trustee, although they are usually ineffective for this purpose.

A Short Introduction to Trust Law

American laws that apply to trusts consist of three categories:

- *Common Law:* We inherited common law from England when our country consisted of English colonies. This is a large collection of legal remedies established by innovations that gradually became tradition, going back to the Norman Conquest or beyond. Common law pertaining to trusts is recorded in Restatement of the Law, Trusts, which we described in the Introduction, and is the basis upon which other forms of trust law have been constructed. The rule against perpetuities is one example of common law that is the starting point for state laws that determine how long a trust may last. Where no new law has been developed, common law still applies.
- *Statutory Law:* This is law created by governmental legislatures. The statutory laws of a particular state apply only to those entities that are subject to that state's jurisdiction, such as a trust governed by a trust instrument that says, "this trust is to be administered according to the laws of the Commonwealth of Virginia." State statutes determine such things as how income and principal are to be distinguished and what principles govern the management of trust property. Another example: some states have statutes that limit a trustee's compensation in terms of percentages or dollar amounts. At the federal level, tax

laws are an example of statutory laws that apply to entities in all states, including trusts.

- *Case Law:* Courts decide cases based upon existing law, and the decisions of appeals courts are written down and published in books that can be found in law libraries, or, with increasing frequency, on the Internet. In this process, old law is sometimes clarified or abolished, and new law is created. Where such new law has sufficiently broad application, it may be codified by statute.

The trust instrument may make its own rules, as long as it doesn't go against state law concerning public policy or other illegal activity. For instance, a state statute that limits the type of assets a trustee can invest in will apply only if the trust instrument doesn't give him or her broader discretion. As a personal trust is a state entity, the trust instrument can't overrule federal laws, such as those that deal with taxation or environmental regulation.

- *Uniform Acts and Uniform Codes:* The National Conference of Commissioners on Uniform State Laws drafts and approves recommended law which may then be approved by states (including the District of Columbia). A uniform act is a particular piece of recommended law, such as the Uniform Transfers to Minors Act, while a uniform code, such as the Uniform Trust Code is a codification of parts of the common law (with some changes) pertaining to trusts. Various states may then adopt these uniform acts or codes, sometimes with substantial changes, as statutes to provide a national uniformity of law. At present we are a long way from national uniformity, although many states have adopted some uniform acts or have used their own modifications of them. For instance, as of this writing only five jurisdictions have adopted the Uniform Trust Code, but many more now have some variation of the Uniform Prudent Investor Act included in their statutes. However, the courts of states that have not adopted unified acts or codes may look to the models for guidance when statutory law is deficient.

1. Compromise Claims

Claims can be against the trust, such as one by an accountant you haven't paid, or they can be on behalf of the trust, such as one where you are trying to collect insurance payments for property damage. It's important for a trustee to be able to adjust, compromise, settle or abandon claims expediently, where it appears that time, effort and expense will outweigh the probabilities of success. Otherwise the beneficiaries might attack you for not recovering the grand sum of $50 on a minor repair job that wasn't done properly, even though the repairman has since taken up residence in Bolivia. Time and effort are also wasted by trips to the courtroom, if you have to defend your actions.

2. Sell Trust Property

This provision typically permits a trustee to sell property publicly or privately for cash or credit, and to give options for sales, exchanges or leases. In the case of real estate, it would normally go on to say that you can do all the things that might be remotely connected to a sale, such as to subdivide, repair, and improve. Unless the sale is necessary to carry out the purposes of the trust, it might otherwise be necessary to find an implication in the trust instrument that a sale is permitted. A provision authorizing the retention of property might be such an implication, because it offsets an assumption that trust assets would be sold.

One of your many duties as a trustee (set forth in Part One, Chapter V) is to make trust property produce income. As a means of carrying out this duty, common law permits a trustee to lease property for such periods and according to such provisions as are reasonable, unless prohibited by the terms of the trust.

3. Allocate Expenses

Serving as a trustee you'll almost certainly incur expenses that are necessary to carry out the purposes of the trust. An expense-allocation provision gives you some flexibility in how you pay these expenses–from trust income or principal. This lets you be fair to different classes of beneficiaries.

As an example, your fee might be allocated 50% to each category so that the income beneficiary doesn't bear the entire brunt of annual fees while the remaindermen are charged nothing. Or take the expense of installing a Jacuzzi in a residence owned by a trust. You might normally charge it entirely to principal. However, if the only tenant is the sole income beneficiary, it might be fairer to charge at least some of the installation expense to that beneficiary's income as payment for his or her pleasurable soakings.

4. Distribute in Cash or in Kind

This provision enables you to distribute trust property to beneficiaries either in kind (the property itself) or in cash proceeds from the sale of it, whichever the beneficiaries prefer. Without such a provision, you would normally be required under common law to distribute the trust property in kind to the beneficiaries, particularly if there is only one of them.

Often distribution in kind is appropriate. Liquidating assets can have adverse tax consequences, and of course a beneficiary may want the property as it is. Sometimes, however, selling some or all of the assets and distributing the cash proceeds might make more sense. Some assets are difficult to divide equally among several beneficiaries, and a beneficiary might also want the convenience of having you sell an asset that he or she doesn't want.

5. Assume the Continuance of Status for Beneficiaries

As trustee, you may need to act on behalf of a beneficiary who can't handle financial matters without your help. For example, you may need to use trust funds to pay his or her bills directly because he or she is ill or incapacitated. This kind of clause relieves you of liability for doing so unless you have reliable information that the beneficiary's condition has improved to the point where he or she can pay their own bills.

6. Borrow Money, Mortgage or Pledge Property

Unless the trust instrument specifically allows it, you can't pledge trust property as collateral for a loan. One exception to this rule is if a change in circumstances requires you to do so in order to carry out the purposes of the trust (in which case court permission would normally be required). Depending upon the type of trust, you might find it convenient to exercise this power prudently to get past a short-term need for cash or to refinance a mortgage at a lower rate.

7. Take Action with Respect to Foreclosures, Mergers, Reorganizations

Companies aren't static. They merge with other companies, reorganize themselves in different forms and can go out of business. Because mergers, dissolutions, and other such changes can affect principal, a trustee should have the ability to deal with them. This provision typically gives you the power to participate in voting trusts and to delegate discretionary duties, such as leaving the voting of proxies to board members.

C. Investment Provisions

Your authority and responsibility to invest trust assets wisely are central to your job as trustee. Investment provisions, usually included among the administrative provisions, address what types of investments are permissible, required or prohibited.

1. Power To Retain Property

This provision allows you to keep certain kinds of trust property, even if you wouldn't be allowed to invest in them otherwise. There could be many reasons why you might want to retain such assets, at least for a while. For instance, the beneficiaries might want a family business retained, if it keeps them employed. Or you might want to dispose of an undesirable piece of unimproved land, but need an extended period of time to do it. A provision authorizing you to retain property without regard to diversification or risk gives you authority to deal on your own terms with a plot of land that consists essentially of a gully, or with that scary interest in a Nigerian pottery factory. Generally a retention power is coupled with language purporting to give you relief from a duty to diversify assets and, depending upon the type of trust, from any requirement to make the assets produce income.

2. Invest in Any Property

Unless the trust instrument frees you to invest in any kind of asset, state law may limit your choices severely. A few states even limit investments to a list of specified types, a holdover from an earlier time in England when government bonds were about the only approved non-land investment. A provision allowing you to invest in any property gives you the opportunity to broaden your choices and to take advantage of new investment vehicles as they appear. Keep in mind, though, that even if you are allowed to invest in all kinds of assets, you still must invest prudently.

3. Buy Investments at a Premium or Discount

The power to buy and sell at premiums or discounts relates primarily to marketable securities. This power, along with others relating to investment transactions, helps to avoid questions of whether paying a premium means that you overpaid, or whether obtaining a discount implies that you made an inferior investment.

4. Hold Property in the Name of a Nominee

Most marketable securities are now held by depository trust companies in their vaults, and are registered in the names of nominees - fictitious names employed for the convenient holding and transfer of securities in place of the names of the real owners. The securities change ownership in huge volume daily, but they never move physically. It's all done electronically by brokers, banks and trust companies.

You would find it inconvenient to register each security in the name of "John J. Doe, Trustee under Agreement dated 1/17/87 with Jane B Roe, Settlor" and have to keep these securities somewhere. If you and a co-trustee at a different location had to each sign a certificate or a stock or bond power for every sale of a security, it would be cumbersome for both of you. Instead, you can buy and sell through a corporate entity, such as a bank or brokerage firm that has an account with a depository trust company that holds the actual certificates. The bank or brokerage firm will keep your trust account separate, and the securities will be registered in its nominee so that it can perform most of the paper work involved in a purchase or a sale. All you have to do is give the bank or brokerage firm a written order to buy or sell.

The nominee provision avoids any possible conflict with common law or outdated statutes. A related provision authorizes the opening of a custody account at an institution so that you can use the nominee registration services of a bank or brokerage firm. Another related provision allows the trustee to hold unregistered property, such as older municipal "bearer" bonds that do not reveal who owns them .

5. Employ and Retain Agents

This provision authorizes you to hire others to perform various duties. It is especially valuable in enabling you to use the services of a professional investment advisor and/or a decision-making money manager. It should specifically include a reference to the types of agents authorized. It addresses a concern in states that restrict a trustee's power to delegate responsibility, especially responsibility of a discretionary nature, such as making an investment decision.

6. Vote Proxies

Your power to vote and exercise other powers for shares of stock owned by the trust arises from your duty to promote the interest of the beneficiary. This provision relieves you of an obligation to vote such shares in person.

7. Specialized Provisions

We have covered only the most frequently included investment powers. Where the trust holds a family business interest, real estate or atypical trust assets, other provisions might be included to enable you to deal with them. We include special provisions relating to the administration of business interests and real estate in the Appendix. If you are asked to act as trustee of a trust that will contain these assets, and the trust instrument does not appear to give you sufficient authority to deal with them, consider asking the settlor to include provisions that would be useful.

D. Miscellaneous Provisions

There is no limit to what attorneys can pack into a trust instrument to cover all kinds of contingencies. Here are some provisions that you are likely to encounter and need.

1. Definitions

Some definitions are merely for housekeeping purposes. For example, singulars include the plural and vice versa, and the term "trustee" means both individual, corporate and successor trustees.

You should be more concerned with definitions that have an impact on your decisions, such as what is meant by the term "education," as we discussed earlier. Another example: a word such as "support" might be amplified beyond its common meaning to include payments to maintain a beneficiary's accustomed standard of living at the time of the settlor's death.

2. Consideration to Be Given to Beneficiary's Other Financial Resources

This provision imposes a duty upon you, but it can avoid an unfair result. Suppose you have an enterprising beneficiary who commutes to college in a Bentley, having already made a small fortune with his or her mail order business, who wants the trust to pay his or her tuition. If the trust instrument required you to look at this beneficiary's resources, you might want to turn down the request and direct trust money toward more needy beneficiaries. However, if the trust were silent on this point, but allowed you to invade principal for education, a court might find some implication in the trust instrument that favored the student.

3. No Responsibility for Payment of Insurance Policy Premiums

Some trusts are designated as the beneficiary of life insurance policies owned by others. If someone outside the trust, such as the settlor, is supposed to pay the premiums but stops paying them, the policies lapse. In these situations, you don't want to contend with beneficiaries who think that it becomes your responsibility to make the payments to keep the policies in force. A provision stating that the trustee does not have this responsibility gets you off the hook.

4. Governing Law

Most trust instruments declare that they are subject to the laws of a particular state–usually the state where the settlor lives and owns property. Your concern in reviewing this provision is how practical will it be for you to comply with the laws of the designated state. It may be inconvenient and expensive to deal with an Alabama trust if you are a resident of California, as you may have to rely on remote Alabama legal counsel, and you may also have to make trips to Alabama to deal with assets, beneficiaries or an Alabama court.

If the trust instrument doesn't say anything on this point, it may not be clear as to which state's laws you are subject. For example, real estate held by a trust is subject to the jurisdiction of the state in which it is located. However, land held in a partnership is considered an interest in personal property in some states, making it subject to the laws of wherever you have your trust "office." A trust holding only personal property normally is considered located where you are.

Movable Trusts

There can be advantages to making a trust subject to the laws of a state that has a favorable tax climate or flexible investment standards. This may be difficult to arrange for a trust created under a will, as it may be under the fixed jurisdiction of a court in the state where the settlor died. But there is more leeway for trusts created under agreements while the settlor is alive, and he may even be able to provide that the trustee can relocate the trust after it is established.

5. Spendthrift Provisions

Under many circumstances a beneficiary may have the right to transfer his or her interest in a trust to another. Some are quite willing to transfer a significant interest for quick cash, and there are people who make handsome livings from buying such interests at carefully calculated discounts - an exalted version of check-cashing services in poor neighborhoods. The interest might be a remainder interest in principal or a stream of income for several years. A spendthrift provision prevents this from happening by taking away the beneficiary's right to sell his or her interest.

The beneficiary's creditors, however, can't normally be prevented from reaching trust income or principal assets once they are in the beneficiary's hands. Depending upon the circumstances, they may even be able to reach undistributed assets in the trust. You can find related information in Part One, Chapter V of this book and Article 5 of the Uniform Trust Code.

6. Settlement by Receipt and Release

Trustees have to account for what they have done before they can be released from their responsibility. Trusts under wills are often under the supervision of courts that require formal accountings approved by them. Although they provide certain protections to trustees and beneficiaries alike, formal accounting procedures are frequently drawn-out and expensive affairs. There may be no practical need for such a proceeding if the administration of the trust has been straightforward and simple, and all of the parties to the trust feel that they don't need court supervision.

The trust instrument may authorize you to terminate the trust or an interest in it without going through the expense and red tape of a court-approved accounting. The beneficiaries can then sign a "receipt and release", relieving you of all responsibility for your administration, and they can receive their shares of what is left in the trust relatively quickly. In doing so, however, they may be relinquishing valuable court protection against your prior mistakes, and you are also foregoing the protection of court approval. Still, it is a convenient provision to make use of, under the right circumstances.

E. Exoneration

Efforts are frequently made to free a trustee from all liability for undertaking risky actions (or risky inaction), as long as he or she either acts in good faith or is not supposed to have any control over an action taken (or neglected) by someone else. Exoneration clauses can offer protection against personal liability in some situations. For example, you might be exonerated for holding unproductive land at the settlor's direction, although it declines in value.

Generally you shouldn't rely on exoneration clauses. Instead, you should act according to what you believe is best for the trust, documenting your reasons, and if you are stymied in this, ask for direction from your lawyer or the appropriate court. There is more on this subject in Part One, Chapter V, where we discuss trustee liability.

F. Compensation

Unless your fees are fixed by statute (as they are in some states) or by a separate agreement, there should be a provision with a heading like "Trustee's Compensation," which sets forth the method of computing your fees. Fees are discussed in Part One, Chapters I and VI.

G. Co-Trustees and Other Consultants

If there are co-trustees or outside advisors for you to deal with, they should be identified in the trust agreement. An oral direction, or a written one that isn't in the trust instrument has no force. While a separate agreement covering certain matters, such as trustee's compensation, may be valid, it is tidier if all of the directions for a trustee are in one place: the trust instrument. Advisors are discussed in Part One, Chapter I.

H. Resignation and Removal

Beware the Shopworn Trust

You should always be leery of a trust that has "made the rounds," especially if it is going to be difficult to separate yourself from it. A trust company, one of the authors once worked for, accepted a cemetery trust that had passed through the hands of three prior corporate trustees. The reason why this trust had careened among various trustees soon became evident: the principals of the cemetery company that had established it were impossible to deal with. The current trust company decided that it, too, wanted to get rid of this trust, but under the trust agreement, it had a duty to find a replacement. Unfortunately, when the music stopped, there were no more empty chairs. No one could be found to take a trust that had been through four prior trustees.

The trust instrument should have a provision that allows you to resign, and there should be no requirement on your part to find a successor trustee to take your place. Without such a resignation clause, you may have to apply to a court for permission to resign, and the court will have to be convinced that your resignation won't be detrimental to the interests of the trust.

Your departure could be a matter left up to others, such as a co-trustee or a majority of the beneficiaries if there is a provision enabling them to remove you. This is becoming more common due to the recent frequency with which corporate trustees change their identities through mergers and acquisitions sometimes diminishing their reputations for good service in the process. Removal provisions don't necessarily require any justification for removing a trustee. All the beneficiaries (or some other authorized party) might have to do is sign a letter telling you that you are removed. Then you would have to carry out the responsibilities explained in the final chapter of this book, Part Three, Chapter VII, Termination Of Your Responsibilities.

Your most concentrated effort in administering a trust will probably be expended in setting it up, and your first year probably will be your least profitable one in terms of hours spent for what you earn. Your investment program will need time to justify itself. It may also take many months to become well acquainted with beneficiaries and make them appreciate your effectiveness. Therefore you might want to try to have a removal provision modified so that it cannot be exercised until a fair trial period has passed, such as three years after a new trustee has assumed responsibility.

Chapter III
Your Investment Authority

Investments or Assets?

The two words are often used interchangeably. Properly speaking, the trust is funded with assets. If these assets (or their replacements) are held by the trustee for income or appreciation, they are investments. Everything owned by the trustee is an asset, whether it is an item of income or principal.

Of all the tasks a trustee must perform on an ongoing basis, investment management is undoubtedly the most visible. Periodic statements keep the income beneficiaries informed as to the changes you make in the investments, how frequently you make them and what it costs to make them. They also show changes in the value of these investments over time. When the trust terminates, or your relationship with it does, your stewardship of many years is recorded not in a narrative relating your selfless service, but in an accounting of what you took in, how you invested it, what you paid out, and what remained at the end. The investment history will be scrutinized the most.

Investment management will most likely be your most controversial responsibility, too. Some beneficiaries may want to know why the trust can't produce more income than a 4% yield, when they can earn 6% on their own certificates of deposit. Others will question why the principal isn't growing faster than an average annual return of 5%. In fact, your trust would have a total return of 9%, according to these numbers. This may be perfectly respectable in terms of the trust's objectives, but beneficiaries may judge you only on their share of what is generated. You may also have been using up some principal for their needs, which they forgot about. You may be alternately criticized for your conservatism or your recklessness, depending upon how assets in the trust are performing relative to irrelevant yardsticks, such as last year's performance numbers for a "go-go" mutual fund.

Routine grousing by the beneficiaries will do you no real harm. However, if they become seriously upset with any aspect of your administration, they can take you to court. The court will review the sources of your authority and determine if you have adhered to the rules that apply. Beyond that, it will ascertain whether or not you have managed the trust property according to the trust's purpose, and followed whatever standards set by applicable law. If the court finds that you are right, your actions will be approved, you'll be able to continue in them and the expenses of your defense will be borne by the trust. If you are wrong, you'll have to desist from whatever actions are at fault, make up any losses from your personal funds, and personally pay the costs of your defense.

You don't necessarily have to please each and every beneficiary, and you aren't in competition with market indices or other investment managers. Your assignment is to manage the investments in terms of the total purpose of the trust. There are certain laws, rules and sources of authority to guide you. If you follow them, act with prudence, and keep good records of your actions, you'll perform your duties with distinction. We'll show you how to do this now, beginning with an explanation of where you should look for direction.

A. The Trust Instrument

This is the first source of authority you should consult, as it can override others. The investment provisions of trust instruments come from three sources:

- the settlor
- the drafter
- state statutes

Provisions dominated by the concerns of the settlor may reflect an interest in retaining certain assets, such as a business interest, a real estate holding or an art collection. They may indicate a preference for certain types of investments, such as bonds with AAA ratings or mutual funds. They may show the settlor's disapproval of other investments, such as securities of companies that produce tobacco products or alcoholic beverages. These provisions might state the settlor's preferences without requiring the trustee to follow them, or they might be mandatory, requiring the trustee to observe them. If the draftsman is skilled, settlor-driven provisions will be accompanied by appropriate administrative powers and exoneration clauses.

An experienced trust lawyer will usually add provisions that give the trustee broader discretion than state statutes do. For example, he might insert a clause allowing you to delegate day-to-day management to investment professionals or invest in the securities of regulated investment companies (mutual funds, *etc.*), if state law makes no provision for this or prohibits it.

Some trusts contain minimal investment provisions or none at all, requiring you to rely on the statutes of the state having legal jurisdiction. It may be that the only "investment" provision is one that identifies the state having such jurisdiction, so that you know that the laws of that state are the ones that govern the investment of the trust's assets. This kind of trust is usually drafted by a do-it-yourself settlor, or an incompetent lawyer, but in some cases a skilled attorney has made a deliberate decision that the state laws are appropriate for a given trust.

In reviewing the trust instrument, you must make your own assessment as to whether the investment provisions are satisfactory. Our view is that a trustee should normally have broad discretion. Just keep in mind that you have the duty to perform in a responsible manner, however broad your discretion is. Leeway to invest in a wildcat oil-drilling program doesn't mean you have to do it. If you lose money, and a court determines it was because you were reckless, you will be personally liable for the loss.

B. State Laws

If the trust instrument is silent with respect to your investment authority, or vague, then you may have to rely on the state laws that govern the trust. You can obtain the current statutes applicable to your trust. Each state has several pages of statutes pertaining to trust investments, but you probably won't find them difficult to understand. A meeting with a lawyer is a better approach, however, because he can explain anything that you don't understand, and his fees can be charged to the trust. Such a meeting is also impressive documentation if you later need to prove that you did your homework. Ask the lawyer to keep you advised of any changes that may occur in investment laws (and other trust statutes, for that matter). Some of these state laws are very old and are being updated.

Finding State Statutes

You can ask an attorney for the statutes. If you and the attorney are on close terms, he or she might even show you where they are on the bookshelves and let you do your own research without charging a fee.

If you have access to the library of a law school, you can find them there without much trouble.

Many states make them available on line.

Statutes fall into three different categories: those influenced by the Prudent Man Rule, those influenced by the more recent Prudent Investor Rule, and those of a few states that have lists of approved investments.

1. The Prudent Man Rule

The Prudent Man Rule, which has been around since1830 (it originated in a court decision in Massachusetts, (*Harvard v. Amory*)) essentially says that a trustee must simply be faithful to the trust and exercise sound discretion. The trustee should invest as other discreet and prudent men invest for themselves (in 1830 men did all the investing), concentrating on the probable income and probable safety of the capital. The trustee should not speculate.

States that Follow the Prudent Man Rule

- Louisiana
- Mississippi
- Wisconsin (limits on percentages of common stock)

Wonderfully vague, the Prudent Man Rule, as the decision came to be called, allows trustees to invest as they see fit, as long as they do so in a prudent manner and in the best interests of the trust. Many states gradually enacted statutes based upon the rule, incorporating the following principles:

- Each asset must be preserved. If one investment declines in value, you will be accountable for the loss unless you can prove that you exercised prudence in selecting and monitoring it. This holds true even if the trust has tripled in value because all of the other investments performed admirably.
- The trustee has no duty to increase the value of principal.
- All of the assets should produce income. Trustees are not encouraged to invest for capital gains in order to use them as a substitute for ordinary income.
- Diversification of a trust's investments is not required in all Prudent Man Rule states. For instance, Pennsylvania statutes used to incorporate the Prudent Man Rule, but they didn't require diversification. This is an example of why you need to review the particular laws of your state in detail.
- You can delegate investment responsibility up to a point. You can retain investment advisors for their recommendations, but you are generally expected to make the ultimate investment decisions, rather than grant discretionary powers to a professional manager. This is true even if your investment skills are no greater than those of an ordinary individual.

2. The Prudent Investor Rule

The majority of states have now adopted statutes incorporating some version of either the "Prudent Investor Rule" or the Uniform Prudent Investor Act (UPIA), either by statute or court action. The Prudent Investor Rule is an updated version of the old Prudent Man Rule, designed to be a better fit with modern investment practices.

Here is the gist of what the UPIA says:

- Each stock, bond, real estate holding or other asset is considered in its relationship to the total portfolio, and also in its relationship to other individual assets. Like members of a basketball team, each component may have a somewhat different role. Some may be more aggressive scorers while others play more supportive or defensive positions. Some investments can be tolerated for being volatile or producing little income, as long as they were bought and held prudently, and the trust's investment objectives are accomplished.
- As trustee, you have a duty not only to preserve the trust property but also to maintain its value in relationship to outside forces, such as inflation and the changing economic scene. If there is inflation that averages 3% annually, trust property values should generally keep up with it, and trust income should also increase. Investment in the stock of a sound company that is expanding is desirable. If the expansion consists of both broadening the company's basic business and also adapting to current trends, so much the better.
- Trusts should produce income, but because assets are considered as pieces of the whole, there is flexibility in how you can accomplish this. You can hold bonds to provide most of the needed current income, and

buy stocks more for capital growth and increased future income. Where you have discretion to distribute income and principal, you might employ increases in trust principal as an income substitute. The Prudent Investor Rule recognizes the concept of total return.

- Diversification is a front-burner issue. Because you are encouraged to take reasonable risks, you need to manage them. The primary way to do this is by diversifying investments and offsetting the characteristics of one asset with those of another. You can practice diversification by balancing different assets against each other within a particular class of such assets, and by offsetting the behavior of one asset class against that of others. For example, emerging growth stocks might work well with blue chips, and both might combine well with an underpinning of mid-maturity United States Government bonds. This is because each of these asset classes tends to behave differently under a given market condition.
- Delegation of investment responsibilities is condoned and even recommended under certain circumstances. If you have only average investment acumen, you may hire outsiders with more expertise, not only to advise you, but also even to act in their own discretion, as long as you select them prudently and supervise them carefully.
- You should incur only those costs that are reasonable in amount and appropriate to carrying out your investment responsibilities. You can infer from this, to the extent it is not spelled out in statutes, that you need to keep control over such items as brokers' commissions, mutual fund charges, the efficiency of executions of sales and purchases, and the fees of independent advisors.

If two mutual funds are essentially similar in terms of performance, risk levels, and investment style, you should select the one with the lower expense ratios and sales charges (if you have the authority to invest in mutual funds). You should compare a bank's bundled fee for investment management and custody, along with its ability to obtain low transaction costs, not only to the fees of other banks for the same services, but also to the fees others would charge for providing these services on a separated basis.

You should shop on behalf of the beneficiaries like an inspired bargain hunter, but you should also keep in mind that cost must be weighed against value. You might save money by executing security trades on the Internet at $7 each instead of through a full service broker at $100, but you might be better off using the broker if you don't know what you're doing.

Trust Provision Designed to Protect the Trustee in Following Authorizations Given in the Trust Instrument When the UPIA Might Impose Liability

The UPIA is a default rule; that is, it applies unless the trust instrument says that it does not apply. Where you want to follow certain authorizations that conflict with those of the UPIA, such as disregarding expense factors when selecting mutual funds, it might be desirable to have the following clauses included in the trust instrument.

Applicability of the [name of state] Uniform Prudent Investor Act (the "Act").

(a) In the exercise of the powers and discretions herein granted to the Trustee, Trustee may reasonably act in reliance upon the provisions of this Trust. In the event of conflict between such provisions and the provisions of the Act, the provisions of this Trust shall control.

(b) The Settlor has discussed the scope of the Trustee's duties with the draftsman of this Trust, especially but not limited to those provisions (list provisions referred to) which might be construed to hold the Trustee harmless in contrast to that standard imposed upon Trustee by the Act. The Settlor, nevertheless, desires that the provisions of this Trust shall control and has initialed the margin of this page to confirm the same. The Settlor states further that he has appointed the named Trustee not for any investment expertise (Settlor deems it highly likely that Trustee will hire investment counsel) but by reason of Settlor" confidence in Trustee" judgment, probity and knowledge of Settlor's intentions as expressed for Trustee.

Settlor's Initials

____

States that Follow the Prudent Investor Rule

Alabama*
Alaska
Arizona
Arkansas
California
Colorado
Connecticut
Delaware*
District of Columbia
Florida*
Georgia*
Hawaii
Idaho
Illinois
Indiana
Iowa
Kansas
Maine
Massachusetts
Maryland**
Michigan
Minnesota
Missouri
Montana
Nebraska
Nevada
New Jersey
New Hampshire
New Mexico
New York
North Carolina
North Dakota
Ohio
Oklahoma
Oregon
Pennsylvania
Rhode Island
South Carolina
South Dakota*
Tennessee*
Texas*
Utah
Vermont
Virginia
Washington
West Virginia
Wyoming

* similar
**substantially similar

This list was considerably shorter when this book was first published in 1999

3. Specifically Authorized Investments

At one time, many states listed the permissible investments for trustees if the settlor did not made broader provisions in the trust instrument. A small handful of such states still have such lists. The lists of authorized investments have been broadened over time, but they remain restrictive. Where common stock investment is permitted, there are limits on their percentage of total assets, for instance.

If you are subject to the laws of a legal list state, your responsibilities are limited and well defined. However the trust may be handicapped in terms of capital appreciation, and you can expect complaints from those who might benefit from broader investment choices.

States that Limit Trustees to Listed Investments

Alabama (combined with variation of Prudent Investor Rule)
Kentucky

C. Common Law

Common law was important for trust investment purposes a long-time ago, but its value in that respect is now primarily for historians. The old common law principles are probably too antiquated to be of much use to a modern investor, although the duty to preserve and protect property and make it productive, coupled with the requirement of prudence, still makes sense. Virtually every state and the District of Columbia have laws governing trust investments that originated from common law in one way or another. It is unlikely that you will need to fall back on common law because state laws or the terms of the governing trust instrument are not sufficiently clear direction for you. In that unlikely event, let a competent attorney decide for you what you should do.

Chapter IV
Your Investment Choices

This book doesn't include chapters on general investment management because the subject is too broad and is very well covered elsewhere. However, we would like you to think about specific classes of assets in terms of their suitability as trust investments. Asset selection may be entirely up to you, or there could be assets that you are required to retain or invest in. There could also be assets that you are merely requested to use or consider using. In each case, you must determine if are they appropriate for the trust, and if you have (or can acquire) the necessary expertise to deal with them. While we can't review all possible asset classes here (some financial planning software provides for thousands), we'll look at a representative group.

The basic common law requirements of trust assets are that they should be:

- transferable
- marketable
- easily valued
- capable of being protected
- productive of income

This doesn't necessarily have to apply to all of the assets of a particular trust, but it should apply to enough of them so that you can perform your duties as a trustee. Holding assets that lack one or more of the above criteria may not have much impact if they amount to less than 10% of the trust property, but beyond that the problems listed below could become significant.

You can't sell or exchange assets that aren't transferable. Someday you'll need to transfer trust assets to those who become entitled to them. An asset that can't be transferred now, because it is under restrictions (such as stock that can't be disposed of until certain conditions are met), may not be a problem if the restrictions are likely to be lifted before the asset has to be sold, exchanged or distributed. Still, a current lack of transferability is a cause for concern, as the timing of the need to dispose of an asset can be unpredictable.

You may need to sell assets to raise cash to meet the needs of beneficiaries and to pay taxes. But while some assets always have a ready market, there may be no buyers for others when they are needed.

Assets need to be valued from time to time in order to execute a transfer, determine the value of the trust, report information to beneficiaries, and comply with tax law requirements. Depending upon how commonly held an asset type is, determining price can be easy and cheap, or difficult and expensive.

You have a duty as a trustee to preserve the trust property–something that will be difficult to do, if you can't provide safekeeping or insurance coverage for it. You could be personally liable if the property is lost, destroyed or stolen.

For most trusts, the assets should produce income. The typical trust is designed to pay a regular income to beneficiaries, and to pay expenses, including your fees. If the assets don't produce enough income to carry out the purposes of the trust, you may have to sell trust property to raise cash to meet various needs, reducing the value of the trust. Beware especially of assets that, while they generate no real income, create a tax liability because they are nevertheless considered to create income for tax purposes. This "phantom" income can arise in a number of ways, such as from making non-deductible mortgage payments on an income-producing property that exceed the income.

A. Cash and Cash Equivalents

You know what cash is. The equivalents are such things as short-term certificates of deposit, money market accounts, commercial paper and other such vehicles. Some can be converted quickly to cash without loss of value. Others may have maturity dates, although not longer than one year, and there could be minimal gains or losses if they are converted to cash (such as a penalty for early redemption of a certificate of deposit) before they mature. Although it's possible for some equivalents to decline in value, careful selection and an emphasis on quality can keep this possibility remote. The purpose of cash and cash-equivalents is for:

- expected expenditures, such as those for taxes, fees and anticipated distributions
- unexpected expenditures, such as sudden needs of beneficiaries
- investment opportunities.

Cash and equivalents are generally safe, easy to care for, present no valuation problems and are readily transferable. There should be a reasonable amount of them on hand, but they should not be used as a long-term investment unless there is a direction to that effect. For a trustee who has to be concerned with maintaining the purchasing power of beneficiaries over many years, cash and equivalents can be a very poor investment, as we indicated earlier.

Not only is there no protection against inflation, but also yields are normally low, and fluctuations in interest rates can result in undependable income. Under most sets of circumstances, an all-cash investment would be not only unimaginative, but also imprudent. If you take this route, someday a judge is likely to say to you, "surely, you could have done a little better than this."

What Are Long-Term and Short-Term Investments?

Most professional consultants say that the dividing line between "long" and "short" is five years. They regard long-term assets as those that may grow in value over several years, but which will fluctuate in value within shorter periods. If you're going to spend a fixed amount of dollars within five years, these consultants recommend investing those dollars in cash or cash equivalents to avoid possible declines in value. In other words, create reserves.

B. Marketable Securities

These are the investments of choice for professional trustees. Marketable securities are publicly traded stocks and bonds, also called "listed" because they are listed in print or electronically at their current values, along with other kinds of information. They are called "marketable" because they can be readily bought and sold for the most part. But "marketable" is not the same as "liquid," as a sale at any time after purchase might result in substantial gains or losses.

There are dozens of sub-classes of listed securities, each of which has different characteristics, and they can be used in different combinations to meet practically any investment objective. For trust investment purposes, it is sufficient in most cases to divide marketable securities into five broad classes, and you might need to use only two or three of the classes listed in the following insert.

Broad Categories of Marketable Securities

- Large cap equity (Standard & Poor's 500 Index type)
- Small cap equity (companies with less than a $500 million market capitalization)
- International equity (securities held by Morgan Stanley Capital International's EAFE [Europe, Australia, Far East] Index)
- Investment grade fixed income (minimum rating BBB)

  short term

intermediate term

long-term

- International fixed income (such as those found in the Solomon Brothers Non-United States Dollar World Government Bond Index)

From an administrative perspective, many marketable securities are ideal investments for a trust, because usually they can be sold quickly with a reasonably good idea of what the sale will bring - very convenient if an unexpected need for cash arises. They are generally easy to value; if quotes are not available from a newspaper, a brokerage firm can find prices for you. You can keep stock or bond certificates in a safe deposit vault, but more likely you will use safekeeping provided by a bank or a brokerage firm. These companies in turn use depository trust companies, where changes in ownership are made electronically. As explained in Part One, Chapter II, it is both efficient and convenient when the securities never have to move physically from the depository trust company, no matter how many changes in ownership or other transactions take place.

From a legal perspective, there is so much information available about individual securities and the securities markets, that it is relatively easy to document investment decisions pertaining to them, using references to authoritative sources.

From the investment perspective, there are more advantages. If you intend to invest in individual issues, there is considerable research available from brokerage firms and investor service providers on marketable securities, particularly on those issued by the larger companies. For most trusts, there is sufficient variety among the different classes of marketable securities for you to create an allocation among them to suit practically any investment or tax objective.

Investing in individual securities normally means working with a broker. It is beyond the scope of this book to go into the details of dealing with brokers, but you should know that it is unfair to expect the average broker to have a comprehensive understanding of fiduciary responsibility. Internal brokerage systems normally protect you against such things as individual brokers mistakenly opening a margin account for a trust, but you need to be careful. Some brokers are more qualified than others with respect to trusts. Ask the brokerage office manager who these might be,

You should do a background check on your broker as a matter of due diligence. You should also make sure that registration of trust securities in the name of a brokerage firm nominee does not violate a duty to keep them registered in your name as trustee if there is no nominee provision in the trust instrument. In managing expenses, you'll have to satisfy yourself that the broker's commission scales are in line for the services received, and that executions are not unfairly benefiting a dealer.

Checking Out Your Broker

Call the National Association of Securities Dealers at (800) 289-9999. You can learn from one of its representatives if a broker is currently registered and if he or she has ever been the subject of an official sanction. You can obtain a written history of a broker's disciplinary record from this source.

Call your state securities commissioner. The office will have information that is more current and complete. You can obtain the telephone number from:

North American Securities Administrators Association (NASAA)
10 G Street, Northeast
Washington, DC 20002
(202) 737-0900.

You don't have to worry too much about your broker's firm failing. Before that can happen, the cash and securities in an individual investor's account, including accounts for trustees, would be transferred to a healthy firm, often with the involvement of regulators. The Securities Investor Protection Corporation (SIPCO) insures accounts for up to $500,000, including $100,000 in cash. SIPCO processing of claims can take three months or so, however, before an investor receives his or her cash and securities. You can insure any excess, which is what many firms do themselves by purchasing "excess-SIPCO insurance." You need to find out what your brokerage firm has to offer along these lines.

If you prefer to hire a professional money manager, such as an independent investment firm or a bank, there are hundreds to select from, but you should try to identify those who understand the particulars of trust investing. Many independent investment firms have managers who formerly worked in bank trust departments, and they may have a number of trustees as clients. Ask about this.

If you are legally able to delegate investment discretion, you should avoid the type of manager who runs all of the accounts according to one model. In the name of discipline (and their own convenience), such managers sell securities in any account that does not fit their model, without regard for the effect on the particular client's tax position or other needs. This Procrustean bed approach is unlikely to suit your trust's objectives. Your agreement with a money manager should confine him or her to carrying out your investment policy and make clear when certain specific actions should not be taken without your approval. You may be permitted to delegate investment management, but generally not the management of investment decisions.

How many different managers should you have? The answer has to do with the size of the trust and the cost-effectiveness of paying for a multi-manager approach. A $50 million trust can justify the use of several managers specializing in different investment styles, although the fees of a single manager would cost less because of the way in which investment management fees are typically scaled. A single manager who runs balanced portfolios should be sufficient for most accounts of up to $5,000,000, although more than one might be justified where there are specialized assets involved.

A Suggested "Appointment of Investment Manager"

Investment managers have their own agreements which you will be required to sign, and which you must review, and modify if necessary, to suit your purposes. The following Appointment of Investment Manager form is something you might consider incorporating in such an agreement or using as a separate document when retaining such a manager.

Appointment of Investment Manager

____________ Date __________

____

____

Dear Sir/Madam:

We are Trustees of the following Trust:

____

We hereby appoint you our agent to perform all necessary, desirable and advisable functions in connection with investing those assets of the Trust which we hereby transfer to you as shown on the attached schedule.

As our agent, you are instructed that the purposes of the Trust are as shown on the attached Investment Policy Statement ("IPS") and, by acceptance of this agency, you acknowledge that you have examined the IPS and that adhering to it will not involve any conflicts with your obligations under the applicable regulations to which you are subject.

Your fee will be:

____

Conditions of Appointment:

1. This appointment is terminable by either of us with or without cause at any time.
2. Our account will be held in our name as Trustees and all securities and other assets in your custody will be protected by SECURITIES INVESTOR PROTECTION CORPORATION up to $500,000 (including $100,000 for cash) and you will provide $49,500,000 of excess protection per account by a private insurer; you have furnished us with a certificate from the insurer evidencing such coverage and will notify us of any change or termination of such coverage no later than 24 hours after such change or termination.
3. You will furnish us with monthly statements of the account in sufficient detail so that we may adequately monitor your performance in compliance with the scope and tenure of this appointment.

Very truly yours,

_________________, Trustee

_________________, Trustee

Accepted this ____ day of __________, 1999,

_________________, Agent

C. Mutual Funds

Mutual funds, one type of marketable security, offer an inexpensive method of obtaining a multi-manager approach. A trustee with limited assets can invest in one or more mutual funds to obtain broad diversification of asset type and investment style, if this is desirable. Investment in different kinds of funds can be used to balance different types of risks, as would be the case with combining a large-cap value fund, a small-cap growth fund and an intermediate term United States Government bond fund in a trust portfolio. A service, such as Lipper or Morningstar, can provide considerable information on each of the several thousand funds that are available.

There are some cautions to observe, however. When you use mutual funds as an investment vehicle, you depend upon fund managers who have no awareness of your function as a trustee. It will be up to you to monitor the funds you select to see that they adhere to the terms of your investment policy, and to make changes when the policies of the fund manager no longer meet your requirements. You'll also have to select and monitor funds with an eye to their expenses, including taxes. No-load funds that are "tax managed" may be preferable in many cases. Furthermore, you will have to manage fund distributions, so far as you are able to, as a fund's timing of these distributions won't ordinarily meet the cash flow requirements of the beneficiaries. The typical single year-end distribution that many mutual funds make would be unsuitable for a beneficiary needing monthly income remittances.

D. Life Insurance Policies

Policies of life insurance are found most often in specialized insurance trusts, but they can be found in other trusts as well. This most often happens in the case of life insurance where a decedent owns a policy on the spouse's life and arranges for it to become part of a trust that won't be taxed as part of the survivor's estate. Because insurers are not always willing to pay claims in full (such as where the insured smoked but just might possibly have lied about it to qualify for cheaper no-smoker premiums), the trustee should be authorized to compromise claims.

You should periodically review life insurance policies for their value and the underlying credit-worthiness of the insurer. This exercise of diligence also applies to annuity policies if your trust holds them. *See* Exhibit I, A Variety of Trusts in the Appendix for more on life insurance where we describe the irrevocable life insurance trust.

E. Real Estate

For centuries after the Norman Conquest, real estate was the only asset held in trust. In all its varieties, real estate is still a frequent holding in trusts, especially those managed by individual trustees. A settlor who has been a successful investor in real estate can hardly be blamed for wanting such an investment to be held as part of a trust for his survivors. It can be a productive asset in terms of income and capital appreciation. A trust may also be a good means of keeping a large real estate holding intact for a family.

However, real estate may not be productive, valuation is often expensive and difficult, and a large holding may pose problems in terms of portfolio diversification. It may also be expensive to manage in terms of special expertise required and its carrying costs, including property taxes, insurance, management fees, and repairs. Sales commissions and closing fees are also high. The taxation of real estate can be complex, too.

Sometimes a decedent leaves a residence in trust for a surviving spouse. This often comes about as a result of "tight" federal estate tax planning, such as when a combined estate of $1,400,000 is divided into two separate shares of $700,000 for each spouse, so that each can create a credit shelter trust for the other. The limited selection of assets in an estate this size may result in shoehorning the residence into a trust. You might also be asked to be trustee of a Qualified Personal Residence Trust (see Exhibit I, Appendix). Whether or not it is a good idea psychologically for someone to live in a home he or she can no longer call their own, isn't always considered, and you might have to deal with a reluctant tenant.

In these situations the problem is that the tenant may consider the residence "his or hers," and this may make it difficult for the trustee to carry out inspections and repairs, and the like. If the survivor grows feeble with age, these problems can become worse, and the trustee might also have to become involved in relocating the tenant. At the least, the trustee should have provisions in the trust instrument enabling him or her to properly manage the asset, and there should be approval in the instrument or in the law for retaining a non-income-producing asset.

More often the real estate is income-producing commercial property, such as that with such improvements as an apartment or office building, or a factory. This type of asset requires varying degrees of attention and special handling. Insurance needs to be kept in force, taxes have to be paid, and even pastures may require maintenance in the way of fencing or flood control.

Environmental Issues

A major consideration for real estate – and residential property is not excluded – is whether or not there are environmental issues to deal with. In terms of liability prevention, there nearly always are. In 1980, the Comprehensive Environmental Response, Compensation and Liability Act (CERCLA) was passed. This gave the federal government the right to clean up contaminated property and recover their costs for doing so from "potential responsible persons," which by now, as the law has evolved, can include individuals and organizations fairly remote in their link to a contaminated property. A related federal act with similar provisions, the Solid Waste Disposal Act/Resource Conservation and Recovery Act (which is referred to here – and only here-as the Tank Act) covers underground storage tanks, which CERCLA does not.

This is serious business. If your trust holds a plot of land next to a chemical plant, and the grass on your plot is growing in interesting shades of orange and blue, the trust, and possibly you personally as the trustee, might be liable for a very large clean up expense.

That a trust might incur such an expense is bad enough. This could seriously impair the trust corpus or even wipe it out. It could injure and stir up beneficiaries damaged by losses in their benefits. From your perspective, what is much worse is that the expense could become your obligation, shared with the trust and others, or just yours alone. There are a number of ways you might become a target for the Environmental Protection Agency, the federal enforcer of CERCLA. One obvious example is knowing that the chemical plant is dumping on trust property and doing nothing about it. Another, slightly less obvious, is being aware that your trust has a potential liability for a cleanup, but going ahead and exhausting the trust assets with payments to beneficiaries. The possibilities for getting into trouble are seemingly endless and the law is a complex tangle and still evolving.

You want to avoid the problem altogether, if you can, and if you can't, you better start talking to specialists. Trust and estate lawyers are not usually also environmental law specialists, but they confront these problems and should know where to find help for you.

CERCLA and the Tank Act are not alone in creating potential liability for those who own and operate real property. State laws also hold them accountable. Trustees also face potential liability from beneficiaries who may take exception to "their" money being spent to comply with federal and state environmental laws. However some states have at least protected trustees from unhappy beneficiaries. These states have passed statutes that authorize such trustees to spend trust money to fix their environmental problems. Some states have also passed legislation to protect innocent trustees who didn't create their problems, but an exemption from personal liability may be conditional upon notifying the state's environmental protection department of a problem.

Early in 1997, a new piece of related federal legislation was created. The Asset Conservation Lender Liability and Deposit Insurance Protection Act (Asset Conservation Act) modified both CERCLA and the Tank Act. Generally this Act limited the liability of a trustee to the assets in the trust, but did continue a trustee's personal liability under certain circumstances, such as a trustee's manipulation of trusts to avoid clean-up costs. More importantly, it withdrew limits on liability where a trustee's negligence contributed to contamination. While you might not be at personal risk for accepting a trust with contaminated real estate under many circumstances, you still can become open to such risk later through negligence.

The Asset Conservation Act also listed eight activities a trustee could engage in or not engage in without incurring personal liability:

- undertaking a response action with respect to CERCLA
- addressing a hazardous substance condition in a legal manner
- resigning as trustee
- providing for environmental compliance in the trust instrument (if possible)
- monitoring or inspecting the asset
- advising other parties to the trust
- changing the relationship of the trustee to the trust
- administering property that was already contaminated when the trustee became owner

Avoiding a problem is the best answer, and it is relatively simple. If you are expected to hold real estate in trust, you should require that an environmental risk assessment be made by qualified experts to determine if there are problems. The property owner can not release you from liability for contamination on an uninvestigated property. If the investigation uncovers problems, you should require that they be remedied before you become involved, and see to it that they are. Otherwise you should decline to accept the asset or decline to serve as trustee. If you are already a trustee and you uncover problems, you can resign if other actions are not feasible.

Sometimes a formal investigation isn't necessary, if common sense tells you to stay away. One of the authors in his capacity as a trust officer once visited a potential property for a trust that was to be distributed from an estate: a bindery in a neighborhood abundant with razor wire and guard dogs. It was next to an abandoned junkyard with pools of oil on the ground. There were underground oil tanks on the property, as well as many half-filled drums of unidentified chemicals. Panels had come off the walls revealing crumbling asbestos. The trust's ownership in this EPA nightmare was to be a one-twelfth interest, and the other owners were not inclined to take on any clean-up expenses. An appointment as trustee was quickly declined.

A trustee should have comprehensive general liability insurance. Most post-1985 policies of this nature have "pollution exclusions," although these may not necessarily apply if the insured is not the polluter or if the problem is not strictly one of pollution. Umbrella policies and excess insurance policies should also be reviewed to see if they cover pollution liability left out by primary policies. Environmental Impairment Liability and Environmental Hazards Insurance may also be available. It is even possible that you, as trustee, might have the good luck to be covered by insurance policies held by other parties, such as a vendor's policy for coverage of you as purchaser. All of these options should be explored.

All trusts with real estate assets should have provisions in the instrument enabling you to deal with the environmental problems. All should also have general provisions that enable you to perform the basics of real estate investing, such as the ability to execute contracts. Depending upon the type of real estate represented, other provisions may be needed. Raw land may need to be subdivided, for instance, and the trustee may need to be exempted from making it produce income.

F. Business Interests

When you consider how many entrepreneurs there are in this country, it is no wonder that trustees are frequently faced with the possibility of holding closely held stock as a trust asset. For some trusts, a business interest may constitute the major asset. Entrepreneurs sometimes look at a trust as a way of preserving a business interest as a lasting monument to themselves, a kind of financial mausoleum. Many of them are convinced that their businesses can be continued successfully by their offspring. This conviction may have no basis in fact, as roughly two-thirds of family-owned businesses fail within three generations. Some business interests end up in a trust only because their owners were unsuccessful in disposing of them before they died.

However, a trust can keep a business interest intact for a family that consists of members with varying degrees of activity in it and passion for it. The trust may be the only means of providing some of them with a lasting job and others with an income while being fair to all. The basic problems for you as trustee are those of income production, marketability and valuation, but the daily responsibilities can be heavy.

A minority interest may leave you with relatively passive duties and a worrisome lack of control. A majority interest may require your full-scale involvement: learning the business, finding, overseeing and retaining managers, dealing with minority interests and determining if, when and how the business is to be sold. A seat on the board may serve to keep you informed and give you some measure of oversight. It may also put you into a conflict-of-interest situation between beneficiaries and non-beneficiary shareholders, because as a director you also have a loyalty to the shareholders. With business holdings in the trust, the beneficiaries are less likely to be isolated from one another and the potential for conflicts rides high. They can fight each other, and they can unite and fight you.

1. Subchapter S Corporations

Some corporations are organized under Subchapter S of the Internal Revenue Code (as opposed to those organized under subchapter C). "S" corporations are taxed in a way similar to the way partnerships are taxed while retaining other desirable attributes of a "C" corporation, such as unlimited life and limited liability. If you hold Subchapter S stock in your trust, it is probable that this was carefully planned for in the estate plans of its owner, but in case it wasn't, the following information may alert you to a problem that can extend beyond the trust. Trusts may be S Corporation shareholders, but only at the peril of destroying the S status of the corporation if they are not eligible shareholders.

A trust can be an eligible shareholder if designed to be a Qualified Subchapter S Trust (QSST) by incorporating these features:

- all of the income must be distributed
- there can be only one current income beneficiary
- the beneficiary must be a United States citizen
- principal distributions must be only to that beneficiary
- the income beneficiary's interest must be for life or for the term of the trust
- the beneficiary must receive all of the assets in the trust if it ends before he dies
- the trust must be a United States trust

Two types of grantor trust also qualify. One is where the grantor is treated as the owner of the trust for tax purposes, because the grantor, not the trust, is treated as the shareholder. The other is a grantor trust controlled by the beneficiaries, because the beneficiaries, who are treated as the owners of the trust for tax purposes, are treated as the owners of the stock.

If your trust doesn't look like any of these, an unqualified trust will work if it is either established at the death of its creator or becomes irrevocable at that time, but there are time constraints. If the trust is included in the settlor's gross estate for federal estate tax purposes, you have two years before you must dispose of the stock, otherwise you'll have to move fast because you have only sixty days. If you do dispose of it, you must make sure that you are complying with the rules regarding ownership of Subchapter S stock currently in effect.

2. General Partnership Interests

A major problem for a trustee who becomes the legal owner of a general partnership interest is unlimited liability for the partnership, which flows to the partners. If the partnership interest is as a general partner in a limited partnership, the trustee has a potential conflict-of-interest problem similar to one that he or she would have as a director of a closely held corporation whose shares he or she holds in trust. As the controlling partner, he or she has a duty of loyalty to all holders of the limited interests.

Another major problem is that the original general partner (the settlor) undoubtedly had special skills and expertise. If you were named as trustee to hold such an interest, it may have been because you have these qualifications; otherwise you would have to retain others who have them. A general partnership interest may find its way into a trust because of an estate plan involving a family limited partnership. You could then have trouble in determining in which direction your loyalties lie if you also hold any of the limited interests for family members.

G. "Nontraditional" Assets

This is a polite term used by bank trust departments to describe assets they don't want. Banks are geared to managing marketable securities, and they tend to discourage the use of other assets, including real estate and business interests, with extra fees or with internal policies prohibiting their use. This is why such assets often end up in trusts administered by individual trustees. They include limited partnerships, tangible personal property, patents, copyrights, and just about anything else that can be owned and transferred to another. If authorized as investments, such assets can be useful in a very large trust that can afford wide diversification. Here are representative examples of less traditional trust assets, with our observations.

1. Interests in Limited Partnerships

These are generally characterized by the potential for big returns linked with high risk and minimal marketability. They used to be more prevalent than they are now because of tax advantages that have disappeared. Where they are marketable, usually in a secondary market, discounts tend to be steep. Finding a value for them on a given date can be very difficult. They might be justified in a large trust, but one has to ask if the potential reward justifies the risk and effort involved.

Assume that the average annual return for your trust is 9%. You are invited to participate in a limited partnership formed to squeeze more oil out of existing wells, and you're told that it should generate a hefty 30% return. The high return appeals to you, but being a prudent trustee you decide that any investment in this asset probably should not account for more than 5% of the trust. Therefore if you buy in, this holding would result in an incremental increase in return for the trust of only slightly better than 1%. This is perhaps less than thirty basis points over what an equal concentration in an investment in an emerging markets mutual fund might provide – an aggressive investment, but at least a more marketable one.

Meanwhile, which asset is likely to be the most troublesome to perform due diligence on and find valuations for? And which is most likely to someday erupt like Vesuvius? This is a good test to apply to other exotic assets, too.

2. Private Equity Investments

Venture capital funds hold unmarketable investments that may be held for several years, and interests in such funds have a limited market. These funds are intended to produce high returns. In most cases you wouldn't exercise your discretion to invest in a venture capital fund. If you did, you would want to carefully review the fund's past record and management qualifications, study the partnership agreement (if any) to see how fees and the allocation of returns are structured, and determine what controls the limited partners have over the general partner.

3. Hedge Funds

Because of increasing interest in hedge funds (despite some recent disasters among them), we'll mention them here. Generally they may have appeal to some trustees because of their historically low correlation to traditional investments. Trustees are always looking for ways to temper volatility. There are many varieties of hedge funds, which typically involve using risky strategies and volatile assets to achieve high returns. These activities are frequently characterized by high turnover (and associated short-term gains and losses), extended leverage, uncompleted deals and uncovered positions. You need to assess the fund manager's ability to compete for deals and the soundness of his or her strategies. Such investments are unsuitable for most trusts.

4. Tangible Personal Property

Sometimes a trustee will have to deal with tangible assets such as antiques or fine art. A Philadelphia bank once held a painting by the artist Maurice Utrillo in trust. The provisions of the trust called for it to be rotated among the beneficiaries on an annual basis, not all of whom held the painting in equal esteem. Interim storage was a problem, but the beneficiaries were a bigger one. It always came back to the bank with nicks in the frame, and once it was returned with a wad of chewing gum attached irreverently but firmly to the canvas. Tangibles can be things of beauty worth preserving, but they aren't easy assets to maintain or provide safekeeping for. They don't produce income and may be expensive or difficult to appraise. Emotional attachments can create problems. Such assets sometimes can be difficult to dispose of, too.

5. Obligations of Beneficiaries and Others

A loan to a beneficiary is an asset of the trust. If a trust lends money to an individual, assuming that this is authorized and prudent, it should be done in the manner that a bank would employ. You should consider having a regular schedule for payments of interest and principal, requiring collateral, and perhaps also requiring credit life insurance on the borrower's life. Taking into consideration the quality of the investment, which is likely to be less than that of the obligation of a sound public entity, the trustee should be concerned that the trust will receive an appropriate yield. If the yield is low or non-existent, then the Internal Revenue Service rules for imputed interest should also be reviewed to see if there would be an adverse tax result. For if you are making a loan below rates which the Internal Revenue Service considers a market rate, the difference will be attributable as taxable income to the beneficiary.

6. Wasting Property

It's possible that you will receive property that can be used up or exhausted, or that expires "wasting property," such as timberland, a gravel pit, annuities, royalties, or patent rights. The obvious problem is that it will be difficult for you to fulfill your duty to conserve trust property if the property won't conserve itself. A present beneficiary could be unfairly favored at the expense of his or her successor, in this case. Without authority in the trust instrument or in statutory law, you would have to sell the property if it is not a proper trust investment. If it is proper, and you decide to retain it, or if it is improper but there is no reasonable market for it, you would have to amortize the depreciation out of income in a manner that is reasonable.

7. Other Asset Types

Copyrights, trademarks, trade secrets, patents, uncopyrighted literary productions, and unpatented inventions can be held in trust with proper authorization in the trust instrument. This is also true of equitable interests. As an example, you could transfer your summer residence to your brother in trust for his two sons. One of the two sons could then transfer his interest in trust to his lawyer as trustee for the benefit of his former wife.

Can a lawsuit be an asset of a trust? One of the authors met a potential trust customer who thought so. He was impoverished, but somehow thought that, after his death, a trustee could sue his doctor and his hospital for infecting him with Hodgkin's disease. He proceeded to point out, almost proudly, certain of his anatomical irregularities, including his obesity and his bulging eyes, which, he assured his listener, were evidence of this disease and grounds for a successful malpractice lawsuit. His idea was that he would create a trust for this claim and that the trustee would institute the suit on behalf of his survivors.

Possibly this individual could have sued the hospital on his own. And if he died before the suit was resolved, an executor could have continued it in a survival action. However, the estate could not have been settled or distribution made to a trust until the lawsuit was itself settled. The suit was not transferable to a trust or anyone else. It had no ascertainable value, and the proposed bank trustee had no trouble in reaching the decision to decline its appointment.

There is always someone who will want to put an unusual asset into a trust, such as a Denver dentist who wanted to fund one with his wine collection (again declined by a corporate trustee). An individual trustee is favored with these kinds of treasures because the banks, whatever else they are, are experienced enough to limit themselves to investment classes they have expertise in.

At least most of the time. Keeping to our subject of wine, the former Crocker-Angelo Bank in California once had to make good large losses, even though it was only a passive trustee of a trust that held vineyards as assets. The investments soured, and the bank reaped the grapes of wrath. The court determined that Crocker had breached its fiduciary duty in not overseeing the actions of the active manager. Don't assume, because your duties as a trustee don't include management of the assets, that you can overlook their mismanagement.

We aren't suggesting that you automatically decline If you are approached about managing a trust that is to be funded with anything other than stocks, bonds or cash, or where a settlor or co-trustees with unusual investment ideas will have control. You can rest assured that somewhere, sometime, another trustee has undoubtedly been confronted with a similar situation and has managed to execute his or her duties. Properly equipped, you can deal with just about any asset. Exercise prudence and reasonable care and seek expert advice, including direction from the court as needed. But before accepting an appointment as trustee of a trust with difficult assets, insist upon proper powers and exoneration, and know your personal limitations.

It is extremely helpful if all nontraditional assets are addressed specifically in the trust instrument, if you are supposed to retain them or invest in them. The trust instrument should address:

- identification of the property, acknowledging its nature and its benefits and drawbacks as a trust investment, its value and proportion of the total trust property, it capacity to produce income
- its role in carrying out the purpose of the trust
- direction or authorization to retain
- direction or authorization to sell
- where wasting assets are concerned, a definition of income and direction as to its application

Chapter V
Dealing With Parties To The Trust

A. Understanding the Beneficiaries

There is a tendency on the part of some trustees to regard beneficiaries only in terms of their equitable rights in a trust. From a legal point of view, this may be acceptable, but you'll be a more successful administrator if you regard them as your clients rather than as mere legal entities. If you take the attitude that you are serving clients, rather than upholding the law, you'll pay attention to their personal attitudes, concerns, preferences and limitations.

A son can be upset that his share of his father's estate wasn't left outright to him. A widow is often concerned about how the trust may support her for many years in the future, and may be inclined to deprive herself rather than ask for needed funds. A shy or reclusive beneficiary may resist invitations to meetings. There may be intense rivalries among family members. Some beneficiaries without financial training may be concerned about an investment policy that they regard as risky. You may need to uncover thought processes so that you can be responsive.

Then there are beneficiaries who may regard you as a minor deity. This can be a problem because they might call upon you for personal advice or assistance that exceeds your authority as trustee. You may want to comply, but you should try to make them understand where your trustee responsibilities begin and end. The important thing is that you not exceed your authority in your capacity as a trustee.

B. Your Responsibilities

Trustees sometimes find themselves in trouble, despite their best intentions. In the heat of taking advantage of a wonderful investment opportunity or zealously straightening out a claim or error with a third party, they don't always stop to think through how their actions might possibly affect a beneficiary in some adverse way. Another hazard, although more of one for corporate trustees, with their higher visibility, is that they have been accused on occasion of being more concerned with doing things to suit themselves than putting the interests of the beneficiary first.

There are certain duties that you must perform. If you perform them, you should have no difficulty defending your actions, if this ever becomes necessary. These duties can be modified by the trust instrument, but no amount of modification can protect you, if you commit a breach of trust.

The 15 Trustee Duties According to *Restatement Second, Trusts*

1. Duty of Loyalty
2. Duty to Deal Impartially with Beneficiaries
3. Duty to Take Trust Property and Keep Control of It
4. Duty to Keep Trust Property Segregated
5. Duty to Preserve the Trust Property
6. Duty to Make Trust Property Productive
7. Duty to Pay Income to the Beneficiaries
8. Duty to Keep and Render Accounts
9. Duty to Furnish Information
10. Duty to Exercise Reasonable Care and Skill

11. Duty Not to Delegate
12. Duty to Enforce Claims
13. Duty to Defend Actions
14. Duty Concerning Co-Trustees
15. Duty with Respect to Individuals Having Control Powers

1. The Duty of Loyalty

You are under a duty to the beneficiary to administer the trust solely in the interest of the beneficiary. Your fiduciary relationship with him or her goes beyond the fiduciary relationship of agent to principal, and is more intensive.

With respect to the sale of trust property, you may not sell such property to yourself, even if you act in good faith and pay a fair price. This includes the sale of such property to an organization in which you have an interest, if the asset's value is substantial enough to influence your judgment in making the sale. Nor can you purchase it from a third party, such as at a foreclosure sale or at an auction on behalf of the trust. The fact that co-trustees consent to the sale doesn't make it permissible. You may not sell property to a third person with the understanding that you'll repurchase the property individually, or that you will receive some kind of bonus, commission or "kickback" for arranging a sale. Neither can you sell trust property to your spouse.

It follows that the same kinds of rules apply to purchases of property for the trust. For instance, you may not renew a lease for yourself individually for an office in a building owned by the trust. Nor are you allowed to purchase for yourself, a lot adjacent to land owned by the trust, if the trust instrument has directed you to purchase it for the trust if and when it comes on the market.

There are, however, circumstances where such sales or purchases might be in the best interests of the beneficiaries, and in such instances these transactions might be completed with court approval. The court won't normally grant approval if there are other buyers or sellers willing to buy or sell at the same price as you or an associated third party are willing to pay. Once the trust has terminated, or you have ceased to be a trustee, the restrictions on purchases and sales for your own account no longer apply.

You may not use trust property for your own purposes. Trustees have borrowed money from trusts that they administer, sometimes paying a generous rate of interest and making repayments of principal on schedule, but this is a breach of trust, unless authorized by the trust instrument.

You must be studiously unconcerned with the welfare of third parties in administering the trust, whether or not their welfare affects you. If you are doing business with a broker only because he or she is a friend who could use the business, you are nevertheless acting improperly with respect to the beneficiaries because you have put his or her interests ahead of theirs.

You may be administering more than one trust. If you enter into a transaction that involves dealing between two trusts, the transaction has to be fair to both. And what you do for one trust with third parties must not favor that trust over the other trusts. The Glenmede Trust Company, of Philadelphia, spent considerable time and money defending its good name because a beneficiary of one of its trusts detected what he thought was favoritism to another trust. Glenmede had sold a large block of a particular stock out of the latter trust without doing the same for the former, and the stock subsequently declined in value. The suit against Glenmede was ultimately unsuccessful because there were circumstances that supported the company's actions, but in the meantime Glenmede had to bear months of unflattering coverage in the press.

It's important for you to keep confidential any information about a beneficiary that would be detrimental to him or her if disclosed. This is why bank trust departments are continually cautioning their employees not to discuss matters concerning beneficiaries in elevators, restaurants and other public places. You should also not undertake any unauthorized credit or medical investigations of beneficiaries.

Should you find yourself dealing with a beneficiary on your own account, you have the duty to be fair and to communicate all the material facts concerning the transaction that you know or should know. You should not deal with an incapacitated beneficiary or one that is not acquainted with his or her legal rights.

2. The Duty to Deal Impartially with Beneficiaries

If there is more than one beneficiary, you have a duty to treat all of them impartially (which is not necessarily equally) and not favor one over the other. This applies not only to beneficiaries who have a concurrent interest in the trust but also to those whose interests may succeed those of others.

We refer again to the classic conflict between beneficiaries, where the current income beneficiary wants all the income the trust can possibly generate, and the future beneficiary wants maximum capital appreciation for the trust property that will eventually be distributed to him or her. Your duty to be impartial would require you to steer a middle course, investing for both a reasonable income yield and moderate appreciation of principal, assuming that you are permitted to invest for capital appreciation. If both beneficiaries are unhappy, you're probably doing well by both of them.

The rule also applies to such actions as applying income and principal at your discretion, your sale of property to beneficiaries and third parties, your willingness to provide extraordinary services, and just about anything that affects their well-being. We are not aware of a trustee being accused of a breach of trust over a difference in his or her courtesy to different beneficiaries, but we suggest that a trustee should be even-handedly polite, punctual, patient and pleasant, so far as possible.

The trust instrument may permit or encourage you to put the interests of one beneficiary over those of another. A settlor might direct you to favor one of his or her children over older siblings who already have had more financial advantages, for example. You could then do more for that child to the extent of your discretionary powers. However you couldn't take this favoritism to the level where it becomes abusive to the others.

3. The Duty to Take Trust Property and Keep Control of It

You have a duty to gather all trust property into your possession and keep it under your control. A collection of silverware earmarked for eventual distribution to a beneficiary must remain in your possession until the distribution date, unless the trust instrument provides otherwise. Land can be leased, if the trust instrument provides for this. If it were already leased before the trust was created, you would have to notify the lessee and see that the rents are paid to you. The requirement for the physical possession of stock and bond certificates for marketable securities has been relaxed in view of modern securities handling procedures, much of which is electronic, but securities must be identified, in one way or another, as belonging to the trust. You should see that the income and principal payments on notes are payable to you and collect any outstanding balances at maturity.

None of this means that you can't transfer assets to a broker, an attorney a bank or other agent, when it is reasonable to do so in order to properly administer the trust.

4. The Duty to Keep Trust Property Segregated

You must keep trust property registered in the name of the trust and keep it separate from other property, such as your own property or that of other trusts under your control. For example, you can't keep cash belonging to the trust in your personal account to suit your convenience, however honorable your intentions.

5. The Duty to Preserve the Trust Property

You must preserve trust property by protecting it from loss or damage. Examples are carrying appropriate insurance coverage, providing adequate safekeeping for such items as securities, important documents or coin collections, and keeping premises safe from intruders. You might have to make special arrangements, such as providing climate control for valuable paintings in storage.

In selecting a bank for establishing deposit accounts, you must exercise reasonable care and skill in selecting one that isn't insolvent or likely to become so. As a further protection against bank failure, you should also not keep large amounts of cash at one institution for long periods of time. Even if an amount doesn't exceed the limits for Federal Deposit Insurance Corporation, you could be held responsible for interest lost while claims are being settled.

A situation can arise where there are insufficient funds available to preserve trust property. Take the situation where a house held in trust has a badly leaking roof, but there is insufficient cash to repair it, and other assets can not be readily sold to raise the needed amount. Here your duty would be to notify the beneficiaries and give them the opportunity to advance the funds for repairs. The same requirement would be made of you if you were pursuing a lawsuit to restore misappropriated property and ran out of funds to continue the suit.

Your duty to preserve trust property obviously extends to your investment decisions, where you should avoid a decline in asset values through careful monitoring and decisive actions.

6. The Duty to Make Trust Property Productive

This rule complements the one just above. If you have received tangible personal property, you have a duty to a beneficiary to sell it and invest the proceeds in income-producing assets, unless required by the trust instrument to deliver it to him or her or to hold it for him or her. Barring an exception made in the trust instrument, you should convert unproductive intangible personal property and real property to assets that produce income, rather than hold it in hopes of future capital appreciation.

7. The Duty to Pay Income to the Beneficiary

Your duty is to pay the income to the beneficiary at reasonable intervals, assuming the trust's purpose is to pay income to him or her for a period of time. This does not mean that you can't retain sufficient income to pay expenses chargeable against income, such as a portion of your fees. You can also withhold income until you determine how much of it a beneficiary is entitled to. Some trusts provide for the accumulation of income for a lawful term, in which case you are relieved of the duty to pay it out during the defined term.

Trusts are often created to provide for individuals who aren't able to take care of themselves, such as minors, or those who may eventually become incapacitated–a parent or an elderly spouse, for example. Where you are required to pay income to a beneficiary and he is under an incapacity, you must pay the income to his or her guardian or other legal representative. Where you are authorized to apply the income for such a beneficiary, you can do so and not pay it directly to the guardian. If you were directed to apply it, you would violate your duty not to delegate responsibility (see below) if you paid it to the guardian. You would also be violating your duty to preserve trust property, if the guardian were charging for services that you were supposed to provide.

A difficult situation exists when a beneficiary is not able to manage for him or herself but has not been declared legally incapacitated. If you have knowledge of his or her condition, it would be reasonable to apply the income for his or her benefit without authorization, at least until a guardian has been appointed, or until authorization can be provided by an amendment to the trust, if possible.

Provision for an Incapacitated Beneficiary

Incapacitated Beneficiaries: Permitted Methods of Distribution

With respect to any sum or property, whether income or corpus, which is required or permitted to be distributed out of any trust hereunder to or for the benefit of any person who, at the time, is a minor or whom the Trustee of such trust, in its reasonable discretion, determines to be under any disability preventing such person from acting properly in his or her own behalf (irrespective of whether legally so adjudicated), the Trustee of such trust may properly make distribution of the same in any one or more of the following ways as such Trustee, from time to time, in its sole discretion, shall deem to be most expedient in the best interests of such person; namely, by paying, distributing, or applying the same to:

(a) such person directly,

(b) the legal guardian of such person,

(c) bank who, in taking the same "as custodian for" such person "under the" state's "uniform gifts to minors act" or "uniform transfers to minors act" indicates that such sum or property will be treated in all respects as "custodial property" for the benefit of such person in accordance with the provisions of the Uniform Gifts to Minors Act or Uniform Transfers to Minors Act of such state (whether or not such act permits custodial property of such origin),

(d) the parent, spouse, or other individual having the care and custody of such person who, as such person's natural guardian, shall preserve the same for the immediate or ultimate benefit of such person (or such person's estate), but who shall not be obligated to qualify as a legal guardian or account to any probate court therefor,

(e) the Trustee or Trustees of any trust, all of the assets of which are then fully and unqualifiedly withdrawable by such person,

(f) the direct payment of any educational, medical or other proper expenses of such person (including expenses, such as taxes, repairs, *etc.*, reasonably appropriate to preserving any assets belonging to such person) as long as such expense is not the legal obligation of any other person,

(g) the purchase of stocks, bonds, insurance (the term "purchase" to include any premium payment) or other properties of any kind, the ownership of which is registered in the sole name of such person, or

(h) the making of a deposit into a bank, savings and loan association, brokerage, or other similar account in the sole name of such person, provided that distribution shall be made in the manner described in subparagraphs (c) and (d) above only if legally enforceable indemnification in favor of such person is received against anyone other than such person (or his or her estate) benefiting thereby. Even in the absence of minority or disability, distributions made in the manner described in subparagraphs (a), (e), (f), (g) or (h) above shall be conclusively deemed to have been made for the direct benefit of such person. The receipt for or evidence of any such payment, distribution, or application, shall be a complete discharge and acquittance of such Trustee to the extent of such payment, distribution or application, and, except for enforcement of any above described indemnification, such Trustee shall have no duty to see to the actual application of amounts so paid or distributed to others.

What is a reasonable interval between payments depends upon the situation. There could be justification for making only annual payments out of a very small trust with negligible income, but if this trust received all of its income in January, it would not be reasonable to wait until the following December to remit it. Corporate trustees are now more inclined to pay income monthly, rather than quarterly as in the past, and this is probably appropriate for most trusts.

8. Duty to Keep and Render Accounts

You are under a duty to keep clear and accurate accounts showing in detail the nature and value of the trust property and how you have administered it. A beneficiary with a present or future interest, including one with only a contingent interest, can compel you to provide the court with an account of your administration. Many states regulate accountings by statute, and some require periodic accountings to the court for approval. Others require them only at the termination of the trust or at the termination of an interest in it.

The trust instrument can provide that a formal accounting to the court is to be dispensed with, if a statute doesn't bar this. It can provide that you merely submit an accounting for approval to a designated individual, such as one or more beneficiaries. If you have made a proper disclosure of your administration, approval would then discharge you for the period covered by the accounting. This "receipt and release" approach has increased in use among corporate trustees in recent years, but it also takes away from both you and the beneficiaries the protection of a court's experience and scrutiny, as we mentioned earlier.

The trust instrument could even state that it relieves you of all accountability, but don't count on this. This provision would not stop the beneficiaries from holding you liable for a breach of trust.

9. The Duty to Furnish Information

Because the trust exists for the beneficiary, it stands to reason that you have a duty to provide him or her with any information he or she requests about the nature and value of the trust property. A beneficiary is entitled to whatever information is needed to enforce his or her rights under the trust, or to deal with or prevent a breach of trust, regardless of what the trust instrument may say on this point. The beneficiary is also entitled to have an accountant examine your accounts, vouchers, securities and other records and documents. This request must be reasonable. For example, a demand for daily information normally would be abusive – but it might not be, if a major event were taking place in a short time, such as the sale of the dominant asset in the trust.

There is no requirement to provide information that hasn't been asked for. However, a silent trustee is eventually going to be asked questions. The best practice is to volunteer reasonable amounts of information in the form of financial statements showing all principal and income transactions and values at regular intervals. Many trust instruments provide that statements shall be given to the beneficiaries "annually or more frequently." Corporate trustees used to provide beneficiaries of modest-size trusts with statements on a quarterly basis, but the trend has been toward monthly statements in keeping with the practice of brokerages, mutual funds, and the commercial departments of banks. This is probably a good practice for an individual trustee to observe.

It is especially important to provide unrequested information to a beneficiary if you plan to enter into an unusual transaction that could materially affect the beneficiary. For instance, suppose that you plan to sell real estate that is a major asset, and it is an asset that would be in the beneficiary's best interests to acquire. You should acquaint him or her with your intentions and your plan for effecting the sale so that he or she would have the opportunity to bid on it.

You are under a duty to provide a beneficiary with any information he or she should have in order to deal with a third party with respect to his or her interest in the trust. This sometimes arises with respect to future interests, where the beneficiary is enticed to assign a right to income or principal of the trust for a fraction of its value because he or she is uninformed as to what the true value of a discounted interest is. You have a duty to inform him or her of the discounted present day value of the interest, if you are aware of the transaction.

It has been a principle of common law that a trustee doesn't have to provide a beneficiary with information obtained at the trustee's expense for his or her own protection. However there is the possibility that this principle will not always hold. In 1993, both the American Bar Association and the American College of Trust and Estate Counsel expressed opinions that an attorney representing a "fiduciary" (the term includes trustees) has certain limited, indirect duties with respect to beneficiaries. When it comes to lawyer-client privilege, some courts have made a distinction between matters concerning trust administration and those concerning trustee misconduct, and there seems to be more inclination to respect the sanctity of lawyer-client privilege involving the latter. However, the conflict between the principle of attorney-client privilege and a trustee's duty to furnish information is something to keep in mind, and perhaps something to consult with your attorney about whenever you are asked to release information arising from any communications between you and legal counsel concerning trust matters.

10. The Duty to Exercise Reasonable Care and Skill

The beneficiaries have the right to expect you to exercise the same skill and care that someone with ordinary prudence would exercise in respect to his or her own property. If you lack this level of prudence, you are not excused for having made your best efforts. And if you have represented yourself as having superior skills before accepting your appointment, the beneficiaries have the right to expect you to use those skills. Banks and trust companies, who hold themselves out as professional trustees, are generally held to a higher level of accountability than ordinary individual trustees; an attorney specializing in trust and estate law would also be held to a higher standard, although perhaps not with respect to purely investment-oriented decisions. If you are a tax expert, presumably your accountability would be higher for that area of your administration.

What is prudent is determined by circumstances at the time that you exercise your judgement, not by a later determination based upon hindsight. This is why it is good practice for you to document your actions and decisions, explaining the circumstances and your thought processes.

11. The Duty Not to Delegate

As a fiduciary, you are under a duty to the beneficiary to personally perform acts which you can reasonably be expected to perform on your own, and not delegate performance to others.

You certainly couldn't delegate the entire administration of the trust to someone else, even if you plan to be out of the country for several months, unless the trust instrument provides for this. You couldn't transfer the trust property to someone else and then resign after the fact, either. However you can delegate certain acts which you can't reasonably perform, such as the management of distant landholdings, or the preparation of fiduciary income tax returns if you have no training as an accountant.

Originally the interpretation of the duty not to delegate was more broadly applied, but over time a distinction between "discretionary" duties and those of a lesser "ministerial" nature has been developed. Generally, ministerial duties don't require decisions based upon analysis of data and don't materially affect the beneficiary. Using a bank for its safe deposit facilities instead of using your own wall safe (cleverly concealed behind a calendar) would be a reasonable delegation of a ministerial duty. Discretionary duties have to do with making important decisions. Determining an investment policy is a major discretionary duty. Exercising a power to use principal for a minor beneficiary's welfare is another example of a discretionary duty. If you had such a power, leaving it up to the minor's parent to determine when principal should be used would be an improper delegation of a discretionary duty. You could ask the parent for advice, but the final decision would have to be yours.

In determining what acts you can delegate, there is no clear dividing line between what is proper or improper. According to *Restatement Second, Trusts*, you should give consideration to:

- the amount of discretion involved
- the value and character of the property
- whether the property is principal or income
- the proximity or remoteness of the subject matter of the trust
- the character of the act as one involving professional skill or facilities you have or do not have

Restatement Third, Trusts, not yet completed, goes further, showing how the law adjusts to changing times. With respect to investment management, it suggests that the delegation of your investment authority to skilled professionals isn't only permissible, but necessary, if you lack the skill and experience to manage investments yourself. However, you should stay in charge of the management of investment decisions and the supervision of your agents. Remember that the investment principles concerning delegation in *Restatement Third, Trusts* still aren't followed in a number of states at this time.

12. The Duty to Enforce Claims

If you hold a claim, you owe it to the beneficiary to take reasonable steps to enforce it. Normally claims are thought of as rights to be enforced against outsiders, such as vendors, businesses, tenants or professionals. With a trust, it's possible that you may need to enforce a claim for trust property against individuals closer to the trust. The property might still be in the possession of a prior trustee or in the hands of an executor of an estate. It might be held by a settlor who has made an enforceable commitment to transfer it to the trust. It might even be held by a beneficiary to whom you made an overpayment, in which case it's your duty to the other beneficiaries to repossess the excess.

In enforcing claims, you should apply the test of reasonableness. You aren't expected to enforce claims that are clearly uncollectible, and you can compromise claims that can't be collected in full. There is no point in taking action against a beneficiary to whom you have paid more than his due, if you can simply withhold future payments, with interest, to make up your mistake.

If a court rules against you in your pursuit of a claim, you have a duty to appeal to a higher court, but not if the process is likely to cost more than the claim is worth, or if it is likely to have some other bad result.

13. The Duty to Defend Actions

If the trust is on the receiving end of an action, you have a duty to the beneficiary to defend against the action to protect the trust property from loss and to appeal to a higher court if you lose. As with the duty to enforce claims, you should apply the test of reasonableness. You can compromise a claim or submit it to arbitration, and pay a claim that may not be enforceable but also not worth the trouble to defend against.

14. The Duty Concerning Co-Trustees

If there is more than one trustee, you are under a duty to the beneficiary to take part in the administration of the trust. You must also exercise reasonable care to prevent a co-trustee from committing a breach of trust, and you must compel a co-trustee to correct a breach of trust. It would be a breach of trust on your part to allow a co-trustee to have so much control over trust property that he or she could appropriate it. However, this wouldn't normally apply where a bank or a trust company is your co-trustee because of the regulatory requirements which they must adhere to. The trust property should be registered in the names of all of the trustees. A reasonable exception would be where a corporate trustee has possession and has registered the property in one of its nominees or where co-trustees have an account for the trust with an institution using its nominee.

Normally when you are co-trustee with a bank or trust company, the corporate trustee will have possession of the trust property and take charge of all ministerial duties. This is proper because a bank or trust company is well organized to provide such services as custody, tax compliance, safekeeping and investment transactions. It is also subject to state or federal laws and examinations that don't apply to individual trustees, and it conducts internal audits, as well. Nevertheless, you can't assume that professional trustees, corporate or individual, never make mistakes, and you must remain vigilant. You can't ignore your own responsibilities because a professional co-trustee is supposed to have more experience and skill.

If you have a duty to exercise a power, and a co-trustee refuses to concur, you can't merely submit to his or her will. If you can't agree on the just exercise of the power, you should turn to the court for direction.

15. The Duty with Respect to Individuals Having Control Powers

You have a duty to cooperate with individuals having control over certain aspects of the trust administration and follow their directions in their exercise of this control, unless such exercise conflicts with that individual's duty to beneficiaries or with the terms of the trust. Two examples might help your understanding of this duty.

First, take the case of a beneficiary who can exercise a power for his or her own benefit. A beneficiary who has the power to purchase a business from the trust at its fair market value would have such a power. You would have to sell the business to him or her if he or she asked you to. You would be responsible only for determining its fair market value and seeing to it that the sale is carried out according to any other terms of the trust instrument.

Secondly, there is the case of a party to the trust who can exercise a power only on behalf of the trust. This individual has a duty to the beneficiaries that is much like your own. Suppose that an expert in oil drilling programs has the power to direct you to invest up to 15% of the trust's principal in programs that he or she selects. Here you have the greater responsibility of reviewing the motives of the oil expert and making a decision about complying. If you think he or she is disregarding the interests of the beneficiaries because he or she wants to profit from selling participations in drilling programs that the individual is involved in, you may need to go to court for instruction.

You may be directed not to take a certain action without the direction of a control person. If you think that the failure of that person to direct you to act would be a violation of his or her fiduciary duty to the beneficiary, you have the duty to recommend that he or she direct you to act. If he or she refuses, you would have to go to court determine what should be done.

C. Duties You Don't Have

It might be well to state here that you have no obligation to beneficiaries other than those stated above. If a family member or friend appoints you as trustee, it might be with the expectation that you will take a personal interest in the beneficiaries. That is to say you are expected to function as a quasi-personal guardian, doing such things as assisting them in applying to a college, filling out their health insurance forms, or helping them find new living quarters. These are personal services that you might be willing to perform, but you aren't required as a trustee to perform them. Your job is to manage the trust, not the beneficiaries.

If you do perform such services, you are entitled to charge for doing so on a basis separate from your fees as trustee. You can bill the beneficiaries directly or charge a beneficiary's share of income with his or her approval or that of his or her legal representative. It would be improper to charge the beneficiary's share of income for such services without approval, as this would be in violation of the Duty of Loyalty.

D. Liability

1. To Beneficiaries

You have no liability to a beneficiary who isn't under an incapacity and consents to an action that is against his or her interests. The same applies where a beneficiary is under an incapacity and his or her guardian consents. However, you must give the consenting parties a full understanding of what they are consenting to, in accordance with your duty of loyalty to them.

Legal Liability

While a beneficiary's interest in a trust is an equitable one, he or she is entitled to legal remedies against you if an interest of his or hers becomes a legal one. If you are required to pay the beneficiary the net income on the first days of March, June, September and December, the net income available at those times is legally his or hers. If you are required to pay the principal upon his or her attaining age thirty, the beneficiary can take legal action against you at that age if you don't pay it to him or her within a reasonable time.

Equitable Liability

A beneficiary can enforce his or her equitable interests in the trust against you for a breach of trust, and in some cases, for unintentional acts even though they don't constitute a breach of trust. If you haven't committed a breach of trust, you aren't liable for a loss incurred by the trust, such as one incurred by an unforeseeable sudden decline in a prudent investment. However, you would be liable for any profits earned unintentionally by you in selling trust property, although this may not constitute a breach of trust.

You commit a breach of trust when you violate a duty:

- through negligence
- intentionally, even when your intentions are good
- through mistaken use of powers or by misunderstanding your duty

If you make an improper investment because you negligently failed to investigate it, you violate your duty to exercise reasonable care and skill. If you are required to pay the income to a beneficiary but intentionally withhold it because you are concerned that he or she will waste it, you violate the duty to pay him or her the income, however good your intentions are. You would violate this duty if you don't pay the income because you mistakenly believe that the instrument or the law gave you this discretion.

However you don't commit a breach of trust if you violate a duty because of a mistake of fact or of law. If you invested prudently in stock of a company because of excellent financial reports issued by the company, and the stock subsequently declined in value because the reports were discovered to be misrepresentations, you wouldn't be liable for the loss. If trust counsel advised you that you could take a certain action based upon a recent court decision, and the decision were reversed by a higher court after you acted, you wouldn't be liable for any resulting losses.

If there are several beneficiaries, any of them can maintain a suit against you. If you commit a breach of trust for which there are two or more alternative remedies, and if none of the beneficiaries is under an incapacity, they are entitled to whatever remedy they agree upon. Otherwise the court will determine which remedy best suits the purpose of the trust.

2. To Third Parties

In the administration of a trust, you will deal with other parties besides beneficiaries and co-trustees. These include the settlor, agents, vendors, government agencies and others. In feudal times, the trustee was held accountable to third parties as if the trust property were his or her own, free of trust. In these times, the tendency is to limit the trustee's liability only to the extent that he or she can be indemnified by the trust. Your liability to third parties can arise in three ways.

You could become liable as titleholder to trust property. As the holder of title to property of the trust, you are subject to personal liability for property taxes, but only to the extent to which the trust estate is sufficient to reimburse you. However, as titleholder to trust real estate, there is an exception to the general rule of limited liability. Depending upon how you violate the laws concerning environmental protection, you could expose yourself to civil and criminal liability, as discussed in the previous chapter.

You could become personally liable for the loss or injury caused to a third party under the law of torts. If you cut down a tree on your property in such a way that it falls on your neighbor's roof, he or she could then sue you for the cost of repairs, and possibly for other expenses. If, as a trustee, you hired an uninsured, unlicensed amateur to remove a tree from trust real estate, you would be liable for any damage he or she caused to others, as this would be a breach of trust. You would also be liable if you carefully hired a qualified agent, and his or her work nevertheless resulted in damage to a third party through no fault of his or her own, but you would then be entitled to indemnification from the trust. Of course, as a prudent trustee, you should have insurance protection against such incidents, in accordance with your duty to protect trust property.

You could become personally liable for not complying with the terms of a contract you execute as trustee, or misrepresenting facts contained in one. You may be protected by a provision in the trust instrument relieving you of personal liability, as long as the third party is made aware of it. You can also provide in any contracts that you shall not have personal liability as a trustee. Further, you would be indemnified by the trust if you incurred the liability in the proper administration of the trust, provided that the trust properties were sufficient to cover the expense.

E. The Costs of Failure to Perform

1. Penalties

The aim of enforcement is to restore the beneficiary's interests to the level they would have remained at, if you had not caused a breach of trust. The beneficiary can prevent you from committing a breach of trust, or make you redress one that you have committed by making you pay money, making you restore specific property or its equivalent, or forcing you to take appropriate actions. You may be required to pay interest to make up a loss of income to the trust, as could be the case where you left large amounts of cash uninvested for an unreasonable period of time. To protect the beneficiary's interests, the court can appoint a receiver to assume your control and administration of part or all of the trust property. If your breach of trust is sufficiently serious, the court will remove you and replace you with a new trustee.

You might think that a loss committed by one breach can be offset by a gain created by another breach, but two wrongs don't necessarily make a right. If the breaches have to do with related transactions, the losses and gains may possibly be combined to arrive at a net result, but much would depend upon how closely the breaches are related. The gains and losses from two unrelated breaches can't be offset. You must restore any losses caused by one distinct breach and are accountable for the profits of another distinct "successful" breach.

In some situations, the court has awarded punitive damages. A trustee in Kansas was required to pay $2,000,000 in punitive damages for violating several duties to beneficiaries by investing in oil programs in which he had an interest.

Trustees are also sent to jail for criminal acts, which would be prosecuted by the County District Attorney. The most frequent crime committed by individual trustees seems to be the misappropriation of trust property, which constitutes embezzlement.

2. Damage to Your Reputation

Personal financial loss is a serious matter, of course, but you should not overlook the damage a negligent act can cause to your reputation as an honest individual and possibly as a skilled professional. As has been said many times, it takes years to build a reputation, but only a single event to lose it. A loss of personal reputation can in turn cause you further financial losses, if your clients and associates turn away from you.

Chapter VI
Your Compensation

A. "Reasonable Compensation"

Absent a provision in either the trust instrument or a separate agreement, a statute or a court determination may set your compensation. It is well established that a trustee is entitled to reasonable compensation for services performed. In an important Connecticut case *Hayward v. Plant*, it was the fee of an executor that was at issue, but the case is looked upon as establishing guidelines for trustees, as well. The court found that the following factors should determine what is reasonable compensation:

- the size of the estate
- the extent of the responsibilities
- the character of the work
- problems and difficulties encountered
- knowledge, skill and judgement required of the executor and his or her use of it
- manner and promptitude of estate settlement
- results

Potential trustees often overlook some of these factors in attempting to estimate reasonable compensation. And if you ever have to defend yourself against claims that you have overcharged for your services, these factors should be the foundation of your defense .

How You Earn Your Fees: Routine Responsibilities

Here is a list of tasks that you can share with anyone who wants to know what you do for your money. You could go into them in more detail, according to the circumstances of the particular trust.

- receive and review the trust instrument;
- receive and receipt for trust assets; have them transferred into your name as trustee;
- verify that you have all of the assets to which the trust is entitled;
- hold initial meeting with the beneficiaries to obtain basic information; inquire as to their resources, if applicable. Determine their requirements within the context of the trust provisions, such as the need for better housing if the trust instrument provides for this; determine their mental and physical health; consider special requests; agree on frequency of payments and statements; obtain any other items of information as may be relevant or advisable;
- analyze the trust assets;
- prepare an investment policy statement;
- invest assets, reviewing and changing them as needed;
- make payments to beneficiaries, possibly exercising discretion;
- plan tax strategies, prepare and file tax returns;
- keep records and provide beneficiaries with periodic statements;
- communicate with beneficiaries periodically through meetings or other means;
- prepare and file accountings; and
- deal with a wide range of potential personal liabilities during your administration.

B. Authorization

Where possible, your compensation arrangement should be agreed upon between you and the settlor and stated either in the trust instrument or in a separate agreement. If you are able to discuss the matter with the settlor, but can't reach an agreement regarding fees, save yourself pain and decline the appointment. Statutes that set trustee fees are generally rigid, seldom taking into account the nature of a particular trustee's responsibilities. The cost of a court determination of a fee is an expense that can be avoided by proper discussion and planning. If you can't make a satisfactory arrangement with the settlor, you can sometimes make one with the beneficiaries, if it is in their interests to pay what you consider reasonable compensation. Such an agreement would apply, however, only to those beneficiaries who sign it. Neither a current beneficiary nor a future beneficiary who refuses or is unable to sign would be held to it.

C. Structuring a Fee Schedule

Your compensation should be sufficient to cover any costs not reimbursed by the trust, such as office supplies and postage. It should also compensate you in some measure for your exposure to liability not covered by insurance. Finally, it should provide you with a fair profit: the payment for your expertise, effort, devotion to the cause, and any aggravation from the beneficiaries or others. But what's a fair profit?

If, for guidelines, you look to what corporate trustees charge, the information is confusing. Victor Whitney, in his two-volume *Trust Department Administration and Operations*, states that a mature corporate trustee should have a profit objective of 25% of gross income. According to this, a trustee's profit should be $4,000 on a $500,000 trust that earns $20,000 annually (at a 4% average yield). However Mr. Whitney is speaking of profitability on a company's total inventory of trusts, not on each trust, and he says that it takes $500 million in assets under management for this objective to be attainable. Keeping in mind that a bank generally provides all required services internally and has economies of scale, this is probably not a good model for the individual trustee, but it provides a useful insight. Banks can make money on volume; you can't.

A more practical approach might be to first determine your costs and the costs of the services you would outsource, such as investment management, tax compliance and accounting. To some degree, your flexibility in selecting outside service providers should help you to minimize these costs–which is also one of your duties to the beneficiaries. Then you might compare these costs to what a corporate trustee would charge the same trust for its bundled services. Can you superimpose a profit on top of your costs and still be within a reasonable range of the corporate trustee's fee?

You have justification for charging a fee that might be higher than what a corporate trustee would charge. First, you have the ability to outsource to investment organizations that may be superior to a corporate trustee's internal investment department (or affiliate). You can also make changes in your selections as often as needed. A bank with a mediocre investment management service is usually stuck with it. Brokerage-affiliated trust companies generally have more investment management choices, and the total fees they charge are consequently considerably higher.

Secondly, you are providing a custom service unlike that of any bank or trust company where services are standardized as much as possible and customer contact is minimized. The claim of custom service is also used by higher-cost broker-affiliated trust companies, if they try to personalize service by keeping the family broker involved as an intermediary between the trust company and the beneficiaries.

We believe that the outer limit on what an individual trustee can charge and still be reasonable is probably as much as 20% more than the fees charged by banks and traditional (non-broker) trust companies.

1. Extraordinary Services

If the trust requires extraordinary service, you should charge additional fees for it. Extraordinary services are those that trustees don't normally perform, but which nevertheless must be provided to carry out the purpose of a particular trust. Examples are the sale of a business or real estate interest, locating a missing remainderman, or any other service that might make unusual demands on your time and skills. These services shouldn't be confused with personal services performed on behalf of a beneficiary, which we discussed in the previous chapter. Fees for extraordinary services often can be charged at an hourly rate commensurate with the type of service, a clerical rate for clerical duties, a higher rate for tasks involving greater responsibility or skill.

We suggest that you avoid referring to fees for extraordinary services as "extraordinary fees."

2. Flat Fees and Itemized Fees

It isn't a good idea to agree to act for a flat fee (for example, $3,000 per year), as the only advantage of flat fees is that they are simple to understand. Conditions and responsibilities usually change over the duration of a trust, and a flat fee that is profitable at the outset can become a losing proposition over time. We also recommend against charging lots of separate fees for each type of service performed, called "unbundling" in the trust industry. Beneficiaries dislike complexity, particularly when it approaches what they perceive as "nickel and diming."

3. Percentage Fees

Annual fees can be charged as a percentage of income, a percentage of principal, or a combination of the two. On trusts worth more than $500,000, you might charge different percentages on a declining scale, such as a fee on principal of 1% on the first $500,000, .8% on the next $1,000,000 and so on. This is the approach used by the majority of banks, trust companies and investment managers.

For the typical trust, we recommend charging fees on the market value of the principal monthly and allocating them equally between income and principal, if you are permitted to do so. This arrangement is simple, it is usually fair to everyone, and it averages the fees on principal over twelve months. However separate fees charged on a percentage basis against income may be more appropriate for a trust with a high-income objective, or where there may be big swings in asset values. An example drawn from one bank's schedule for annual fees is a fixed percentage of 6% of income collected and a declining fee on principal beginning at 6/10 of 1% on the first $500,000.

Are you a co-trustee? When you serve as a co-trustee with a bank or trust company, the corporate trustee will insist upon a full fee based upon its fee schedule. It will explain that, if anything, working with a co-trustee actually increases its workload, and that it provides all of the basic services. However as a co-trustee with a bank or trust company, you still must review, analyze and make decisions, and you have the potential for liability. Depending upon the circumstances, a charge for your services of between a third and a half of what the corporate trustee charges should be reasonable, whether or not there are other individual co-trustees.

If you are a co-trustee with other individuals, the work and responsibility isn't always divided on an equal basis. You may have greater or lesser skills than the others, or you may be physically closer or more closely associated with the beneficiaries. An individual co-trustee we know of bore the brunt of having to deal with a mentally-challenged beneficiary in constant need, who was his niece, while a non-family co-trustee in a remote state collected 50% of the fees. Because of moral obligations to a deceased sister, the related trustee did not feel that he could resign, but his share of the fees should have been much higher. Your share of fees as a co-trustee should depend upon what part of the total work and responsibility you bear.

4. Corporate Trustee Fees as a Starting Point

The rates of a large corporate trustee, in this case those of a major East Coast regional bank, may be helpful to study. According to its recent fee schedule, these rates cover investment management (including the daily investment of cash and execution of transactions), the collection of income, the preparation of periodic distributions and the distribution of income and principal. The bank charges separately for extra service, such as "excessive" bill paying, handling special assets, or the sale of property or a business. Its fee schedule doesn't reveal if a fee is charged for a tax advice letter to beneficiaries, or how many remittances, bill payments or remittances are included in the standard rates. Brokerage fees are presumably charged separately to the trust.

According to the bank's schedule, its annual charges are based upon market values and are (or at least used to be) as follows:

$11 per $1,000 on the first $500,000
$9 per $1,000 on the next $500,000

$7 per $1,000 on the next $1,000,000
$5 per $1,000 on the next $1,000,000
$3.50 per $1,000 on the next $7,000,000
$2 per $1,000 over $10,000,000

Therefore the fees for the following selection of account sizes, stated as a percentage, are these:

$100,000	$1,100	(1.1%)
$500,000	$5,500	(1.1%)
$1,000,000	$10,000	(1%)
$2,000,000	$17,000	(0.85%)
$5,000,000	$29,000	(0.58%)
$10,000,000	$46,500	(0.465)
$20,000,000	$66,500	(0.333+)

For your trust, investment management is likely to be the most significant expense if you outsource it. If you used a no-load, low-cost mutual fund family, such as the Vanguard Group, your average investment management cost for investing a $500,000 account in their funds might be no more than .50%, and probably even less, depending upon the funds you selected. If you were to use only one independent investment manager employing a balanced style (stocks and bonds), the minimum acceptable account would likely be higher. In that case, the fees might be something like those that Pitcairn Trust Company charges in a non-trustee role for its investment management services for balanced accounts, which are (or used to be):

First $1,000,000	.60%
Next $4,000,000	.50%
Next $5,000,000	.40%
Next $10,000,000	.30%
Next $20,000,000	.25%

Now we are ready to look at what a full service trust department charges for our selected array of accounts above, with the likely cost of outsourced investment management subtracted. Assuming you wish to charge no more than a full-service corporate trustee, this shows what is left of your fee to cover other expenses (such as hired tax services), your exposure to liability and your profit.

It may help to explain the first line (which we state without regard to any minimum fees a bank or investment manager might charge). The account value here is $100,000, and the bank charges an average percentage fee of 1.1% of the account value, or $1,100. The investment cost, which is taken from the Pitcairn Trust Company schedule above is .60% of the account value, or $600. Assuming that you are subtracting from your fee the investment management fees that go to an outside investment manager, the remainder of your fee is only 46% (approximately) of what a bank charges, or $500.

		Investment	
Account value	Bank Fee	Costs	Your Margin
$100,000	$1,100	$600	$500
$500,000	$5,500	$3,000	$2,500
$1,000,000	$10,000	$6,000	$4,000
$2,000,000	$17,000	$11,000	$6,000
$5,000,000	$29,000	$26,000	$3,000
$10,000,000	$46,500	$46,000	$500
$20,000,000	$66,500	$76,000	($9,500)

Interesting! It is clear from this example that you will have to charge more than what a representative corporate trustee charges (especially if you have a very large trust, in this example at least). This is particularly true if you use more than one independent investment manager, each charging fees that are structured like Pitcairn's regressive schedule, because the total investment costs will increase sharply. Probably no more than one manager is justified for accounts under $5,000,000.

Less clear, but still apparent, is that banks recognize how little difference there is in the non-investment costs of managing a small account and managing a large one. They make their money on investment management, pretty much the same money as the independent investment managers, and they make it on volume, as we explained above. Without a volume of accounts and the capability to manage the investments yourself, you can not hope to make a fair profit unless you charge more than corporate trustees.

Using the rates of other corporate trustees and investment managers will yield somewhat different results, so you might experiment with various fee schedules. We suspect that in most cases, though, you'll need to charge a premium over corporate trustee rates if you are to have a fair profit remaining after paying for all outsourced services and other expenses, unless you assume full investment management duties. We aren't able to recommend a fee arrangement for your particular trustee responsibilities, but the above information may help you to design one–or to decide to turn down an appointment that will not compensate you fairly.

If you wish to charge a fee that is in excess of those normally charged where the trust is situated, keep in mind that you may be opposed by state statutes limiting such fees, courts that may have to approve them, or beneficiaries who object to them. Ideally, your fees should be authorized by the settlor and any conflict with statutes or courts resolved prior to your appointment. Approvals from beneficiaries, if needed, can be difficult to obtain. We hope that the material in this chapter will aid you in presenting a good case for reasonable compensation, *however much it might vary from the norm*, to any and all parties concerned.

PART TWO

Organizing And Taking Control

Chapter I

Accepting Your Appointment And Setting Up The Trust

A. Your Acceptance or Declination

Until you accept your appointment as a trustee, you are under no duty to administer a trust. A settlor may have named you as a trustee in his or her trust agreement or in his or her will, and may have notified you of this, but this in itself doesn't make you a trustee or make you responsible for his or her trust. You can disclaim your appointment and are under no liability. The vaults of bank trust departments hold thousands of wills of living testators who think they have taken care of the matter of trusteeship, but the banks are under no legal obligation to accept when the trust is activated by the settlor's death. They can wait until that time to see if they want the appointment and the obligations that go with it.

A disclaimer may take various forms, which you should be aware of so that you do not disclaim accidentally. A failure (as opposed to a refusal) to accept an appointment for a long period of time after property has been transferred to you in trust, or a refusal to give bond, if required to do so, are indirect disclaimers. Obviously it is better under most circumstances to actively decline the appointment in writing, in a timely manner to the appropriate persons or to the court. This can consist of a simple statement.

Example (for a Will): Written Declination of Appointed Trustee

To: (Beneficiary)
(Address)

Whereas I have been appointed as Trustee under Article ____ of the Will of (Decedent) dated ____________ of the Trust established under Article ____ of said Will, and

Whereas I have not accepted this appointment to date,

I hereby decline said appointment.

Dated at (town or city, state) this ____ day of (month, (year).

(Signature of named Trustee)

Acceptance can also take more than one form. Your performance of the acts of a trustee before your formal acceptance may imply that you have accepted. If you promised to serve as trustee before the trust was created, your failure to disclaim the appointment within a reasonable time may indicate acceptance. As with a declination, a prompt acceptance in writing is the best procedure.

Example (for a Trust Agreement): Appointment of and Acceptance by Successor Trustee

Appointment of Successor Trustee

To: (Named Trustee)

Whereas, in accordance with Article _____ of that certain Trust Agreement dated ______, _____, between (Settlor) and (original named Trustee), we, (names of those entitled to appoint a successor Trustee) are given the power to appoint a successor Trustee if (original named Trustee) resigned his appointment or was unable to act, and

Whereas (original named Trustee) has resigned his appointment in accordance with Article ____ of said Trust Agreement,

We, the undersigned, hereby appoint (name of appointed successor Trustee) as Trustee of the Trust established under said Trust Agreement, effective upon your acceptance hereof.

Dated at (city, state) this _____day of (month, year).

(Signatures of those authorized to appoint successor Trustee)

The above Appointment as Trustee is accepted.

(Signature of appointed successor Trustee)

Date of Acceptance: ________, _____

Once you have accepted the appointment as trustee, you can not disclaim it, and you are under a duty to administer the trust. However lax the standards may be for qualifying as a trustee, the standards applied to your performance as one are quite high. You are now in a fiduciary relationship with the beneficiaries, with all the responsibility that this implies. Some trustees find that it is more responsibility than they had anticipated. If it is too late for you to disclaim, you might still be able to resign, which we cover in the final chapter of Part Three, Chapter VII "Termination of Your Responsibilities," but the process is not always easy or without exposure to liability. It is better to disclaim and not get into a situation that you think you might not want to be in, than to have to find a way out of it later.

B. Bond or Other Security for Performance of Duty

A bond protects the trust in the event that you are unable to make good any losses arising from your negligence or criminal acts. The trust instrument may relieve you of the requirement that you be bonded, but under certain circumstances, such as where you are to serve as trustee of a trust located in another state, you might have to post bond anyway. Therefore your next step after acceptance could be applying to an agency that offers fiduciary bonds. This would be an expense of the trust, but as you would not have any assets in hand at this point, you might have to pay the bond premium and reimburse yourself later from the trust.

C. Receipt of Documents

You should obtain these documents and maintain them in a convenient file:

- The trust instrument. This would be one of the following: a signed original copy of the trust agreement, of which there may be more than one original copy, a certified copy of the original will, or a certified copy of a court decree establishing the trust.
- An original of your written appointment as trustee, if provided under a document other than the trust instrument. This might be a written appointment by a settlor or beneficiaries having the authority to appoint a trustee, or a court document.
- An original copy of your acceptance of your appointment.
- An original of the resignation or removal of a prior trustee.
- Death certificates if needed to transfer title to assets.
- Deeds to real property.
- Original agreement concerning your compensation executed by the appropriate parties, in the absence of a provision for this in the trust instrument or in the applicable state statutes.
- An original power of attorney if you are exercising one on behalf of the settlor to fund the trust with his assets.
- Copy of the federal estate tax return, if assets are being distributed to the trust from an estate subject to such taxes.
- A copy of that estate's tax determination letter from the Internal Revenue Service.
- Copy of executor's final accounting for an estate distributing assets to the trust.
- Copy of a prior trustee's accounting for your approval.
- Copies of your receipts for assets received.
- A federal employee identification number (EIN) for the trust (this is not the estate's EIN if the trust is a testamentary trust); if no EIN has been issued, you must apply to the Internal Revenue Service for one. (*See* Application for Employer Identification Number (Form SS-4) in Appendix)

D. Gathering Assets

1. From the Settlor or Settlor/Trustee

As soon as possible after your acceptance, you should identify all assets that constitute the trust property, locate them and take them under your control. This should not be difficult if you are acting as trustee of an *inter vivos* trust and the settlor is alive and competent. He or she would transfer assets to you against receipt, either as settlor, or as the prior trustee if you are his or her successor. You might need to obtain some missing cost basis information, but the collection of assets should be otherwise uncomplicated. If you are succeeding an incompetent settlor who was his or her own trustee, you may have more work to perform in terms of determining what assets belong to the trust, locating missing assets and gathering them from other locations and holders.

Powers of attorney, if you are relying on these to fund a trust, can be difficult to use if they are not "fresh." The holder of assets may question if the power is still valid if it was executed more than six months ago, as the issuer of the power may have revoked it or rendered it void through his death. Powers of attorney can be "durable" or "non-durable." The former remains valid while the grantor of it is living, even if he becomes incapacitated, while the latter becomes invalid in such an event. If the power is "non-durable power," you may have to prove that the issuer is still able to act on his or her own behalf. If the power is a "springing" power, one that becomes valid only if the issuer becomes incapacitated, you may have to produce proof, such as a doctor's certification, that the settlor is under an incapacity.

As an aside, a bank clerk the authors know of, who was unfamiliar with power of attorney terminology, once made reference to a "durable power of eternity." Now that would be a power with power!

If you hold a power of attorney, or know that you are appointed under one not yet in your possession, you should attempt to see that the grantor of it periodically updates it by re-executing it at least annually.

2. From an Estate or Prior Trustee

If you are trustee of a new trust created under a will, you'll have to determine if you are receiving all of the assets to which the trust is entitled. You would first ascertain what specific assets or what share of the estate is distributable to the trust, according to the will. You would then determine if the taxes on the assets of the estate were allocated and paid properly according to the tax payment provisions in the will or state law. This is why you should see the executor's tax determination letter from the Internal Revenue Service. The executor's final accounting would show the amount due to the trust net of any taxes or debts. You would need to either approve this accounting, insist on any corrections, or require a formal accounting supervised by the appropriate court if the accounting were an informal one.

You would also approve a satisfactory accounting if you were succeeding a prior trustee. It would be the responsibility of both an executor and a prior trustee to transfer all trust assets to you, and you should not have to deal directly with other holders of these assets unless the prior trustee has died or become incompetent. If he or she has been removed and refuses to cooperate, you will need to seek legal assistance promptly.

You will need proof of your authority as trustee, as well as proof of your identity in order to satisfy institutions and individuals that you have proper claim to assets in their possession. You should be able to provide certified copies of the trust instrument, or at least those pages evidencing your appointment together with signature pages and notarizations, or other evidence of your appointment/acceptance. You will need death certificates for a deceased settlor if you have to collect assets for a testamentary trust.

You would transfer assets into your name as trustee of the named trust. Examples of typical registrations are:

"John J. Jones, Trustee u/TA (under Trust Agreement) of William Smith , Settlor, dated March 3, 1998,"
"John J. Jones, Trustee u/W (under the Will of) William Smith, deceased, for Susan Smith,"
"John J. Jones, Trustee of Marital Trust u/W William Smith, dec'd."

You may want a more precise title for legal documents such as deeds of conveyance, but for everyday purposes it will be more convenient to use a reasonably short registration that is sufficient to identify the trust without confusing it with a separate but possibly related trust. A registration such as one of those above would also serve for an account title at a bank, brokerage firm or other financial institution.

3. Cash and Equivalents

You should have a checking account in the trust's name for the purpose of collecting initial cash balances from other sources, depositing trust income and writing checks to pay expenses and remittances. This need not be an interest-bearing account, as you will maintain only the minimum balances necessary to eliminate bank charges and execute routine transactions. You can hold additional cash in interest-bearing accounts.

We recommend gathering all cash, regardless of amount, into this account and using it as a conduit to other accounts, so that there is a clear record of all such receipts and disbursements in one place. Amounts of cash in excess of those needed for frequent routine transactions should be transferred to a money market account or other interest-bearing cash-equivalent vehicles. Total cash on hand should be in relation to the size of the trust and its needs, but $5,000 to $10,000 would be a reasonable amount for a $200,000 trust. You will have to furnish the usual proofs of your authority as trustee, as well as an EIN, to open deposit accounts.

4. Marketable Securities

Before you take in stocks, bonds, mutual fund shares or other such securities, you will need to decide how you plan to manage the investments. Generally your choices are:

- brokerage accounts
- accounts with independent investment managers

- investment advisory or custody accounts with banks
- mutual fund accounts

If you are undecided, a brokerage account is a good starting point. Custody is generally free of charge for active accounts, and the brokerage firm will likely be able to provide you with access to independent managers and mutual funds, as well as to traditional brokerage services. An account with a broker can buy time while you sort out other permanent alternatives.

5. Non-Marketable Securities and other Intangibles

You should place personal loan notes, mortgage notes, accounts receivable papers, documents for patents and other such papers in a safe deposit box in the name of the trust.

6. Tangible Personal Property

You should also hold collections of art, jewelry, stamps, and other tangibles in a safe deposit vault, unless the trust instrument provides for other arrangements. Such property should be itemized and properly insured. Large items may have to be placed in a non-bank storage facility, in which case you must take steps to assure that the assets will be safe and insured, documenting these actions. Obviously you should take additional steps to protect assets that deteriorate easily, such as animals and crops (or that wine collection we warned you not to take).

7. Real Estate

You should inspect each property and make sure that it is in compliance with Environmental Protection Agency rules, arranging for any needed professional inspections. Determine what repairs and maintenance need to be done and how often, and what insurance needs to be in force. Arrange for transfer of title, using the usual proofs of your authority, and have bills for utility services sent to your attention as trustee. You should hold deeds and other related financial documents, in the trust's safe deposit box.

Real estate in states other than where the trust is located can be a problem. Most states have an income tax. Income from real estate may be taxed in those states, and you may have to file tax returns in those states for it. If the state where the trust is located has an income tax, you may have to pay tax on property located within a different state that has no income tax. You may therefore want to consider sale of out-of-state real property. This also applies to tangible personal property that is income producing, if it is located in another state.

8. Business Interests

You will need to determine the extent of your ownership, your rights and restrictions. You will also need to determine what is the best way to represent your interests, if you are not the 100% owner. This might be by holding a seat on a board of directors or by being appointed an officer of a corporation. Your stock or other evidence of ownership participation should be held in a safe deposit box held by the trust.

9. Benefits

Some trusts, particularly those created by settlors for themselves or those for beneficiaries of special needs trusts, can be the recipients of Social Security benefits, pension benefits, annuities or other scheduled payments. You may have to communicate with the payors to have such payments directed to your attention. Each payor will have its own requirements for complying. The Social Security Administration will require direction from the beneficiary or his or her legal representative to make you the Representative Payee, for instance.

10. Inventory

You have to prepare an inventory of the trust assets. This is a record showing an ascertainable description of the property, the date received, its adjusted cost basis and its market value as of the date it legally became property of the trust, which is not necessarily its value on the date received by you. However, the date of receipt or some other convenient date may have to serve in the case of tangibles, real estate, business interests and other property that can not be appraised or valued readily.

E. Organizing Files

You can keep your records in whatever way works best for you. There is no requirement that you keep records in a particular manner, other than observing recommendations for the length of time certain records must be retained. However a typical system for keeping trust files, other than original documents, would consist of the following files:

1. A Permanent File or Legal File, for use from year to year, would contain:
    - a certified copy and extra copies of the trust instrument, necessary information for each party to the trusts, such as address and telephone number, certified social security number and date of birth,
    - copies of approval letters and agreements
    - investment policy statement
    - copies of legal opinions
    - insurance policies carried by trustee
2. Annual Files with separate folders for:
    - documentation file - of investment decisions and documentation of discretionary distributions, calculations for fees, distributions, *etc.*
    - trust statement file
    - tax file - returns and related documents or information
    - correspondence file
    - supporting records file - statements from brokers, banks, *etc.*, canceled checks, vouchers
3. A Tickler File, in the form of a desk top calendar or an electronic file in your computer, to remind you of important dates, such as tax return filing dates, insurance premium payment dates, maturity dates for fixed income securities, and significant event dates (such as the date at which a beneficiary attains an age entitling him to a distribution).

F. Record Retention

How long should you retain records? Here is a suggested guide.

1. Permanent Retention
    - original or certified copy of trust instrument
    - approved accountings
    - receipts and releases
    - deeds and other proofs of property ownership
    - evidence of the final conclusion of legal actions
    - contracts with vendors and agents
    - tax returns

Some say that tax returns can be discarded three years after the April 15 deadline or the later filing date for an extension to file. However, the Internal Revenue Service has six years to audit a return on which it thinks income has been underreported by 25%, and there is no statute of limitations to prevent it from auditing a return that it thinks is fraudulent. It can also audit for a year in which no return was filed if it thinks one should have been. We recommend permanent retention for all tax returns.

2. To the Date Accounting or Receipt and Release Is Approved
    - documents relating only to the period covered, such as investment reviews, statements, agreements, letters of approval, general correspondence, bills, vouchers, and canceled checks
3. To the Date a Legal Action Is Concluded
    - all related correspondence and legal documents except proof of the final conclusion, which should be held permanently
4. Until Their Expiration Date
    - product warranties
5. Insurance Policies
    - liability policies should be retained at least until every statute of limitations applicable to the risks covered in the policies has expired
    - fire, homeowners, and like policies should be held for at least three years after their expiration

Subject to space limitations, disposing of records is one activity you need not pursue with diligence. There is always the possibility that some old, unessential record may be a helpful source of information for a needed name, address, amount, or example.

G. Documentation

Your nemesis is out there somewhere, waiting for his opportunity. Perhaps he was that man that you saw with the rumpled suit in your doctor's waiting room, only he wasn't waiting. He had commandeered the receptionist's window and was pressing her for all kinds of records. As soon as she produced one document and he had reviewed it, he asked for more. You guessed that he was somebody's lawyer because of the briefcase at his feet. All eyes in the room were focused on his back, but he was oblivious to everything except the task in front of him. He had the concentration of someone who was going to win his case. And he was going to win it with documents, whether they were faulty, missing, or evidence of actual wrongdoing.

It's important to keep good records and keep them carefully. You never know who will attack you, regardless of how conscientiously or selflessly you have performed. You need to record not only what you have done, but also why you did it. For instance, if you help a beneficiary out-of-debt with a discretionary distribution, record in your files that you explored other avenues, such as a loan from the trust, and that your use of principal accomplished a true purpose of the trust.

When you obtain necessary approval for an action from beneficiaries or others, you should retain it in your files. Make use of certified mail where important documents or requests are involved. Make more than one attempt, if necessary, to obtain responses to important requests. There should always be a trail of evidence back to any transaction to show that you have performed diligently and faithfully, to confound that persistent inquisitor in the rumpled suit, should he ever come calling.

One of the most important records you should maintain are those that document periodic reviews of trust investments. These reviews should indicate that you have adhered to your investment policy or that you have modified the policy to adapt to changing times or needs. You should take into account the nature of the trust when scheduling reviews, especially the size and volatility of the portfolio. Larger trusts may contain more asset classes, some of them volatile, and more volatile portfolios may require frequent reallocations. We recommend that you perform reviews at least quarterly for most trusts. File with most recent list of assets attached.

Example: Investment Review Document

Investment Review for Jones Family Trust Date: 6/30/2001

Time Horizon: 25+ years

Distribution Requirements:
- Annual fees and expenses of approx. $7,000
- Balance of net income paid monthly to beneficiary
- Income beneficiary has $5000/5% withdrawal right over principal
- Principal distributions at trustee's discretion

Liquidity Needs: Cash to cover unanticipated principal invasions and withdrawal rights

Tax Considerations:
- All income payable to beneficiary in 39% combined federal and state tax bracket
- Realized capital gains taxed to trust

Investment Objective

____ Total Income (Approx. 20% cash, 80% Fixed income, 0% equity)
____ Conservative/ Income (Approx. 20% cash, 55% Fixed income, 25% equity)
____ Balanced/Income (Approx. 5% cash, 50% Fixed income, 45% equity)
_X_ Balanced/Growth (Approx. 5% cash, 30% Fixed income, 65% equity)
____ Aggressive Growth (Approx. 5% cash, 95% equity)

Risk Tolerance

____ Less than 5% decline in value in one year
_X_ Approx. 5-15% decline in value in one year
____ Approx. 15-25% decline in value in one year
____ Up to 35% decline in value in one year

Current Asset Allocation

	Amount	Percent	Within Acceptable Range
Cash	27,000	5	yes
Fixed income	162,000	30	yes
Domestic equity	324,000	60	yes
International Equity	27,000	5	yes
Total	540,000	100	

Current Yield .025

Current Equity Holdings:

Domestic Common Stock*	% of Category	S&P 500
Autos & Transportation	0	1.9
Consumer Discretionary	8.6	12.9
Consumer Staples	24.8	9.8
Integrated Oils	5.4	8.4
Other Energy	1.0	2.1
Financial	11.7	19.1
Health Care	19.5	12.8
Materials & Processing	5.6	2.8

Producer Durables	3.0	3.0
Technology	15.4	11.8
Utilities	3.0	8.7
Other	2.0	6.7
Total	100.0	100.0

S&P categories represented 9

Other diversification guidelines met? Yes

Recommendations: Convert taxable bonds to Pennsylvania tax-exempt issues, now that we have clearer picture of income beneficiary's tax situation, maintaining current after-tax yields.

Trustee

Record keeping means more than making records of your actions, your reasons for them and their results. It also means keeping those records safely somewhere. In case you need to produce records, they should be at hand. Original documents, such as the trust instrument, death certificates, letters of approval and agreements between you and parties to the trust, should be kept in a bank safe deposit box. Other important documents, even if replaceable, should be kept in a fireproof file cabinet that is locked when you aren't using it. These include certified copies of documents, copies of tax returns, vouchers, canceled checks, bank statements, brokers' statements, statements for the trust and correspondence. If your desk is accessible to others, keep it locked when you are not seated at it.

With the universal use of computers, many trustees rely on them for record keeping as well as for performing administrative tasks. If you are a computer-literate trustee, keep in mind that hard drives can crash, and floppy disks and tape can deteriorate. It is advisable to have printed copy to back up your electronic files. Your computer should also have a security system to prevent others from accessing information or unintentionally erasing it. One good feature of using outside accountants and other providers of services is that they will have off-site back up for the paperwork, such as statements and tax returns, with which they provide you. At least they should have; ask to make sure.

H. Obtaining Essential Information

Under ideal circumstances, you would have some background information about the beneficiaries before a first meeting with them so that this initial encounter does not bog down in a quest for data. To this end, if you do not already have it, you should telephone each beneficiary, introduce yourself, and explain that there will soon be a meeting for which you will need information in advance. Here what you should ask for, offering to mail a form for this purpose.

- Full name
- Address, home and business
- Dates of birth–copy of proof of date of birth is desirable
- Telephone numbers, home and business
- Fax numbers and e-mail addresses, if available
- Social Security numbers
- Tax bracket
- Important dates that may trigger a lifestyle change, such as estimated retirement date

- Personal information about health status or financial situation that could bear on the beneficiary's interest in the trust
- Name, address and telephone numbers of whom to contact in an emergency

You could also gather this information by just mailing the questionnaire, which is less time-consuming, but also less effective. A telephone conversation gives you an opportunity to "read" an unfamiliar beneficiary for apprehensions, attitudes and personality – and become better acquainted.

I. First Communications with Beneficiaries

If at all possible, you should meet with the beneficiaries, singly or in a group, when you first assume your responsibilities, or even before. In preparation for this meeting, you should send them an agenda of what topics you would like to cover. Generally the agenda would include the following:

- a review of the terms of the trust;
- an explanation of the duties of a trustee, particularly that of treating all beneficiaries equitably – with special reference to their possibly conflicting personal objectives for current income, capital appreciation and tax treatment;
- an explanation of any applicable restrictions on investment, and the need for an investment policy, a financial review of the trust assets, and anticipated income;
- appreciation, and fees and other expenses;
- a discussion of how remittances, statements and special requests for funds should be handled; an explanation of how the beneficiaries and the trust will be taxed; and
- any recommendations the beneficiaries might have with respect to methods and timing of communication (including confidentiality requirements) and their needs for information.

We prefer individual meetings over group meetings because beneficiaries are likely to be less inhibited if others aren't present.

The purpose of an agenda is to provide structure to the meeting and keep everyone on track, but you should not be too rigid in conducting a meeting like this. Some beneficiaries may be corporate employees, business owners or professionals, but others may be students, homemakers, artists, and such, with not much sophistication about financial matters or how business meetings should be run. Your common sense will aid you in dealing with different levels of sophistication. However, we'll comment on two special beneficiary types that you may encounter, where your attributes of patience and empathy will be tested.

1. The Resentful Beneficiary

We have already introduced you to one of these types: the beneficiary who feels that he or she has been alienated from what should have been "his or her" money, and that you are his or her adversary. It is important to recognize and deal with this attitude as early as possible. It may not be readily apparent, and you may have to probe a bit to uncover it. You might explain that the beneficiary's reaction is a common one when the purpose of the trust has not been properly communicated by the settlor in advance.

Where you detect this attitude, you should make every effort to explain the beneficial aspects of the trust and your duty and desire to make the trust work for the beneficiaries. You should also explain that you have to work within the constraints imposed upon you by the trust instrument and the law. You may not always be successful in convincing a beneficiary of the need for the trust, but you should at least succeed in demonstrating, over time, that you are a fair and reasonable steward.

2. The Grieving Beneficiary

The other special case is bereavement. The trust may have been activated by a recent death, or it may happen that, at some point in the existence of the trust, a beneficiary loses a close relative or friend who may or may not have had involvement with the trust. Therefore you should try to understand the process of grief. Individuals may make a transition through three stages of grief, not necessarily distinct.

First there is a period of denial that proceeds into numbness, a kind of psychological protection from shock. The individual can't accept what has happened, but may go through the motions of daily living. This period can last weeks or even months. The second stage is one of psychological disorientation, which may express itself in feelings of anger, resentment, deprivation, or guilt. The bereaved may undertake actions to atone for the loss, such as self-improvement in relationships to God or to family members, but as reality creeps into the consciousness, depression may become strong. This stage, which may continue a long time, is eventually followed by a gradual acceptance of the loss and a return to normal mental functioning. The lost one is not forgotten, and there may be a recurrence of sharp feelings of loss, but a basically healthy individual regains a comfortable perspective on life.

For you, the grief process of a beneficiary may result in dealing with someone who doesn't respond to requests or recommendations, or who may act erratically, such as by making extravagant gifts to relatives or organizations. The bereaved may seem to alternate between good and bad days. You will need to be patient and understanding, and may need to be resourceful in cooperating with others to circumvent problems arising from the grief process. Sometimes it may be best to put any long-range planning that involves the beneficiary on hold, and stay with temporary arrangements that are most comfortable for him or her, if not the most practical, such as putting off relocation to a more affordable home.

When you conclude your first meetings with beneficiaries, you might help them organize themselves to deal with the trust. The beneficiaries might be especially appreciative if you were to give each of them an inexpensive accordion-type folder containing pre-labeled file folders for correspondence, statements, copies of documents, and tax information. This is not only a thoughtful gesture, it could also help you, in your later dealings with the beneficiaries, if they are able to find papers easily.

It is a good idea to summarize what is covered in the initial meeting and subsequent ones with a follow-up letter. It may seem like extra work, if the meeting seemed to be a resounding success, but such documentation avoids possible misunderstandings of what may have been stated or agreed upon, and it provides a reference point for those times in the future when recollections have faded.

Chapter II
The Business Aspects Of Acting As Trustee

A. Licenses and Permits

As a trustee, you are a self-employed individual in a separate business activity, regardless of whatever other occupation you have. If you are a partner in a law firm, even if there is an arrangement where your fees as a trustee are shared with the firm, the job of trustee can not be shared with any entity other than an appointed co-trustee. The question is, does serving as a trustee mean that you are in a business that requires a license?

We don't believe that acting as a trustee for only one trust or a few related trusts constitutes carrying on a business for license purposes. If you act as trustee for a number of unrelated trusts, then you are most likely engaging in a business or profession. If you do this in your residence, you may need zoning or other permission, as well as some type of license. In a large city, a department in charge of licenses and inspections would be the place to ask what is required of you. A small township might have an officer in charge of licenses or it might outsource this responsibility to an individual who performs licensing together with other services, such as collecting local business privilege and merchant taxes for a number of townships. In a rural area there may be no licensing requirement. The annual cost in a small township, if a license is required, is likely to be nominal, and there may be favored treatment for the kind of business that trust administration is. We are not aware of any state licensing requirements.

It might occur to you that, as a manager of investments for a trust, your activity would be of interest to the Securities & Exchange Committee, but this is not the case. You don't have to be a Registered Investment Advisor to be a trustee. You are the legal owner of the investments you manage and are beyond their purview for that reason. There are enough other remedies available to the beneficiaries from the court if you mismanage the investments.

B. Income and Expenses

You might want to open a separate demand deposit account at a bank or other financial institution for purposes of depositing your fees in it and paying any of your business expenses out of it. Having such an account isn't a requirement, but we recommend it because it keeps your trust business activities separate from your personal ones. It also makes it easier for you to calculate profit and loss. When it is time to pay taxes, canceled checks and a record of deposits for your business are all in one place. Whether or not you open such an account, you must not commingle the trust's money and yours. We recommend opening accounts for the trust in a different bank from the one you use for your personal accounts, so that the banks can't confuse them.

Avoid the check safekeeping type of account, where your checks are recorded at the bank instead of being returned to you, unless you want to risk delays or possible loss of your checks. An account that offers check imaging as an alternative to returning your checks is acceptable. In any event, retain checkbook stubs showing check numbers and payees, as well as all statements.

You can charge to the trust any expenses that are necessary or appropriate for the trust's administration, unless specifically forbidden by the trust instrument. These include the costs incurred in judicial proceedings, the employment of agents, for management (such as the expenses of running a farm) and the maintenance and repair of assets (such as farm machinery). The trust instrument can also authorize expenses that might otherwise be questionable, such as those of landscaping improvements to enhance the sale value of real estate.

We know of one instance where a guardian charged one-half of the cost of his new Mercedes sedan to a guardianship (not the same thing as a trust, but similar). He justified this action to concerned parties by his regular use of the car to take his elderly ward for therapeutic rides. We don't know how the court will view this when the guardian ultimately files the account required of him, but this use of funds would clearly need the approval of the trust instrument if it had been arranged under a trust.

Expenses of trust administration should be paid directly by the trust. If necessary, you may pay them out of your own pocket initially, but you should document them properly before reimbursing yourself from the trust.

The cost to you of traveling to meet with beneficiaries or to periodically inspect and maintain trust-owned real state is a reimbursable expense. If you pay real estate closing expenses from your personal account because the trust temporarily has insufficient funds to do so, you can charge the trust later. We earnestly suggest that you make every effort to have all payments made directly from the trust to the extent possible.

However, there will be other expenses that are a cost to you, personally, for doing business as a trustee. These include the costs of maintaining a home office or other office, supplies, postage, the acquisition and maintenance of computers, copiers, printers and other office equipment, software, instructive material (such as this book) or courses, routine travel, and any entertainment. License fees and taxes are part of your cost of doing business. Legal fees incurred on a personal basis, such as those for advising you on the subject of accepting your appointment, or for defending you personally against beneficiaries, are also expenses of your trustee business. So also are the salary and benefit expenses of an employee, such as a secretary, to the extent they apply to your trust work.

C. Protection against Personal Loss

You should protect yourself against personal liability for losses. Such losses can occur if you breach one of your many duties. You may do something you should not have done or neglect to do something you should have done. You might just say something misleading that results in loss to the trust. Your wrongful act may be either negligent or deliberate.

Many states have statutes that either require an individual trustee to be bonded, or provide that the appropriate court shall have the discretion to require the execution and filing of a bond with sufficient surety, in such amount as the court determines to be appropriate. This protects the trust if you do something illegal that causes loss to the trust, but it doesn't protect you from being surcharged if losses result from your negligence.

Unfortunately you won't have the same kind of access as corporate trustees to certain types of insurance and blanket bonds that protect them from the financial hazards of serving as a trustee. A fiduciary liability insurance policy, which covers errors and omissions, is an example. It differs from a general liability policy, such as an individual's umbrella policy, which covers losses from unanticipated occurrences that result in personal injury or damage to property. A typical fiduciary liability policy will provide protection against losses arising from claims made during the period of time stated in the policy.

It defines what constitutes a claim (a threat to sue for a possible future loss is not a claim; a threat to sue for a perceived loss is). It is also defines what a loss is. One policy may define a loss as a single amount arising from a series of claims or related claims, as when an inappropriate investment strategy turns into a prolonged disaster. A different policy may define a loss as each separate amount arising from the application of that strategy. The distinction can lead to much different outcomes in terms of the insured's responsibility for the deductible amount (called a "retained limit") for each loss that the trustee assumes, as fiduciary liability policies have deductible provisions similar to those in automobile collision and homeowner property damage policies.

Typically, the trustee will be responsible for defending itself against wrongful act claims, and it may have to obtain approval to do so from the insurer if the expense of defense is covered. This expense will usually be applied toward exhausting the retained limit.

Professionals, such as attorneys and doctors, have access to professional liability insurance that takes into account their long professional training in providing them with protection against malpractice. As trustees, lawyers are usually covered under professional liability insurance policies. These offer the same kinds of protection afforded corporate trustees under their specialized policies and bonds (for negligent acts or omissions but not for embezzlement).

If you are a co-trustee with a corporate trustee or a professional, it may be that, if your co-trustee has to defend itself against an action, it may also defend you. However you may be required to pay certain expenses even if this is the case. And if all of the trustees are found to be at fault, don't expect any protection from insurance policies that cover only your co-trustee.

As a sole trustee who may not be a professional, you'll find it costly to obtain the kind of insurance coverage you need, and your choice of policies will be limited. There does appear to be a trend of making liability insurance available to more quasi-professionals. At this writing, there are now approximately fifty types of quasi-professionals included in this category who can obtain some form of insurance protection, including bookkeepers, brokers, consultants, and tax return preparers. The individual trustee is nevertheless generally excluded, as is the individual executor.

It seems that, unlike the highly trained professional or even a quasi-professional engaged in a full-time activity, the individual trustee is regarded by insurers as an amateur pursuing a part-time activity at which he or she has little opportunity to gain expertise. Accordingly insurers consider him or her more likely to make costly mistakes and therefore categorize him or her as a high risk. This description might not fit you, but unless more insurance companies compete to cover individual trustees, you will continue to have little selection and high cost in acquiring effective coverage. With respect to the cost, nothing would be lost in asking the settlor to include a specific provision in the trust instrument enabling you to charge the trust for payment of premiums on a fiduciary liability policy.

Our search for appropriate coverage for individual trustees resulted in referrals to just three companies: First State Insurance Company, Legion Insurance Company and Lloyds of London. You would need to obtain coverage from these companies through a general agent with some degree of specialization. The only one we found willing to make these recommendations was Fidelity Liability Insurance Co., of Wilmington, Delaware, who informed us that the annual premium for a policy covering the trustee of a $1 million dollar trust would be approximately $2,500. We obtained applications through other agents from additional companies, but they were clearly geared to corporate trustees and could not be satisfactorily completed by an individual trustee

Your exposure will be lessened in important areas if you delegate duties to attorneys, investment managers, tax consultants and others who qualify for coverage of their own. You can require in your contracts with them that they have the kinds of insurance that will make good any losses to the trust through their malpractice or negligence. In fact, your own limited access to fiduciary liability insurance makes a good case for outsourcing to competent parties who are insured, as long as you select and monitor them well. Don't entrust custody of trust funds to anyone, professional or otherwise, who is not bonded.

While careful delegation is helpful (to the extent not limited by local law or the trust instrument), you will always be at some risk. If you make payments to the wrong beneficiary, or fail to insure a rental unit against fire and it subsequently burns down, it will be your fault. You should practice risk management by taking all of the precautions that we recommend throughout this book. These include meticulous research, documentation, and the exercise of prudence. Don't fail to maintain good relationships with the beneficiaries. It may also be a good investment to hire an expert to advise you specifically on risk management with respect to your particular trust. The most likely candidate is an experienced trust attorney who has served in the capacity of a trustee.

D. Taxes

When you have earned money, paid expenses, and protected yourself as well as you can, you will need to file tax returns. We hope that you will have taxes to pay, as this would indicate that you are making money. What follows is from the federal income tax rules for 2002.

For tax purposes, a trustee is a self-employed individual. This means that you will likely have to file Schedule C - Profit or Loss From Business (or Schedule C-EX - Net Profit From Business, if you qualify) with your federal income tax Form 1040. If you have other self-employment activities, you will need to file a separate Schedule C for each. On this form, you will report your earnings after deducting expenses. You will be able to deduct certain expenses in full on this form, depreciate others, or choose between depreciating and Section 179 expensing for still others. You would have to attach Form 4562 Depreciation and Amortization to report any depreciation.

Any net profit in excess of $400 as calculated on Schedule C, is subject to a self-employment tax. This tax is calculated on a separate Schedule SE - Self Employment Tax, which is essentially the combined amount both you and an employer would pay for social security tax on your earnings if you earned them working for another employer. There is some relief in that you can deduct one-half of this tax on your Form 1040.

If you lose money serving as a trustee, you may be able to take the losses on Form 1040, but you will be subject to the same rules that apply to all self-employed individuals. If you have too many loss-years, and not enough profitable ones, the loss deductions may be recaptured. The Internal Revenue Service offers no encouragement to wealthy trustees who want to offset other income with continuing unprofitable trust activities. Schedule C, by the way, could be a good document to use in convincing beneficiaries (who usually see only your gross fees on their statements) that you aren't making a financial killing by managing their trust.

If you use your office or incur expenses for other business activities in addition to your administration of a trust, you will need to keep careful time sheets and other expense-allocation records to determine what portions of your expenses are attributable to your trust activities for tax purposes. However, if you manage more than one trust, your business expenses for acting as trustee can be combined on one Schedule C, on which you list your "principal business or profession" as "trustee," entering your Social Security number and leaving the employer ID number section blank.

If you are collecting Social Security, you may want to consider how your trustee fees, which are earned income, affect the amount of your Social Security benefits. Depending upon your age and the amount of your earnings, earned income in excess of certain levels could reduce your benefits. Also, for federal tax purposes, your trustee fees could push your total income to a level where you would not only pay taxes (or higher taxes) on your benefits, but also expose a greater percentage of them to tax.

If your role as a trustee terminates, you should be aware that depreciation deductions you have taken for computers, fireproof filing cabinets, and other depreciable property, may be recaptured, to some extent, in the year following termination. Therefore you should consult with your tax advisor as to the management of such deductions.

Chapter III
Establishing An Investment Policy

A. Why an Investment Policy Is Essential

Before you can get on with the day-to-day administration of the trust, it's time to create an important document of your own: the Investment Policy Statement (IPS). Every investor should have a written policy that governs the investment process, but most especially a trustee, whether the trust is worth $50,000 or $50,000,000. There are several reasons for this:

1. The process of developing policy forces the investor to examine investment objectives, risk tolerance, and any rules or constraints that may limit investment activity. The act of committing thoughts to writing sharpens the focus on them.
2. A written policy provides the investor with a blueprint to adhere to when abnormalities in the securities markets or the economy might tempt an investor to stray from a program designed to carry out long-term goals. This is especially so in bad times, when it is difficult to resist doing something in the way of a "quick fix" to prevent a slide in asset values or in yields.
3. A policy clarifies what is supposed to be done and why, not only for the investor, but also for anyone else who might have to substitute for him or her. This could be someone acting as the investor's agent or attorney-in-fact, his or her guardian or successor as a trustee, or the executor of his or her estate. Of course a substitute might have to change the policy, but existing policy provides a solid stepping-stone to a revision.
4. An investment policy provides the means by which to review and measure investment performance. Are objectives being met employing current strategies? If not, should changes be made in them? A policy helps determine the answers.
5. Objectives can change. The objectives of an IPS can be reviewed periodically in terms of changes in the investor's requirements, changes in tax or other laws, or gradual, long-term changes in the investment climate.

For you, as a trustee, all of these reasons are valid ones to have a written IPS in place, but you are more than an ordinary investor who is accountable primarily to himself. The rules and restrictions governing your actions are more numerous and complex, and they can change, as has happened in a major shift in state law from The Prudent Man Rule to The Prudent Investor Rule. You may have to serve multiple beneficiaries of varying levels of sophistication, all with different personal requirements, including both those with a current interest in the trust and others with a future interest in what will be left when the trust ends. Consequently the list of reasons why you should have an IPS expands.

6. In its positive application, an IPS is a document that you can use to explain to beneficiaries why you are adhering to a particular investment program when it may not seem to them like the appropriate one to follow. You can also use it to educate them about multiple objectives that may not exclusively benefit one party, such as the need to preserve or build the principal of the trust for the remaindermen. In this use, it is something of a relationship management tool.
7. In a defensive role, you can use the IPS to defend yourself against parties who accuse you of improper actions. It can show in court, if necessary, that you analyzed the purpose of the trust, its constraints, and the needs of the beneficiaries, in order to construct a suitable investment program. Further, it can show that your subsequent investment decisions and transactions adhered to this map, uninfluenced by short-term changes in the markets or the economy. Finally, it can reveal how you modified it when the original objectives or constraints changed. As you can see, an IPS is your guiding star over what can be a long voyage, as well as a structured defense against any mutinous passengers making the trip with you.

B. Structuring Your Investment Policy Statement

Trustees of a very large trust, such as those who administer a Fortune 500 company pension plan, would engage major consultants to assist in the preparation of a lengthy and highly sophisticated IPS. The IPS for such a trust might include detail on how many different asset classes should be employed and how each should be compared to appropriate indices or peer groups. There would be sections devoted to portfolio optimization and risk management, as unintelligible to the layman as the tax provisions in wills. There would be a long section on how multiple money managers would be monitored. The cost of its preparation would be considerable, although not in relation to the size of the trust, and policy administration might require a staff of experienced hands. The average personal trust can't justify an effort like this.

It is your responsibility to prepare the IPS. You should make all decisions, once you have good information and recommendations, and the final product should reflect your judgment. If you have no experience in putting one together, by all means enlist the help of an investment manager who has done this for his or her clients. Ask to see samples of his or her work. Ask if he or she would be willing to explain his or her recommendations in a courtroom if you are ever required to defend them. This last question can bring a touch of reality to the process.

Be careful about obtaining IPS advice from anyone whom you might also employ to manage the investments. An advisor/manager should not be self-serving in recommending policies that are tilted toward his or her particular investment style or method of operation. He or she should not de-emphasize or omit factors that would work against him or her in listing criteria for selection. For example, it would be tempting for a manager who has recently lost key clients, to trivialize client continuity in recommending standards for selecting managers.

How, then, do you prepare an IPS for a trust? Although all have common elements, there is no required format. Furthermore, each trust's policy will be unique in terms of its requirements and applicable state law investment rules. The size of the trust alone will have much to do with how elaborate the IPS should be. Any IPS should be specific enough to address the trust's needs and be consistent with the terms of the trust. At a minimum, it should cover:

- goals and objectives
- time frames
- acceptable levels of risk
- risk management
- liquidity and income needs
- asset classes to be employed
- asset allocation strategy
- selection of financial advisors
- procedures for monitoring and evaluating any managers
- procedures for reviewing and amending any of the above

Here we give you one example of a middle-of-the-road IPS for a modest trust subject to broad investment powers. Obviously, the General Objective stated in this policy would contrast considerably with one that had to closely follow the Prudent Man Rule or a legal list.

Example–Investment Policy Statement

INVESTMENT POLICY STATEMENT

DATED MARCH 1, 2002

I. ESSENTIAL INFORMATION

Name and Description of the Trust

The William Jones Family Trust under Agreement dated 4/12/94

This is a testamentary trust for the residue of the estate under Article V of the Trust Agreement of William W. Jones, who died March 31, 1997. The Trust is for the benefit of his wife, Elise Jones, for her lifetime. The Trust was funded by transfers from Mr. Jones' estate. Mrs. Jones is to receive the net income annually in monthly installments. She may withdraw up to the larger of (a) $5,000 or (b) 5% of the principal each year. Additionally the Trustee may invade principal for her maintenance, support, health and welfare, and for that of the settlor's children, Andrea Jones Smith and William W. Jones, Jr., who are also the children of Mrs. Jones.

Upon her death, any assets remaining in the Trust are subject to a limited power of appointment by Mrs. Jones' will, which she may exercise in favor of the children or their issue. In the absence of her exercise of her power of appointment, the Trust continues for the benefit of the children in separate trust shares, one for each living child and one for the surviving issue of each deceased child. Each child receives his or her entire share at age 35. The issue of a deceased child would receive their shares at age 21.

Sources of Authority

This state's Law:

Prudent Investor Rule

Uniform Principal and Income Act

Investment in mutual funds permitted

Trust Agreement:

Trust to be administered under the laws of this state.

Broad investment powers under the 1994 instrument are consistent with this state's current Prudent Investor Rule. Specific authorization to invest in mutual funds.

Corpus

Trust assets consist of cash and marketable securities worth approximately $540,000. This amount could be increased by distributions from the Marital Trust at Mrs. Jones' death, and could be reduced by invasions for the beneficiaries.

Current Beneficiaries

Elise Jones, born 5/1/34, is in good health, and her normal life expectancy exceeds 20 years.

Her other sources of income are personal investments of approximately $200,000 consisting primarily of certificates of deposit, and a Marital Trust established under Article IV of approximately $590,000, invested with emphasis on income. The Trustee of The Family Trust is also the Trustee of the Marital Trust, and investments are coordinated. Mrs. Jones has survivor pension benefits of $17,000 annually with no cost-of-living-adjustment. She has Social Security benefits of $12,400 annually. Her combined federal and state tax bracket is 36%.

At this time, both of the children are living and adult. Andrea is 32 and William, Jr. is 36. Both are in good health. Neither child anticipates requiring principal invasions currently.

Fees and Expense Factors

Annual Trustee fees of .65% of the market value are provided for by letter agreement (attached), estimated at $3,500, and charged entirely against income as agreed upon by the income beneficiary.

Other routine expenses for investment management, custody, tax compliance and accounting services are not included in the Trustee's fee and are estimated to be an additional $3,500 annually. These are also charged against income, per agreement with the income beneficiary.

Total annual routine expenses chargeable against income are therefore approximately $7,000.

Tax Status

The Trust is a simple trust for federal tax purposes. All income is distributed. Capital gains are taxable to the Trust.

II. OBJECTIVES

General

- To invest prudently. Given the authorization in the trust instrument, to invest the principal so as to achieve objectives for the total portfolio rather than for each individual component of it.
- To produce moderate income.
- To meet the periodic need to invade principal through marketability and reasonable liquidity of investments that have an appropriate element of co-variation.
- To increase the value of principal over time.
- To minimize expenses to the extent appropriate for efficient administration of the investments.

Specific

- To maintain cash and cash equivalents at not less than $40,000 for the first year while Mrs. Jones adjusts to possible changes in her standard of living.
- To provide Mrs. Jones with a moderate income of not less than 2% of the annual market value of the principal to supplement her other, currently adequate, sources of income.
- To preserve the principal, and to the extent possible, without reducing Mrs. Jones's income or taking imprudent risks, to increase it at an average annual rate of not less than 5%.
- To minimize taxes for Mrs. Jones.

III. POLICY

Time Horizon

The term of the Trust is expected to be in excess of twenty-five years, allowing for a long-term investment program, but as the need for principal invasions could arise, a prudent approach is to regard 5% of the portfolio as requiring a short-term objective.

Performance

The portfolio is expected to provide a moderate income-yield of approximately 2.5%. The principal is expected to appreciate at a rate of approximately 5.5% on an average annual basis so that the total return should be approximately 8%. This objective has in mind that the related Marital Trust, which may be taxable at Mrs. Jones's death, will be invested to place more emphasis on income than on capital appreciation. This Trust, which will not be subject to further estate taxation, will therefore have a somewhat more growth-oriented objective.

Risk

Some risk must be assumed in order to grow the principal modestly, and the portfolio can withstand periodic short-term changes in asset values and yields to attain longer-range goals. The risk tolerance for this portfolio is established as moderate. Declines in market value of principal should not exceed 15% in any year.

Asset Classes and Allocations

The following asset classes are selected in view of the above guidelines, based upon the Trustee's review of how various asset classes have performed over long periods of time, with attention given to how they tend to offset each other in terms of market fluctuations:

Cash and Cash Equivalents–The purpose of these investments is to provide reserves for short-term anticipated expenditures and unanticipated needs as well as for investment opportunities. Short-term investments shall consist of FDIC-insured certificates of deposit, individual obligations of the United States government and United States agencies, and corporate issues of one-year maturity or less, as well as repurchase agreements and the two highest grades of commercial paper. Additionally, any good quality money market fund, or savings, checking or similar account insured by the FDIC or SIPCO may be used.

Domestic fixed income securities–The purpose of the fixed income segment is to provide reasonable stability for the principal and most of the required income flow for the trust. Any individual fixed income securities shall have maturities of less than ten years, be rated "A" or better by Moody's and Standard and Poor's, be limited to 10% of the portfolio in any one issue or issuer (excluding the United States government and agencies issues). Unit investment trusts may be used if the individual securities within them meet these guidelines. Such securities will generally be held to maturity and diversified by maturity date, as well as by issue. Actively managed diversified portfolios of fixed income investments may be used for fixed income securities. Not more than 15% of the Trust assets (at the time of investment) may be invested in any one of the following categories:

- portfolios that have over 30% of their assets with average quality ratings below "A",
- portfolios that invest primarily in instruments of foreign issuers, and
- portfolios with average maturities in excess of ten years.

Domestic equities–The purpose of the domestic equities portion of the portfolio is to provide a level of total return consistent with that of the Standard & Poor's 500 Index over a full market cycle while maintaining a total level of risk consistent with the return received. The creation of current income shall be incidental to this portion of the Trust's assets. No more than 15% of the Trust's assets (at the time of investment) may be invested in any one of the following categories:

- portfolios that have foreign or global investing as a primary objective,
- portfolios with average capitalizations of less than $1 billion,
- portfolios which are specialized by industry sector, and
- portfolios with less than a five year history of investment results.

At least eight of the industry groups represented by the Standard and Poor's 500 Index shall be invested in at all times, but no more than 20% of this segment of the Trust portfolio (at the time of investment) shall be invested in any one company.

International equities–The purpose of the international equity portion of the portfolio is to provide another dimension of diversification in order to dampen volatility of the major portion of the portfolio and provide another avenue for growth, while maintaining a total level of risk consistent with the return received. The creation of current income shall be incidental to this portion of the Trust's assets. No more than 30% of this segment of the Trust portfolio (at the time of investment) shall be invested in equities issued by industries, services or governments of any one country. Investment shall be restricted to those companies with average capitalization of $1 billion or greater. Foreign currency speculation is prohibited, but foreign exchange contracts limited to hedging currency exposure within a portfolio are permitted.

The following asset allocations are based upon an efficient portfolio for the Trust.

	Lower Limit	Target Level	Upper Limit
Cash equivalents	2%	5%	7%
Domestic fixed income	25%	30%	40%
Domestic equities	45%	55%	60%
International equities	5%	10%	15%

General Guidelines

There shall be no margin or short-sale transactions, no unregistered securities, no commodities or commodity contracts, and no securities lending or related activities.

No holdings in the securities of any one issuer, other than the United States government or United States government agencies, shall exceed 10% of its asset class.

All individual issues held shall be in denominations large enough for efficient liquidation.

Cash equivalents shall have a minimum rating of A-1, P-1. Uninvested cash shall be swept into interest-bearing vehicles.

IV. SELECTION OF INVESTMENT MANAGERS

As the Trustee is not an investment expert and does not have ready access to the kinds of information necessary to manage the assets in a professional manner, the Trustee shall select professional investment managers with ability and experience.

In view of the size of the Trust and its desired asset classes and allocations, a single investment manager specializing in balanced portfolios shall be retained. Such manager shall be a bank or investment management company defined in the Registered Investment Advisers Act of 1940.

The Trustee shall review a profile of any proposed manager that describes its history, good standing, principals, equity and fixed income styles, a list of important clients, its schedule of fees, and its insurance covering the account (including a certificate of its effectiveness). The Trustee shall review the following data provided by the manager or by other available sources:

- Historical performance compared with managers having a similar investment style, time weighted and net of fees.
- Risk/reward measurements compared with other managers having a similar investment style and/or appropriate indices, including but not limited to the S&P 500 Index, the Morgan Stanley EAFE Foreign Equity Index, and the Lehman Government Corporate Intermediate Bond Index.
- Explanation of the investment strategy to be followed and how adherence to it will be documented.
- Familiarity with the applicable rules for fiduciary investing.

The manager will accept its responsibility as a fiduciary to carry out the investment policy and observe its guidelines, using the same skill, prudence, care and due diligence that professional managers would use for trustee clients under similar circumstances. It will exercise investment discretion subject to the duties of carrying out the investment policy and working within its guidelines. It will inform the Trustee of any significant changes in:

- its own organization or effects thereon by regulators or legal proceedings
- structure of the portfolio
- investment strategy
- circumstances that it believes should make the Trustee reconsider its guidelines, such as cancellation or other alteration of its investor protection insurance

It will vote all proxies in such a way as to carry out the objectives for the Trust. It will execute transactions as cost-efficiently as possible. It will keep all records and documentation of its actions that demonstrate it has faithfully executed its duties and provide them to the Trustee as requested.

As an alternative to a bank or independent investment manager, or as a supplement to one, the Trustee may invest in mutual funds. In doing so, it shall rely upon each fund's prospectus and reports, and upon reports issued by generally recognized rating services, such as Lipper, Morningstar or Value Line, to select and replace mutual funds represented in the portfolio.

In such case, the Trustee shall adhere to the stated investment guidelines as much as is practical, with the understanding that mutual funds will not necessarily provide the same conformity to these guidelines expected of a bank or independent manager.

If investment in mutual funds results in insufficient monthly income flow to meet income requirements of beneficiaries, the Trustee shall arrange to maintain sufficient cash reserves in a manner consistent with the above guidelines and provisions in the Trust Agreement respecting the remittance of income and distribution of principal.

V. MONITORING OF INVESTMENT MANAGERS

The Trustee shall review the performance of the investment manager or mutual funds quarterly with respect to the long-term meeting of objectives. Attention will be given to performance as it compares both to market indices and managers or funds with similar investment styles.

The Trustee will ascertain if the investment manager or fund is meeting the IPS guidelines. The Trustee will also determine on a quarterly basis if there have been changes in the manager's or fund's organization, ownership, personnel, legal standing and investment philosophy. The Trustee will consider losses of accounts by the manager, as well as exceptional acquisition of new accounts that could adversely affect service or performance.

The Trustee will consider replacement of an investment manager or fund if its performance is consistently below the median of its peer group over rolling three year periods. He will also consider replacement if the manager has provided a return below that which the trust would have received if invested in appropriate indices for rolling three-year periods.

VI. EVALUATION AND PERFORMANCE CRITERIA

The Trust's total portfolio will be judged over a full-market cycle, primarily on whether the income needs of Mrs. Jones have been met while maintaining the desired liquidity reserves and preserving the purchasing power of the Trust's corpus.

The liquidity reserve's yield shall be expected to equal or exceed that on ninety-day United States Treasury bills and shall be measured against that index.

The Trustee may value any individual fixed income investments and unit investment trusts at amortized cost, if they were purchased with the intent of holding them to maturity, if that continues to be a reasonable expectation. In such case, that portion of the portfolio shall be expected to provide rates of return equal to or exceeding those of comparable United States Treasury maturities at the time of purchase.

The managers of actively managed diversified portfolios shall be selected on the basis of their ability over time to deliver above-average risk/return characteristics of their category of portfolio, and each shall be measured against the index deemed most appropriate for that category.

Reports of the portfolio's periodic and calendar year-to-date performance shall be prepared and reviewed at least quarterly by the Trustee. At least annually, the Trustee shall examine the relative and absolute performance of the overall portfolio, each asset class and each of the component portfolios and individual investments over the past year and since inception. The asset allocation shall be reviewed relative to the needs of the Trust and the diversification standards, and any adjustments shall be made.

In reviewing the actively managed component portfolios, the emphasis shall be on rolling three-year results. The expectation is that each manager will be able to consistently produce an above-average return adjusted for risk over those periods, as measured against an appropriate index (which may be constructed from multiple indices). It would be expected that the absolute returns over that cycle would equal or exceed those of the index used to measure the overall asset class of which the component portfolio is part.

As you can see, it takes thought and effort to assemble an IPS, and also to implement one. This example could be expanded to suit a larger or more complex trust. It could also be pruned back to fit a very small trust by omitting the selection process for an outside manager and by limiting asset classes to domestic stocks and United States Treasury bonds, or perhaps limiting investment to just a balanced mutual fund or two.

In a sense, an IPS is a trustee talking to him or herself, but the content must be understandable to others. If the meaning of what you have said is clear only to you, you may have lost its use as a defense if one is needed. Also, an IPS should not be so broadly stated as to be meaningless. As an extreme example of this, it should not allow you to invest cash in a range between 0% and 100% of the total portfolio.

A problem is that despite all of the reliance on quantitative input, such as the measurable returns for different classes of investments over long periods of time, establishing investment policy is a very subjective exercise. In the IPS example above, a different trustee might have relied more on stocks that pay high dividends instead of on fixed income issues to meet income requirements.

Even the input can be subjectively selected. To determine probable returns for large-cap equities, for instance, what time periods should you consider? Should you look at the last thirty years, or the last ten? Arguments could be made for either period, but the average annual returns would have been much higher for a ten-year period ending in 2002. If used, the assumptions based upon the shorter period would result in a much different asset allocation than those based upon thirty years. A conservative approach would therefore be to assume that, in the future, large-cap equities will have the lower average annual returns of the past thirty years.

The importance of an IPS, despite its subjective elements, is that it demonstrates the sincere effort you have made to weigh different approaches and outcomes and to arrive at rational conclusions, in the best interests of the trust. It clearly establishes that you don't lack a plan. If you document your subsequent investing with written explanations, you should be able to demonstrate that you have followed your plan.

PART THREE

Administration

Chapter I
Communications

Now that you are organized to carry on your work, it's time to discuss the work itself. Trustees, if asked, would say that this consists of investing, generating statements, making discretionary decisions, distributing money to beneficiaries, and paying bills and taxes. Most of them probably wouldn't include communicating, taking it for granted. However, we think that how you perform this part of your job is vital to your success, which is why we open Part Three with this chapter.

A. The Importance of Good Communications

The way communication takes place among the parties to a trust can make or break you, even when you aren't the one communicating. The creator of the trust might not inform you of why you were selected and what is expected of you, or even let you know in advance that you have been selected. He or she may also leave his or her beneficiaries in the dark about his or her intentions in creating the trust, making them resentful of you and the trust. Beneficiaries may talk to each other, encouraging group dissatisfaction with your management of the trust or your treatment of them.

A trustee who communicates effectively can offset damage done by others. The good news is that, unlike some other functions that you must perform, communicating effectively doesn't usually require much specialized knowledge, just common sense, sensitivity and an ability to say things clearly.

Individual trustees can learn many lessons about communication from corporate trustees, both from those who do it well, and others who don't. All are adequate at the basics, such as providing statements and annual information for preparation of tax returns. They have automated accounting systems that are generally reliable in producing the necessary data for these reports, something unavailable to most individual trustees. The weak point, for those institutions that fail to communicate well, is at the human level.

Take the reporting of annual tax information by trustees as an example. Beneficiaries often complain about receiving their tax information late, although it can't be passed along to them until the trustee receives all of it first from original sources. Furthermore, unlike a 1099 form, which individuals receive, tax information sent to a beneficiary by a trustee is not subject to a January 31 deadline. However, many beneficiaries assume that it is. We mention this to illustrate a point: the beneficiaries would grumble less if the trustee would only explain why tax information is sometimes slow, not "late," in coming. Many bank trustees, relying on automated output, fail to do this.

Those institutions that are good at the art of communicating look beyond a narrow concentration on cost-cutting and time-saving to focus on the perceptions of their customers. They know that, in the long run, it is more efficient – and not incidentally more profitable – to deal with beneficiaries who are satisfied with good service. Consequently the superior corporate trustee spends money on an annual mailing to beneficiaries, early in January, to remind them that it wants to provide them with tax information as early as possible, but that it must first receive necessary information from other sources. It encourages its trust officers to make personal calls to beneficiaries who are particularly sensitive, and offer to expedite matters, if possible.

The superior corporate trustee also understands the importance of first impressions. When it first receives a trust instrument naming it as a future trustee, it thanks the settlor for the appointment. It offers to have a representative meet with other members of his family so that the institution and these family members are not strangers to each other when its services are required. Thereafter, it keeps in touch with the settlor, offering to assist in updates of his estate planning and informing him of important developments. And when its services are activated, it provides similar continuing attention to family members who become beneficiaries, regarding them as valued customers.

Unfortunately, the definition of superiority implies that most members of any group are mediocre or worse. With the pressure on corporate trustees to be increasingly profitable, quarter by quarter, relatively few of them worry much about answering for much longer term results. Communication, which takes time and money, often suffers. We know that you can be a better communicator than most of your corporate competitors.

B. How the Settlor Should Communicate with You and the Beneficiaries

The settlor of a trust is probably not reading this book, although it might provide him or her with useful insights if he did. In the event that perhaps you can influence him or her, we'd like to talk to you about his or her role as a communicator.

He or she should acquaint you with the fact that you are being named as a trustee, and tell you why you were selected. The settlor should explain what the assets are likely to consist of, what problems may arise, and what he or she expects you to do that might go beyond the normal functions of a trustee. He or she should not expect you to take directions from him or her or any other party not specifically authorized to do so by the trust instrument.

You and the settlor should have an opportunity to talk about what provisions you might like to have included in the trust instrument that could make your administration easier and more effective. You and the settlor should also reach an agreement as to what constitutes fair and reasonable compensation for your services, and this should be arranged for in the trust agreement or in a separate letter agreement.

The settlor should explain to future beneficiaries why he or she is creating a trust for them instead of leaving them money directly. He or she could explain the tax reasons, his or her desire to assure that assets pass to future generations, or his or her concern that the survivors will otherwise lack financial management and protection. If the beneficiaries understand why the trust was created, they may be inclined to regard trust assets less as "their" assets and more as the settlor's.

We understand that there may be exceptions to this recommendation, as in the case of an incapacitated beneficiary who wouldn't understand, or where advance knowledge of the estate plan might precipitate intolerable family discord. In the latter case, the settlor could explain his or her decisions in a letter to be opened at some future time, such as after his or her death.

The settlor can make it clear in the will or trust agreement that he or she wants certain beneficiaries favored over others in terms of income or invasions of principal. He or she may direct or state or ask that a residual trust should be managed so as to put the maintenance, welfare and support of the surviving spouse ahead of any interests of their children. A direction would have more force than a request (which has no legal force, other than as an aid to interpretation of the settlor's intentions). But both could provide a trustee with some relief from the problem of trying to serve beneficiaries with opposing needs for current income versus growth of principal.

Definitions–Directives and Precatory Clauses

One of the most frequent and most serious mistakes that unskilled drafters of wills and trust agreements make is stating as a wish or a request—what they intended as a directive or a command.

A wish is stated in a clause that is precatory (derived from the Latin word for "pray"), such as "I would like my trustee to give preference to my wife's need for income over the needs of other beneficiaries."

A command is expressed in a direction, as in "my trustee shall give preference to my wife's need for income over the needs of other beneficiaries."

C. How You Can Communicate with the Settlor

It would be wonderful if you could discuss with the settlor all of the matters concerning you that are mentioned above. You should also politely but firmly acquaint him or her of your intentions to act as a trustee should act, if you accept your appointment, without influence or direction from those who have no authorization to provide it. In this best of all possible worlds, no one would ever ask you to do anything improper, but people who create trusts are not always highly educated as to the meaning of "fiduciary responsibility."

D. How You Can Communicate with Beneficiaries

1. Initial Meetings

We have already discussed in Part Two, Chapter I, how you might conduct your first meetings with beneficiaries at the inception of your administration. However, there may be subsequent occasions when you meet with a new beneficiary for the first time. An event such as the death of one beneficiary or his or her attainment of a certain age could cause him or her to be replaced by a successor you haven't yet met, or you may find yourself dealing with a previously unknown contingent beneficiary or remainderman. What we said earlier might also apply here.

Each of these occasions is an opportunity for you to make that important first impression a favorable one. Try to avoid the Zeus-like demeanor of some bank trust officers who conduct meetings in terms of "this is the way we do things here." If you can, arrange such meetings to suit the convenience of the beneficiary in terms of time and location, and be hospitable. Explain the purposes of the trust and your role as trustee, but put the emphasis on the beneficiary's equitable interests in the trust rather than on your legal ones. Find out how you can accommodate him or her. Consider such matters as whether you can schedule remittances to suit his or her needs, and whether confidentiality would be a problem in sending mail to a particular address. Ask him or her to call you when he or she receives the first statement so that you can go over it with him or her. Explain in advance what kind of information you will need if he should have to ask you to exercise a discretionary distribution power.

2. Investment Policy

Assuming that the IPS was not completed by the time of the initial meeting, you should communicate it as soon as it is convenient for you. This isn't required of a trustee, and most trustees don't bother to do it. However, we think it is advisable for you to do. It lets everyone know that you are taking your responsibilities seriously. It gives everyone a common point of reference in terms of what you intend to accomplish on a long-term basis, regardless of shorter term developments in the securities markets or the economy. It also gives you an opportunity to defend your policy before it is implemented, and it also aids in the defense against beneficiaries who criticize it only after it has long been in effect.

Because the full IPS may be more technical than most beneficiaries are equipped to comprehend, your communication should be an abbreviated version of it. You'll have to exercise your own judgment about making available the complete version to beneficiaries who may have the sophistication to follow it. The danger is that the finer details in the complete statement may raise more questions than a simplified version. You should also be careful not to divulge confidential information about any beneficiaries that may be contained in the full IPS.

You shouldn't encourage the beneficiaries to believe that they are being invited to reformulate your policy. There should be an accompanying explanation discreetly to the effect that, while you want to share information with the beneficiaries, decisions must be solely your responsibility according to the trust instrument.

Sample Letter–Investment Policy: The following explanation is a simplification of the sample IPS found in Part Two, Chapter III

To the Beneficiaries of the William Jones Family Trust:

I am writing to the beneficiaries of the Family Trust to explain the policy that will govern my management of the investments. Longer-term objectives for the trust, such as increasing income and the preservation and enhancement of the underlying assets, are only achieved through consistency of investment management. Having a policy to adhere to helps me maintain this consistency through both favorable and unfavorable times, when there would otherwise be temptations to overreact to short-term conditions.

I have created this policy for administration purposes, which is my sole responsibility, but I thought that it would be helpful if I were to share an abbreviated version of it with you.

1. Sources of Authority and Limitations

The trust instrument gives me broad authority to select investments.

This state's law for trust investments requires prudence, and the broad investment provisions in the trust instrument can not be considered a license to disregard this aspect of this state's law.

2. The Purposes of the Trust

a. To provide income to Mrs. Jones.
b. To enable Mrs. Jones to withdraw the larger of $5,000 or 5% of the principal annually, if she so desires.
c. To pay, to or apply for their use, such amounts of principal as are needed by Mrs. Jones, Andrea J. Smith and William W. Jones, Jr. for their maintenance, support, health and welfare.
d. To conserve principal for distribution at Mrs. Jones' death to those appointed in her will, or otherwise to Andrea J. Smith and William W. Jones, Jr.

3. Current Considerations

Mrs. Jones has adequate income from other sources.

It is unlikely that either this trust or the Marital Trust will be subject to transfer taxes at Mrs. Jones' death, under current tax law.

All of the beneficiaries are in good health and none anticipates any needs for principal invasions.

4. Investment Objectives

a. To maintain sufficient liquidity for the first year in case it is needed to assist Mrs. Jones in making adjustments to her style of living as a recent widow.
b. To produce moderate income as a supplement to Mrs. Jones' other adequate sources of income.
c. To meet possible future needs of the beneficiaries for principal by maintaining appropriate levels of liquidity and marketability.
d. To preserve the original value of the principal for eventual distribution.
e. To prudently enhance the value of total principal over time.

5. Duration of the Trust

The trust is expected to exist for more than twenty-five years, permitting a long-term approach to investing. However any anticipated needs for funds within a five-year period will be held in cash-equivalent reserves. Additionally, to meet unanticipated needs, approximately 5% of the total assets will be maintained in short-term investments having excellent marketability and reasonably good liquidity.

6. Performance

The total average annual return for the trust, including both income and principal should be at least 8%, taking into account an emphasis on safety of principal. Of this, the average annual income yield should be approximately 2.5%, and the average annual capital appreciation of principal should be approximately 5.5%. This objective may appear modest in terms with the past performance of an all-equity index, but it is a suitable one in terms of risk management for this particular trust.

It is understood that there will be fluctuations in return from one year to the next, and that these should be tolerable for the beneficiaries in terms of their needs. However declines in the market values of assets should not exceed 15% in any twelve-month period.

7. Asset Selection

Cash equivalents, for purposes of meeting anticipated cash needs within a five-year period, shall consist of funds on deposit in FDIC insured accounts, individual obligations of the United States government and United States agencies of six-month maturity or less, and high quality money market accounts, or equivalent vehicles.

Short-term investments, for the purpose of maintaining permanent reserves, shall consist of FDIC insured certificates of deposit, individual obligations of the United States Government and United States Government agencies of five-year maturity or less, and short term government bond mutual funds, as well as repurchase agreements and the two highest grades of commercial paper.

Long-term investments shall consist of the following:

a. Domestic bonds rated "A " or better by Moody's or Standard & Poor's bond rating services.

b. Domestic equities, the majority of which shall be representative of those issues listed in the Standard & Poor's 500 Index.

c. International equities having an average capitalization of $1 billion or greater.

As permitted by the terms of the trust, mutual funds may be employed by the terms of the trust for each category.

In the interest of diversification, I have imposed limitations upon concentration of investment in a number of ways. For instance, no more than 10% of the trust's assets may be invested in any one bond issue or issuer, other than United States Government and United States Government agencies, and at least eight of the S&P 500 industry groups must be represented at all times in the domestic equity holdings.

We will use the following asset allocations to meet the trust's objectives:

	Lower Limit	Target Level	Upper Limit
Cash equivalents	2%	5%	7%
Domestic fixed income	25%	30%	40%
Domestic equities	45%	55%	60%
International equities	5%	10%	15%

I shall select such independent investment managers and mutual funds from time to time, as are eligible in terms of experience, skill, continuity and performance, to assume responsibility for the day-to-day management of the trust's investments. Each will be required to adhere to the formal version of the policy I have outlined above. I will monitor each manager and mutual fund, and I will remove and replace any manager or fund if necessary in the best interests of the trust.

Sincerely,

Your IPS is not a short course in investing. If you use technical terms in it, leave explanations of them for later discussion if and when the beneficiaries raise questions.

3. Financial and Investment Projections

You aren't required to prepare projections for beneficiaries. Nowhere does it say that this is a specific duty of yours, although keeping beneficiaries informed is. As an investment manager for the trust portfolio, however, you should at least construct investment projections for your own planning purposes, otherwise how will you have any kind of an idea of what the trust may look like in the future? And if you prepare projections for your own enlightenment, you aren't investing much extra time if you share these efforts with the beneficiaries. Other kinds of projections may be more for their benefit than yours, such as those that project increases in their expenses. If they need these, a qualified financial planner can calculate them at the beneficiaries' expense. It might be beneficial for you as well as them if the trust is permitted to pay for this service.

We all know that projections are double-bladed tools. They are useful planning devices, but a projection that is too optimistic can arouse later anxiety and disappointment. We favor them with respect to trust beneficiaries, however. Most beneficiaries live in the present, and may have little understanding of their own future financial needs, let alone what should be expected of a trust over the course of several years. Projections of cost-of-living increases or decreases, trust asset appreciation or depreciation, and changes in income can be very helpful in giving beneficiaries the longer-view perspective. They should be presented with the caveat that projections are only straws in the wind, not fact or certainty. You want to be able to prove later, if necessary, that you didn't present the projections in a misleading way.

A short-term projection covering a few months or a couple of years might be called for when a trust is encountering temporary changes. For example, this kind of projection might address the implementation of a new investment program and the shift from a temporary cash position to longer-term investments. A short-term projection might conceivably deal with a situation outside of the trust, such as a surviving spouse's transition from one financial life style to another over the first year and the need to make personal adjustments in spending habits. Such projections should be fairly detailed, as they concern changes in specific assets.

Long-term projections are more useful for explaining likely trends over future years, where a decade or more may be covered. With such things as investment projections, the interesting thing about them is that for each year, they can be wildly inaccurate, but tend to become more dependable over a succession of years. The performance of the Standard & Poor's 500 Index may fluctuate from positive to negative over a pair of years. A long look backward tells us a different story: that it settles down to an *average* annual return (from both dividends and capital appreciation) that is within a positive range of 9% to 12%, depending upon the period selected. Therefore, it would be reasonable to assume at least an average annual return of 9% for trust portfolio stocks with Standard & Poor's 500 Index characteristics.

It may be interesting to look at the following projection, published in the earlier edition of this book. We made it in 1999 without any advance warning of the subsequent sharp decline in technical stocks, the general market decline that accompanied it or the terrorist attack on the World Trade Center on September 11, 2001. The projection applied average annual rates of return for different classes of securities for each of ten years (of which only six are shown). This is a reasonable approach for a long-term projection, but in this case it would have greatly overestimated the performance of stock capital appreciation for the years 2000 and 2001 unless stock selection had been uncommonly fortuitous. Significant declines in value in the early years of this projection would make it difficult for the portfolio to meet a performance objective over the period that ends in 2010.

Example of a Long-Term Projection (First 6 years of 10)

Jones Family Trust (Growth and Income Objective)
Investment Projection

Initial Value of Trust $540,000

Projected Annual Returns
Cash interest: 3%
Bond interest: 6%
Stock dividends: 1%
Stock capital appreciation: 9%

Year	1999	2000	2001	2002	2003	2004	2005
Mrs. Jones' age	64	65	66	67	68	69	70
Cash	27,000	27,000	28,580	30,252	32,021	33,894	35,878
Bonds	162,000	162,000	171,476	181,508	192,127	203,366	215,263
Stocks	351,000	382,590	404,972	428,662	453,739	480,283	508,379
Total	540,000	571,590	605,028	640,422	677,887	717,543	759,520

Interest income	10,530	10,530	11,146	11,798	12,488	13,219	13,992
Dividend income	3,510	3,826	4,050	4,287	4,537	4,803	5,084
Gross income	14,040	14,356	15,196	16,085	17,026	18,002	19,076
Less: fees/expenses	7,020	7,431	7,865	8,325	8,813	9,328	9,874
Net income	7,020	6,925	7,330	7,759	8,213	8,694	9,202

Notes:

1. Rebalancing of cash, bonds and stocks according to a 5%/30%/65% allocation is based upon the prior year-end total value.
2. Fees and expenses are estimated to be 1.35% of asset market value.
3. This projection is based upon historical average annual returns. Actual future returns may vary, and there could be substantial differences from year to year.

With this particular projection, the fees and expenses are more than half of the net income. Therefore it would be a good idea for the trustee to remind the beneficiaries that all of the fees and investment expenses are being charged against income with the approval of the income beneficiary, so that the principal can grow at a faster rate. Fees are more typically allocated between income and principal for most trusts.

For a trust, a long-term projection can help a beneficiary understand the wisdom of sacrificing some current income to achieve more financial protection at a later date when it is likely to be more needed. Projections that compare the differences between hypothetical portfolios, one slanted toward fixed income securities and one more concentrated in equities, may be particularly helpful here.

The actual length of a projection will depend upon its purpose. The longer a projection is, the more dramatic the end results will be because of the effects of compounding. However, a projection should not be longer than is relevant to the beneficiary. They should not be overly complex, either; an investment projection limited to broad asset categories, such as cash, stocks, bonds, is adequate for illustrating basic principles over an extended period of time. Of course, for your own purposes, you might want to build a model that is more refined, such as one that includes separate categories for stocks of large, medium and small size corporations.

4. Statements

We have explained earlier what information beneficiaries are entitled to, and in Part Three, Chapter III, we tell you what information that statements to beneficiaries should disclose. All we want to do here is make the point that statements are a form of communication. In fact, they may be the most frequent means of communication from their trustee for many beneficiaries. You may therefore want to do a few things to make them more effective as a communication tool.

You should report financially to the beneficiaries reasonably often. Even if there is no requirement for frequent accounts, we think that a trustee should voluntarily provide beneficiaries with frequent statements that disclose all financial activity in the trust. An uninformed beneficiary can become, by turns, anxious, wary, suspicious and finally antagonistic. For a trust that is small or relatively inactive, a quarterly statement may be adequate, but most individuals today have been conditioned to receiving statements monthly from their banks, credit card issuers and brokers. Therefore you should probably meet their expectations and provide a monthly statement if the trust is active and of any size.

Have you ever cursed the newspaper carrier for not being "on time" because your paper didn't come when it usually does? Perhaps all the other times it was delivered were early! If you are reporting more often than required, let the beneficiaries know that you are doing this voluntarily for their benefit. You might remind them of this annually, as they'll otherwise assume that unnecessarily frequent reporting is an entitlement.

Because fiduciary accounting is not easy for the average beneficiary to fathom, you should provide beneficiaries with a general explanation of how statements are to be read, advising them to keep this explanation for permanent reference (in the file folder you gave them for statements, if you did this). It would be best if you used one of your actual statements for this purpose. Points to explain are:

- the difference between income and principal and a general explanation of why certain items are allocated to each
- carrying costs
- fee calculations
- reasons for fluctuation in income from one statement to the next

Make the statements reasonably attractive and convenient to read. Use a good grade of paper that will endure, and use a type font that is large enough for beneficiaries with weak eyesight to read comfortably. You will avoid the stock complaint that "it's obvious you don't want me to know what's going on, when I can't read what my statements say." Provide your beneficiaries with statements that have a good appearance. An attractive statement implies quality service. Just don't overdo it. If they look too extravagant, someone is sure to assume that you are wasting trust money (although statement paper is your expense).

You might be able to offer statements on-line to computer-literate beneficiaries, but we don't think that this is a good idea for reasons of confidentiality.

5. Getting the Right Answer

Sometimes you will expect a beneficiary to give you the answer you want in response to a written inquiry. You may be asking him or her to comply with a legal formality or to an arrangement that you have agreed upon but did not document. A good example is the notice you might have to send to beneficiaries of certain types of irrevocable life insurance trusts, where you must advise them that money has been added to the trust to pay insurance premiums, and that they have the right to withdraw these funds. For tax reasons, this notice is required, but it is definitely not intended that the beneficiaries exercise their right, because if they do, the objectives of the trust would be impaired. They should have been acquainted with this procedure (by you, if not the settlor or settlor's attorney), but they may be careless in replying. You need to make it difficult for them to give the wrong answer.

Again, a bad example might be instructive. If you want to wreck the trust, try sending them a response to fill out that looks like this:

I do ___ do not ___ exercise my right to withdraw the funds recently placed in the trust.

Now if an unalerted beneficiary checks the first box, it may be all over.

It would be far better to acquaint the beneficiary with his or her right to withdraw funds, ask him or her to acknowledge in writing that he or she has received your notice, and if he or she intends to exercise the right of withdrawal, to do so in a separate written communication. These instructions make it more difficult for him or her to commit an unintended act, because he or she would need to perform a separate act to commit an error. (See the Appendix for a complete form letter concerning irrevocable life insurance trusts that avoids an unintended response.) This principle can be applied to other situations where you want the right answer.

6. Postage Courtesy

While we are on the subject of requests for information, how many times have you received such a request from your bank, your insurance agent, or someone else who needs the information primarily for their own purposes, and you are expected to reply at your own expense? This expense may be only the cost of a postage stamp, but it would seem only good manners for the sender to facilitate his or her request with a stamped return-addressed envelope, or the equivalent, such as an invitation to call collect.

Most beneficiaries can afford a stamp or a telephone call, but they also appreciate small courtesies. The cost of these items is a small price to pay for good relationships, particularly when it contrasts with the practice of banks and trust companies that seldom observe such niceties. Provide return postage. Not only will the beneficiaries appreciate it, but they will also be more cooperative about responding, and you'll spend less time following up. Just don't undo the gesture by including an entry on the beneficiary's next statement that says "postage charges: $0.37 for return mail."

7. Bad News

Eventually something will happen that will affect the beneficiaries in some adverse way. This may be something that you are not personally responsible for, such as a stock market crash, or a serious illness of the accountant upon whom you rely to prepare your statements. Then again, it may be an oversight or mistake that is entirely your fault. Too late, you have caught an error in statements that have already gone out. Or, much worse, you have cost the trust real money, such as by paying a bill that should not have been paid, or by giving a broker an order to sell the wrong security.

You can compound the effects of bad news by failing to communicate it. You may hope that the beneficiaries will not notice or will not care, or that subsequent events will offset earlier ones. You might count on the stock market and your accountant recovering, and on no one noticing the statement error or your correction of it. However there are beneficiaries who do pay attention to what is going on, and they become concerned if events adversely affect them, particularly when they feel that they have been blind-sided.

In bad-news situations, your best defense is a good offense. If possible, contact your beneficiaries personally and explain the nature of the problem and any reasons for them not to become disturbed. If the stock market has crashed, reassure them that your investment policy takes such times into account. If the statements will be late, promptly explain why and what you are doing about it. It is always best if you can do this before the beneficiaries learn about the problem on their own or from some other source. Even those who don't call you may be simmering about an unexplained problem.

If the mistake is your own, you may, subject to our warning below, even enhance your reputation by being forthright about it. Admit the error or oversight with an apology, explaining how it occurred and explain how you will correct it. Of course, you don't want to call attention to every little error or omission on your part, or the beneficiaries may begin to wonder about your competency.

Warning

If there is the possibility that you may be sued and suffer personal financial loss because of a mistake, it is not a good idea for you to admit to any blame from the point of view of a legal defense. An admission to error on your part may strengthen an opposing party's case even though other factors may weigh in on your side.

Suppose beneficiaries accuse you of negligence for acquiring, and continuing to retain, an investment that has deteriorated in value. To try to appease them by admitting that you could have made a bad decision would be a mistake. You should review the matter with your attorney (your personal attorney, not the attorney who represents the trust) if it appears that a lawsuit may be in the offing. He or she may be able to tell you that you acted within the boundaries of your authority, and that your documentation provides evidence that your decisions were prudent in view of the facts available to you at the time you made them. He or she may want to review your insurance policies before formulating any strategy.

Even if you are at fault, an early admission of guilt may make it difficult for your attorney to negotiate a settlement out of court that might otherwise be agreeable to opposing parties.

Chapter 11
Distributions Of Income And Principal

A. Required Distributions

Payments to beneficiaries usually consist of regularly scheduled income remittances, discretionary distributions of principal to meet particular needs, and mandatory distributions, either scheduled or triggered by an event, such as the attainment of a certain age or the termination of the trust. But there are other variations. Sometimes income accumulated over more than one year must be paid out at the happening of an event, such as the attainment of a certain age by the beneficiary. Or a beneficiary might have the right to withdraw principal at his or her own discretion, such as a right to withdraw $10,000 annually from principal.

Making required distributions is relatively easy, because you merely have to follow the instructions in the trust instrument without making any decisions (in most cases) but there are a few cautions. You want to be sure that you are making them to the right individuals. If a distribution is contingent upon an event, you want to be certain that the event took place. For example, if a beneficiary is entitled to a share of principal upon attaining a specified age, you should see that he or she furnishes you with proof of his or her age, if you don't already have it in your files, before making any distributions,.

Occasionally you might have to exercise your judgment. For example, if you have reason to believe that payments to a beneficiary are being neglected or misappropriated, you should use reasonable care to remedy the situation. This may include obtaining legal advice, as you do not want to overstep the limitations on your authority.

B. Discretionary Distributions

One of the most important powers that can be granted to you by a trust instrument is to pay out income or principal at your discretion. This power is frequently given to trustees because it is the nature of trusts that they are often established for beneficiaries who need the benefit of the trustee's judgment. These beneficiaries include incapacitated adults, minors and spendthrifts, but they also include average individuals who are not financially astute or who need the protections a trust affords against the designs of others. Trustees are also given discretionary powers to limit a beneficiary's control over the trust assets when such control would cause an adverse tax result, such as inclusion of trust assets in the beneficiary's estate at his or her death.

The power can take various forms. At one extreme, you might have absolute discretion to determine the amount, timing, and frequency of a distribution, as well as the purpose for it. At the other, you might be restricted in all of these factors. A problem, of course, is that a distribution to one beneficiary can negatively affect others. You have a duty to be loyal and impartial to all beneficiaries. You also have a duty to preserve the trust property. Making discretionary distributions is therefore a balancing act.

A beneficiary who believes he or she was negatively affected by how you exercised your judgment can force you to prove in court that you exercised it in the best interests of the trust. If you can't do this, you would have to remedy your error. This might result in financial loss to you, if you have to make good a similar loss to the beneficiary. Therefore you should exercise a discretionary power carefully, gathering all the information you need to make sound determinations, and you should keep records showing why you made the distributions or declined to make them.

You should have a clear understanding of why you might have to make the distribution. If there is a request for one from a beneficiary (usually the case), you should make sure that you understand:

- how much money is needed
- what it will be specifically used for
- when it will be spent
- how the expenditure will be accounted for

For example, a request for college tuition should state the amount of the tuition and any related expenses, the type of education (so that you can determine if it meets a definition in the trust instrument), and the timing of payments to the college. It should explain how the beneficiary will provide you with bills that you will pay directly or with receipts for bills he or she has paid. The request should be something like a mini-business plan.

If you are initiating the distribution, the process would be similar, except that the description of the above points would be yours, and you would include the reasons for why you are initiating it.

You should review your specific discretionary power in context with other provisions of the trust instrument and any amendments or codicils to it. You'll have to take into account the nature and size of the trust, as well as the circumstances that surrounded its creation in order to determine whether to distribute a specific amount, or to meet a specific purpose such as maintenance and support. You may also have to make inquiries about a beneficiary's other sources of funds. Often a discretionary power is accompanied by a provision that either requires this of you or frees you from the obligation.

Where the instrument is silent on this last point, you'll have to determine the extent of your discretion before deciding whether you either must make such an inquiry, can make it at your discretion, or are prohibited from doing so. Your obligation to consider a beneficiary's outside sources of funds falls into three categories:

- You have full discretion. In this case, you could take into account the beneficiary's other income or resources, but you wouldn't have to.
- You are authorized to exercise your discretion to distribute only a specific amount, or meet only a specific purpose. Here you would be prohibited from considering the beneficiary's other sources of funds because the language of the provision makes this irrelevant. An example is discretion to use principal to maintain and support the beneficiary if the trust income is insufficient for this purpose.
- You have discretion to supplement support rather than provide it. This would require you to investigate and consider the beneficiary's access to other means of support. For example, if you can exercise your discretion to provide "as necessary" for a beneficiary experiencing a major illness, you would have to consider the beneficiary's financial circumstances and medical insurance coverage.

Form - Documenting Your Discretionary Action

Trustee's Discretionary Action

Trust Name:____

Initiated by: ____

Description of need for distribution:

Purpose — Amount

Timing of need for funds:

Trustee's duty to inquire as to beneficiary's other sources of funds:

None ___ Other: ________________________________

Beneficiary's other sources of funds (if information is requested)

Description — Amount

Possible adverse effects on other beneficiaries:

How proposed distribution is to be made:
To beneficiary or his legal representative (identify) ___________
Directly to payee (identify):_____________________________

Proposed source of funds:
Discretionary income ___
Principal cash___
Sale of principal assets ___
Other (describe): ___________________________________

Action Taken:

Reason for This Specific Action:

Date __________ Trustee________________

Chapter III
Trust Accounting

A. Principal and Income Distinctions

Individuals don't generally distinguish sharply between their capital and income, except when they have to file tax returns. Because an individual investor is the legal and equitable owner of both, there is no compelling need to separate one from the other. Generally excess income is added to and becomes capital, and in times of need income is exhausted before selling capital assets, but there is no requirement that this order take place. Vacationers can "fly now and pay later" out of income, but they can also sell securities or hock the family heirlooms to subsidize a trip. Either way, they aren't accountable to anyone else.

However where you are the legal owner as trustee and the beneficiaries have varying equitable interests, a distinction has to be made between what is labeled "principal" (capital) and "income" for trust accounting purposes. The best source of instruction for this lies in the Uniform Principal and Income Act which most, but not all, states have adopted in some form. The original Uniform Principal and Income Act was drafted in 1931 in an effort to promote continuity of fiduciary accounting law among the states. It was revised in 1962, and then further revised and modernized in 1997. Two states still cling to the original version, eighteen follow the 1962 revision, and twenty-five have now adopted the 1997 revision.

States That Have Adopted *the Uniform Principal and Income Acts*

1931 Act States

Pennsylvania	Vermont*

1962 Act States

Alaska	Nevada
Florida	North Carolina
Georgia	Ohio
Illinois	Oregon
Indiana*	South Dakota
Kentucky	Texas
Michigan	Utah
Mississippi	Washington
Montana	Wisconsin*

1997 Act States

Alabama	Minnesota
Arizona	Missouri
Arkansas	Nebraska
California	New Jersey
Colorado	New Mexico
Connecticut	New York
Delaware	North Dakota
District of Columbia	Oklahoma
Hawaii	South Carolina
Idaho	Tennessee

Iowa	Virginia
Kansas	West Virginia
Maryland	Wyoming

*State with Bills introduced to Adopt the 1997 Revision

Indiana	Rhode Island
Maine	Vermont
Pennsylvania	Wisconsin

B. Summary of the Uniform Principal and Income Act of 1997

In this Chapter, we refer to the 1997 version of the Uniform Principal and Income Act as "the Act." The Act defines principal as "property held in trust for distribution to a remainder beneficiary when the trust terminates." What is left is the income, or "money or property that a fiduciary receives as current return from a principal asset." A commonly used analogy is that principal is a fruit tree and income is the fruit that it bears.

The Act and its two predecessors deal with four important questions concerning the rights of beneficiaries:

(1) How is income earned during the settlement of an estate to be distributed to trusts that receive outright bequests of specific property, gifts of money and the residue?

(2) When an income interest in a trust begins, what property is principal that will eventually go to remainder beneficiaries, and what is income for the beneficiaries of the income interest?

(3) Who receives the income that has been received but not distributed when an income interest ends?

(4) While an income interest exists, how should trust receipts and disbursements be allocated between principal and income?

Not all trusts receive distributions from an estate, but most trustees will have to answer all of these questions. Therefore what follows is a summary of the answers as provided by the Act, without adhering to the logical but somewhat complex form in which the Act provides them. Please keep in mind that only in those states that have adopted it is the Act authoritative, and some of those states have modified what they adopted. Remember also, that state statutes (or common law to the extent there are no statutes), can be overridden in most cases by the trust instrument. However because there is a strong trend of states adopting the Act, we include this summary. Our intention here is only to heighten your understanding of trust accounting. We encourage you to read the Act itself, with its many definitions, valuable commentary and sections that may have no direct relevance to trustees.

1. Decedent's Estate or Terminating Income Interest

If you are a trustee receiving distributions from an estate, you will need to know which distributions constitute income and which constitute principal. You will need to know if the executor or administrator of the estate has acted properly in paying claims from either ledger and if you have received the proper amounts in each category. You will also need to ascertain if the beneficiary has made payments that improperly reduce a distribution, such as paying expenses that would cause a reduction in a marital or charitable deduction.

2. Apportionment at Beginning and End of an Income Interest

The Act speaks of beginnings and ends of income interests rather than the beginnings and ends of trusts because a trust does not necessarily end when an income interest does. One beneficiary's income interest may be succeeded by another. A trustee first has to determine when a right to income begins and ends.

A beneficiary is entitled to net income from the date on which the income interest begins, according to a date specified in the trust, or otherwise when an asset becomes subject to the trust (or the income interest if it starts later). An income interest ends on the day before the death of the beneficiary or some other terminating event (such as his or her reaching a specific age). It can also end on the last day of a period during which there is no beneficiary to which a trustee may distribute income, as may be the case of a trust created for unborn children.

A trustee should allocate a receipt or disbursement of income to principal if its due date occurs before the beginning of the income interest. For example, a dividend payable to stockholders of record on March 14, 2002 would be a principal receipt if included in assets received by a trust under which no income interest exists until March 15, 2002. If the due date of the receipt or disbursement occurs on or after the beginning of the income interest, it should be allocated to income. If there is no due date or if a due date is non-periodic for a receipt or disbursement, it must be treated as accruing from day to day. The amount accrued to the beginning of the income interest is principal and the rest is income. This is similar to the federal tax rules that apply to income received by an executor or an administrator of an estate for determining what constitutes an estate asset and what constitutes income earned by the estate.

When an income interest ends, the same considerations hold. When a mandatory income interest ends, the trustee should pay to the beneficiary of that interest (or to his or her estate, if his or her death caused the interest to end) any undistributed income received before the date of termination. An exception would be where the beneficiary has an unqualified power to revoke more than 5% of the trust principal immediately before the income interest ends. In this case trustee should credit principal with the undistributed income earned on the principal that is subject to the power of revocation. None of this applies where the trustee has discretion to distribute or accumulate income and the beneficiary has no right to receive mandatory income payments.

Sometimes a trustee has an obligation to pay a fixed annuity or a fixed fraction of the value of the trust assets (as in the case of a charitable remainder trust). If so, he or she must prorate the final payment when his or her obligation ends, if and to the extent necessary to accomplish a purpose of the trust or its settlor relating to income, gift, estate or other tax requirements.

3. The Allocation of Receipts - to Principal

Certain receipts are allocated entirely to principal; these include:

(a) Some receipts from entities. Entities are corporations, partnerships, limited liability companies, regulated investment companies, real estate investment trusts, common trust funds, or any other organization other than trusts and estates, specialized businesses and activities, and asset-backed securities (all discussed separately below). The following receipts from entities constitute additions to principal:

- Property other than money
- Money received in one distribution or a series of related distributions in exchange for part or all of a trust's interest in the entity
- Money received in total or partial liquidation of the entity
- Money received from a regulated investment company or a real estate investment trust if the money is distributed as a capital gain for federal income tax purposes

The Act defines a partial liquidation as a distribution described by the distributing entity as a partial liquidation, and one that will exceed 20% of the entity's gross assets in terms of total assets distributed in one or a series of related distributions. Money is not received in partial liquidation to the extent it does not exceed the trust's income tax on taxable income received by the entity.

(b) Assets received from a transferor during the transferor's lifetime, a decedent's estate, a trust with a terminating income interest, or a payer under a contract (such as a life insurance policy) naming the trust or trustee as beneficiary.

(c) Money or other property received from the sale, exchange, liquidation or change in form of any principal asset, including realized profit, subject to other provisions of the Act.

(d) Amounts recovered from third parties to reimburse the trust because of disbursements, such as those related to environmental matters, or for other reasons to the extent not based on the loss of income.

(e) Proceeds of property taken by eminent domain, other than awards made for loss of income during a period in which a current income beneficiary had a mandatory income interest.

(f) Net income received in an accounting period during which there is no income beneficiary to which a trustee may or must distribute income.

(g) Amounts held subject to the terms of a lease received as refundable deposits, security deposits or a deposit to be applied as rent for future periods (such amounts are not available for distribution to a beneficiary until the trustee's related contractual obligations have been satisfied).

(h) Proceeds received from the sale, redemption, or other disposition of any obligation to pay money to the trustee that is more than one year after it is purchased or acquired, including such obligations acquired on a discount basis, such as a zero coupon bond.

(i) Proceeds of a life insurance policy or one that insures the trustee against damage to, destruction of or loss of title to a trust asset, including dividends paid on the policy if the premiums are paid from principal.

(j) Proceeds from the sale of non-income producing property, subject to the exception listed below under "Receipts Normally Apportioned Between Income and Principal."

(k) Proceeds from transactions involving derivatives, meaning contracts or financial instruments giving a trust the right or obligation to participate in some or all of the changes in the price of a tangible or intangible asset or group of assets, or changes in a rate, an index of prices or rates, or other market indicator for an asset or group of assets. Examples are futures, forwards, swaps and options. This rule is subject to the exception listed below under "Receipts Normally Apportioned Between Income and Principal."

(l) Proceeds from the granting of an option or a gain realized upon the exercise of an option must be allocated to principal. Options in this case include those which give a buyer the right to purchase real estate from a trustee, a put option purchased by a trustee to protect against a decline in value of a large block of stock intended to be sold to meet an estate tax obligation, and call options regularly sold by the trustee.

(m) Amounts received as distributions of principal from a trust or an estate (but the trustee should determine what the terms of the distributing trust or estate say about the distribution).

(n) Any other receipts to the extent not covered by a rule in a trust instrument or the Act.

4. The Allocation of Receipts - to Income

Other receipts are normally ones that a trustee would add to income. These include:

- Receipts from entities in the form of money, such as interest and cash dividends, except those listed above as allocations to principal.
- Proceeds of property taken by eminent domain constituting a separate award made for the loss of income with respect to an accounting period during which a current income beneficiary had a mandatory income interest.
- Amounts received as rent of real or personal property, including an amount received for cancellation or renewal of a lease.
- Amounts received as distributions of income from a trust or an estate (but the trustee should determine what the terms of the distributing trust or estate say about the distributions).
- Receipts from principal.

5. Receipts Normally Apportioned between Principal and Income

1. Deferred Compensation, Annuities and Similar Payments.

Trustees receive payments from such sources as deferred compensation plans, IRAs, annuities, and insurance renewal commissions, to name a few. These payments arise from contractual arrangements involving services rendered (as by an employee to an employer) or purchases from the payer (as by an annuitant from an insurance company). They may be payable in installments, over one or more lifetimes or in a lump sum.

Any such payment, to the extent it is characterized as interest or dividends or is in lieu thereof, is allocated to income, and any payment not so characterized is allocated to principal. If no part of a payment is characterized as interest or dividends (or equivalent), and all or part of the payment is required to be made, 10% of the payment is allocated to income and the balance to principal. If no part of a payment is required to be made, it is all allocated to principal. If a payment is the entire amount to which a trustee is entitled, it is also all allocated to principal. A payment made subject to a trustee's exercise of a right of withdrawal is not considered a payment required to be made.

In working with the federal estate tax marital deduction rules, a trustee may have to allocate more of a payment to income than the above rules of the Act permit. In this case the additional amount is a proper allocation to income.

2. Certain assets, such as patents, copyrights, royalty rights and leaseholds and lottery prizes, lose their value or terminate because the payments they generate are expected to last for only a limited time. A trustee must allocate 10% of the payments from such "liquidating" assets to income and the balance to principal.
3. Receipts from an interest in minerals or other natural resources must be allocated as follows:
   - (a) those constituting nominal delay rental or nominal annual rent on a lease are income.
   - (b) production payments are income if and to the extent the underlying agreement creating them provides a factor for interest or its equivalent. The balance is principal.
   - (c) more than nominal amounts of royalties, shut-in-well payments, take-or-pay payments, bonus or delay rentals are allocated 10% to income and 90% to principal.
   - (d) an amount received from a working interest or any other interest not provided for in (a), (b), or (c) above is allocated 10% to income and 90% to principal.
   - (e) receipts on account of an interest in water that is renewable are income. If the water is not renewable, 90% of the amount is principal and 10% is income.

Separate provisions apply to the natural resource timber.

- (a) to the extent that timber removed from the land does not exceed the rate of growth of the timber during the accounting periods in which a beneficiary has a mandatory income interest, receipts from the sale of timber are income.
- (b) to the extent that the amount of timber removed exceeds the rate of growth, or the net receipts are from the sale of standing timber, they are principal.
- (c) for net receipts from a lease of timberland or from a contract to cut timber the rules under (a) and (b) apply with respect to the amounts of timber determined to have been removed under the lease or contract; but to the extent that such receipts constitute advance payments, bonuses and other payments not allocated under (a) and (b), they are principal.
- (d) in determining net receipts to be allocated above, a trustee shall deduct and allocate to principal a reasonable amount for depletion.
- (e) the same rules that apply to trustees concerning the application of the rules for other natural resources before or after the effective date of the Act apply to the rules for timber.

The above provisions pertaining to natural resources apply to interests acquired by the trustee after the effective date of the Act; for interests owned by the trustee prior to that date the trustee may continue using whatever allocations were previously applied or apply the above provisions. The Act applies whether or not a decedent or transferor was extracting minerals, *etc.* before the effective date of the Act.

4. Receipts from asset-backed securities are income to the extent they are identified as interest or other

current return of the collateral assets, and the balance is principal. Asset-based securities area assets whose value is based upon the right they give the owner to receive distributions from the proceeds of financial assets that provide collateral for the security.

5. Non-income producing property in a trust, or trust property that produces negligible income, can result in the loss of a marital deduction. In this situation, the Act provides that the beneficiary spouse may require the trustee to make the property produce income, convert it to income-producing property, or make adjustments between principal and income to the extent necessary to provide the spouse with the level of beneficial enjoyment needed to qualify the trust for a marital deduction. The trustee may then decide which of these actions or combination of them to take, and apportion accordingly.

6. Sometimes a trustee operates a business or other activity in proprietorship form rather than in a wholly-owned corporation. The Act provides that a trustee may account separately for such a business or other activity instead of accounting for it as part of the trust's general accounting records (the trustee could account in a sub-trust, for example). The trustee must first determine that this is in the best interests of all of the beneficiaries. Such activities include:

   - mining
   - retail, manufacturing, service, and other traditional business activities
   - farming
   - raising and selling livestock and other animals
   - management of rental properties
   - extraction of minerals and other natural resources
   - timber operations
   - investing in derivatives and options

In engaging in such activities, the trustee may determine the extent to which net cash receipts must be retained for working capital, the acquisition or retention of fixed assets and other needs of the business or activity, and the extent to which the remaining net cash receipts are accounted for as trust income or principal. If a trustee sells assets of the business or activity, he or she must account for the net amount received as principal to the extent it is no longer required in the conduct of the business or activity.

7. Allocations that are insubstantial may be allocated entirely to principal. Such would be the case if the amount in question would not increase or decrease the net income in an accounting period by more than 10%, or if the value of the assets producing the receipt is less than 10% of the trust's assets at the beginning of an accounting period.

6. Disbursements - Allocated to Principal

Disbursements that are charged against principal are as follows:

(a) One-half of the regular compensation of the trustee or any person providing investment advisory or custodial services to the trustee.

(b) One-half of all expenses for accountings, judicial proceedings, or any other matters that deal with both income and remainder interests.

(c) All of the trustee's compensation calculated on principal as a fee for acceptance, distribution or termination.

(d) Disbursements made to prepare a property for sale.

(e) Expenses of a proceeding that concerns primarily principal, including a proceeding to construe the trust or to protect the trust or its property.

(f) Premiums paid on any insurance policy other than those covering the loss of a principal asset or loss of the income it generates.

(g) Estate, inheritance and other transfer taxes, including penalties, apportioned to the trust.
(h) Taxes based on receipts allocated to principal, even if they are characterized as income taxes by the taxing authority.
(i) Disbursements related to environmental matters.
(j) Amounts equal to the income paid to a creditor to reduce the principal balance of an obligation of a principal asset that is encumbered with an obligation requiring income from the asset to be paid directly to such creditor (the trustee transfers the amount to income).
(k) Disbursements to the extent not covered by a rule in a trust instrument or the Act.
(l) Disbursements made in connection with transactions in derivatives.
(m) Amounts paid to acquire options involving purchases or sales of trust property.
(n) Any other disbursements to the extent not covered by a rule in a trust instrument or the Act.

7. Disbursements - Allocated to Income

A trustee must normally make the following disbursements from income:

(a) One-half of the regular compensation of the trustee or any person providing investment advisory or custodial services to the trustee.
(b) One-half of all expenses for accountings, judicial proceedings, or any other matters that deal with both income and remainder interests.
(c) Any other ordinary expenses for the administration, management or preservation of trust property and the distribution of income. These would include the expense of interest, ordinary repairs, regularly recurring taxes assessed against principal and expenses of a proceeding that concerns primarily the income interest.
(d) Recurring premiums on insurance covering the loss of a principal asset or loss of the income it generates.
(e) Taxes required to be paid based on receipts allocated to income.

8. Disbursements Normally Apportioned between Principal and Income

A tax required to be paid by a trustee on the trust's share of an entity's taxable income must be paid from income to the extent that the receipts from the entity are allocated to income. To the extent that such receipts are allocated to principal and the trust's share of the entity's taxable income exceeds the total receipts from the entity, the tax must be paid from principal. Receipts allocated to principal or income must be reduced by the amount distributed to a beneficiary from principal or income for which the trust receives a deduction in calculating the tax. (*See* Part Three, Chapters IV and V for an explanation of a trust's deduction for distributions under the federal income tax rules).

9. Permissible Adjustments between Principal and Income

1. A trustee may transfer to principal a reasonable amount of the net cash receipts from a principal asset that is subject to depreciation, but this does not apply to:
   - Any portion for real property used by a beneficiary as a residence,
   - Any tangible personal property used by a beneficiary for personal enjoyment,
   - Any asset used in a business or activity for which the trustee is accounting for separately as allowed by the Act.
2. Under certain circumstances, and according to lengthy and specific rules, the Act allows a trustee to make adjustments between income and principal to the extent he considers necessary. This provision has been brought about largely due to the greater emphasis on total return as an investment concept, and the corresponding decline of income returns in investment portfolios. The provision allows the income benefi-

ciaries to be treated more equitably where this has resulted. For a trustee making such adjustments, there are several requirements, however. The trustee must be investing and managing trust assets as a prudent investor. The terms of the trust must describe the amount that may or must be distributed to a beneficiary by referring to the trust's income. The trustee must determine that he is otherwise unable to administer the trust impartially, based upon what is fair and reasonable to all beneficiaries. The intent of the Act in this regard is to give a trustee operating under The Prudent Investor Rules the leeway to select investments without having to realize a particular portion of the portfolio's total return in the form of traditional trust accounting income.

This ability to adjust can create extra work for the trustee, as he must document the reasons for the adjustments he makes. In general, it may not be necessary to make deep inquiries into individual needs of income beneficiaries, but at the very least there should be documentation showing that the income generated by the trust he is administering is well below that historically generated by trust portfolios.

Some states have introduced the unitrust concept as an optional method the trustee can use to increase the pay-out for income beneficiaries. These states include Delaware, Maine, New York and Missouri; Iowa and Pennsylvania have proposed legislation in progress. Where the unitrust election exists, the trustee may elect to pay some percentage, fixed by statute, of the annual market value of the trust to income beneficiaries if the income generated by the trust is deemed insufficient. For example, Delaware allows a range of three to five percent of the annual market value to be paid to the income beneficiaries in lieu of the actual income. It is a sort of "no brainer" approach to resolving income inequity. It relieves the trustee of extra discretionary decisions (and accompanying exposure to liability) that go with making adjustments between income and principal when income is inadequate. However the trustee would have to make this election in a responsible manner and document the reasons for doing it. It might also be difficult to undo, once the election is made, and there could be hazards to making an arbitrary percentage pay-out, as it may be too much or too little in some time periods.

The power to allocate income, in whatever form and alternatives, can vary widely among the states that have made this possible. The trustee operating under such statutes, where the trust instrument has not overridden them, will most likely have to do some research, and because the statutes are often new, there may be some legal questions with which to wrestle.

So much for the Act. As we said, you should look to the trust instrument and your own state law for the specific accounting rules that apply to your trust. We hope that this section has helped your general understanding of fiduciary accounting principles.

C. The Daily Work

When it comes to data processing, banks and trust companies have big advantages over individual trustees. In their Operations Departments, transactions are posted daily using automated trust accounting systems which take the information entered into them and sort it for various purposes. Later the information is retrieved and used for such different purposes as preparing statements, filing tax returns, notifying beneficiaries of income and deductions for their own tax filings and for keeping the corporate trustee's books in balance.

These systems are remarkably efficient because they not only digest transactions and regurgitate them in different forms for various purposes, but also because they can do many other things as well. They can print complete statements in many formats, cut checks for remittance purposes, track investment performance, and keep many levels of company employees separately informed of things they need to know about a particular account or a group of accounts. For an account that has been on a system since its inception, some can reassemble years of information for the preparation of a formal accounting. There are even provisions for disaster control through the automated safekeeping of duplicate information at remote sites. Obviously, information has to be entered correctly, but another marvel of a good system is that erroneous entries, if they are caught in time, can be reversed without the beneficiary ever knowing, and the system can even help catch them.

Unless you act in the capacity of a professional trustee and are administering more than one very large trust, you aren't likely to have the benefits of an automated trust system. Even the simplest automated system is expensive when the volume of accounts is small, and you wouldn't need special features required by a corporate trustee, such as profitability or compliance reporting.

If you don't have a financial background, you could delegate a major part of your record keeping and reporting to an accountant, preferably a CPA in an established firm. You would arrange for him or her to receive copies of broker and bank statements, and he or she could provide you with completed statements for the trust to retain in your files and send to beneficiaries. The accountant could also perform the tax work. But you would still be left with a certain amount of data processing and filing.

If you do your own record keeping, you can do it all by hand, as trustees have done for several hundred years. However if you are computer-literate, you can imitate an automatic trust accounting system to some degree with one of a number of available spreadsheet applications. With one of these, you can build templates that can be reused as often as needed. Information can be entered in several places simultaneously to serve different purposes. Mathematical functions can be recalculated automatically as you revise entries. Templates can be formatted for whatever purpose you have, such as worksheets or final statements.

If you are only semi-literate in front of a computer, you could have a consultant create templates to your specifications, so that you would need only to put information into them and tap the "Enter" key to perform a number of instantaneous calculations for your purposes. You will see an example of a few templates further on in this chapter, after we have covered the basics of trust record keeping and accounting.

Where a template is to be used as a statement for a beneficiary statement, it can be formatted for that purpose by deleting the grid lines and labels and adding appropriate headings and other improvements. Here are very basic examples of trust accounting procedures you could use.

1. Income Receipts Ledgers

For each income-producing principal asset, you would have a separate ledger listing the asset, the number of units, the character of the income receipt, and the date received.

XYZ Corporation Common Stock Dividends

Date	*Units*	*Amount*
3/5/02	*200 shares*	*$40.00*

Entries could be transferred to monthly or quarterly statements. These amounts could be totaled periodically for various purposes, such as transferring annual totals to a tax report. They could provide the basis for an accounting covering several years.

2. Income Expense Ledgers

For each type of expense chargeable to income, you would have a similar ledger.

Trustee Fees

Date	*Description*	*Amount*
3/31/02	*Trustee's Fees 1/1/02 - 3/31/02*	*$1,250*

3. Principal Assets Ledger

For each principal asset, you would create a separate ledger, showing the date the asset was received and its inventory value (which could be the market value when received at inception of the trust, its value fixed for death tax purposes if received from an estate, or its cost basis if received subsequently).

XYZ Corporation Common Stock

Date	*Transferred Units*	*Inventory Value*
4/10/96	*received 200 shares*	*$55,000*
3/22/02	*sold 100 shares*	*-27,500*
Balance	*100 shares*	*27,500*

There would also be a ledger for principal cash to keep track of changes in this asset due to purchases and sales and other changes with respect to principal assets. The original entry would show the cash at inception of the trust. In most cases this would be frequently added to or subtracted from as the account is credited due to cash receipts from sales, maturities and other cash-producing changes, along with cash disbursements associated with the acquisition of new principal assets, the payment of expenses, and cash distributions to beneficiaries.

Principal Cash
First National Bank Money Market Account

Date	*Description*	*Amount*
3/1/98	*Beginning Balance*	*$4,500*
3/22/02	*Proceeds of sale, 100 shares XYZ Corp Common*	*27,500*
3/30/02	*Trustee's fee 1/1/02*	*1,250*
3/31/02	*Ending Balance*	*$30,750*

If there were more than one cash account, as would be the case with multiple bank deposit accounts for principal cash, you would maintain separate ledgers for each, which would be consolidated on a separate single cash account ledger.

Entries into an electronic spreadsheet could be linked to other spreadsheets for other purposes. One purpose would be the preparation of periodic statements for your own records and for distribution to the beneficiary. These statements, in basic form, consist of one for income and disbursements to the income and principal accounts, and one which is a schedule of the principal assets showing their inventory values, and usually also their current market values.

For statement purposes, you could have a separate template with places for the entries you make in your ledgers. For example, the amounts you enter in the income disbursements ledgers for trustee's fees principal cash could also be entered simultaneously in a statement for receipts and disbursements.

Receipts and Disbursements

	Income	*Principal*
3/31/02 Trustee's fees 1/1/02-3/31/02	*-$1,250*	*-$1,250*
3/22/02 Sold 100 shares XYZ com. stock		*27,500*

The change in the holdings of XYZ shares would be reflected in the most recent schedule showing the current inventory of principal assets, called (what else) Principal Assets.

At a bank or trust company, there would be a code entered for each type of transaction description, so all the account administrator or other employee would have to do is enter it once, and the description would be automatically entered in different forms in different places for various purposes. You, unfortunately, will probably have to revise descriptions frequently and enter them by hand, but at least you will not have to consult a code sheet and try to figure out which code best suits an odd transaction - one of the reasons for "automated errors" at banks.

D. Preparing Statements

Under the terms of the trust instrument or prevailing statutes, you may not be required to provide a beneficiary with periodic statements or to render accountings. However, you are not relieved of the duty to keep clear records of your administration or of the duty to furnish such information requested by the beneficiary as he or she needs to enforce his or her rights or protect him or herself against a breach of trust. Therefore you should always have the information for these purposes at hand, and it should be current.

Financial statements prepared on a monthly basis are a practical method for keeping the record of your administration up to date, whether or not they are provided to the beneficiary that frequently. As explained above, these normally consist of a Statement of Receipts and Disbursements and a Statement of Principal Assets in the basic assembly, although they can also include additional reports for such information as performance measurement and investment operating costs.

1. Statement of Receipts and Disbursements

This is a record of the cash value of all incoming and outgoing assets for a period of time. The cash values of principal assets are shown at their inventory value, which is generally the value at the time these assets were received by the trust. This point may be lost on beneficiaries, who may think that they are looking at market values or cost basis values on this schedule, so it is advisable to explain it.

The descriptions should be brief but clear. Many of the problems that beneficiaries and others have with the statements of corporate trustees is that the descriptions produced by codes in automated systems are more oriented toward computer and formatting (space) requirements than they are toward the reader. A description such as "Div 1000shs IBM com" is easily decipherable by the average beneficiary into "a dividend on 1,000 shares of IBM common stock." But, "Andorra NsHome dues/rec," is less so. What has happened is that a payment has been made to the Andorra Nursing Home for dues and "recreation" because there is no code for the beneficiary's liquor bill.

You can select from a wide variety of terms and formats, as long as you remember that your duty to keep accounts includes making them clear. In the format shown in the following example there are columns for Income Cash, Principal Cash , Invested Income, and Principal Investments. The principal investments are shown at their inventory value. Each column begins with a balance from the end of the previous period, describes credits and debits chronologically and arrives at a balance for the end of the period.

In this example, the intent has been to simplify a typical statement. An actual statement might have shown the charges for trustee fees and investment advisor fees as allocated 50% each to Income Cash and Principal Cash, the charge for safekeeping might have been charged against Income Cash, and the timing of income payments to the trustee, advisor and the beneficiary might not have captured all of the income receipts for the statement period.

Example–Statement of Receipts and Disbursements (.00s omitted)

William Jones Family Trust — Statement of Receipts and Disbursements

December 1, 2002 to January 1, 2003

Descriptions	Income Cash	Invested Income	Principal Cash	Principal Investments
Ending Balances 11/30/02	$17	$10,000	$12,400	$524,738
12/01/02 Interest on FNB Tax-Exempt Money Market Fund		32	30	
12/02/02				
12/10/02 Sold 100 shs XYZ Corp common			5,200	-3,800
Purchased 100 shs ABC Corp common			-4,900	4,900
12/15/02 Dividend 2,000 shs XYZ Corp common	520			
Dividend 1000shs DEF Industries	250			

12/26/02 First National Bank Fee for safekeeping			-36	
12/28/02 Interest 1,112 units Calvert Municipal Bond Fund	412			
12/31/02 Transfer interest FNB Money Market Fund	62	-32	-30	
Trustee's fee 1/12 of 1% on market value, Principal as of 12/30/02	-304			
Trent Investment Advisors Fee, 1/12 of 1% on market Value as of 12/30/02	-304			
Paid to Elise Jones	-653			
Ending Balance 12/31/02	$0	$10,000	$12,664	$525,838

2. Schedule of Principal Assets

This statement would list principal assets by category. The category headings can be broad, such as Cash, Fixed Income, Common Stock, Real Estate, etc., but each category is often divided into subcategories, such as industry groupings for common stocks. The statement should provide carrying values, but it is helpful if you also show market values. Some statements also indicate estimated dollar income and percentage yields. Total values are shown for each category and for the entire portfolio.

The following example is, again, simplified, so don't look for a close correlation with the earlier IPS example provided for the William Jones Family Trust. Because of the relatively few stock holdings shown here, they are not separated by industry.

Example - Statement of Principal Assets

William Jones Family Trust — Statement of Principal Assets
December 31, 2002

	Inventory Value	Market Value	Estimated Income	% Yield
Temporary Investments				
FNB Tax-Exempt Money Market Fund	$12,664	$12,664	$367	2.9

Fixed Income Investments				
1,112 units Calvert Municipal Bond fund	95,550	98,880	2,966	5.0
Equity Investments				
100 shs, ABC Corp common	9,600	9,700	242	2.5
1,000 shs DEF Industries common	97,000	100,000	1,000	1.0
2,000 shs GHI Company common	187,888	191 200	5,162	2.7
1900 shs XYZ Corp common	135,800	138,666	4,079	3.0
Total Equities	$430,288	$439,566	$10,483	2.4
Total Principal Assets	$538,502	$551,110	$13,816	2.5

3. Performance Reporting–An Option

Performance measurement is complex and is often proof of the adage that "figures can lie and liars can figure." The selection of time periods, time-weighting or dollar-weighting, index comparisons and measurement factors can all be manipulated. Corporate trustees generally adhere to ethical standards drafted by the Association for Investment Management and Research (AIMR). However the AIMR standards in many cases are either irrelevant or too impractical for you, as an individual trustee, to apply. For the average trust that has more than one investment objective, it is probably inadvisable to make performance a major issue, and it would be enough to let the standard-issue financial statements speak for themselves.

However, it might be helpful to the beneficiaries if you were to provide them periodically with a reminder of what performance means in a trust context. The following message is an example of such a reminder for a trust with balanced growth and income objectives. It could be enclosed with the year-end statement mailed to a beneficiary.

Example–Explanation of Trust-Oriented Performance

Dear (beneficiary):

With the closing of the past year, I once more wish to remind you that the long-term objectives of this trust are to provide reasonable current income consistent with moderate growth of both the income and the principal over time. We are also governed by the requirements of trust investing to invest prudently, and not take the kinds of risk that are associated with large returns but also with volatility and loss.

Accordingly this portfolio is a blend of securities in different asset categories that may not compare favorably with a particular market index, such as Standard & Poor's 500 Index, which is comprised entirely of stock in large companies. However, we think that the portfolio is designed to best meet the often conflicting objectives of this particular trust and enable me to fulfill my duty to the beneficiaries as Trustee of treating all of you, present and future, with impartiality and fairness.

Over the past three years, the trust has, as a matter of fact, exceeded the objectives established for income yield and capital appreciation as stated in the Investment Policy Statement summary that I provided you with at the inception of the trust.

Chapter IV
Taxation—In General

For those who relish elaborate puzzles, federal taxation can be the greatest game ever. The instruction manual for this game is the Internal Revenue Code (the Code), which sets forth rules, exceptions to the rules and exceptions to the exceptions. Adding to the complexity are interpretations of the rules from various levels of authority from both within and without the Internal Revenue Service. For trusts, federal taxation is governed by rather daunting Subchapter J of the Code. Many professionals find the tax laws relating to trusts intriguing and challenging, but few trustees are enthusiastic about games where missteps and lack of expertise can result in extra taxes, interest costs and penalties.

We'll ease you into tax waters in this chapter and immerse you in them in the next. The purpose of these two chapters is not to equip you to file fiduciary tax returns. You'll do this work yourself only if you have the necessary specialized training and experience; otherwise you'll farm it out to experts. Our intention here is to provide you with an overview together with a number of trust tax concepts and insights that will help you to understand what your experts are doing. Where we enter into detail (like that in our explanation of the nearly obsolete throwback rules), it is mainly to give you some sense of how complex tax compliance can be.

It may also help you if we explain in general terms to beneficiaries some of the mysteries of the tax interplay between themselves and their trust, such as why the trust income they receive may not match the trust income they are taxed with. More importantly, it may give you some understanding of how a trust's tax liability interacts with the tax liability of income beneficiaries and remaindermen, so that you can coordinate the trust's tax returns with theirs. Finally it may help you to avoid missteps that could result in financial liability for you.

Except where we specifically refer to state or local matters, all references are to taxation at the federal level. Because of the special connotation the term "grantor" has for tax purposes, we use it in lieu of the term "settlor" in this chapter and the next one.

A. The Trust as a Taxable Entity

A private trust is a conduit in the sense that, barring some sort of calamity, every asset that goes into it eventually comes out again (although some tax attributes, such as certain tax carryover credits can be lost forever if not used). Income that is received is paid out; even income that is accumulated is eventually distributed. To the extent that principal assets transferred to the trust are not distributed or used for beneficiaries during the term of the trust, they are distributed at the end of it. However what goes into a trust does not always come out with the same characterization, as we shall explain later.

The income of trusts is subject to taxation, just like the income of other tax entities, such as individuals, partnerships and corporations. The rates of the regular tax are progressive and are currently the same as for individual taxpayers. The brackets are punishingly compressed, however, so that the top tax rate of 38.6% for 2002 applies before taxable income exceeds $8,500.

Tax Rates for Trusts - for Years 2002 and 2003

(The following taxable income brackets will be adjusted downward annually through 2006. In 2006 the rates will be 15%, 25%, 28% 33% and 35%.)

For taxable years beginning in 2002, the following rates are in effect:
(Computed using the formula provided in Code Sec. 1(f))

If taxable income is:	The tax is:
Not over $1,850	15% of taxable income
Over $1,850 but not over $4,400	$277.50 plus 27% of the excess over $1,850
Over $4,400 but not over $6,750	$966.00 plus 30% of the excess over $4,400
Over $6,750 but not over $9,200	$1,671.00 plus 35% of the excess over $6,750
Over $9,200	$2,528.50 plus 38.6% of the excess over $9,200

For taxable year beginning in 2003:

If taxable income is:	The tax is:
Not over $1,900	15% of the taxable income
Over $1,900 but not over $4,500	$285.00 plus 27% of the excess over $1,900.00
Over $4,500 but not over $6,850	$987.00 plus 30% of the excess over $4,500.00
Over $6,850 but not over $9,350	$1,692.00 plus 35% of the excess over $6,850.00
Over $9,350	$2,567.00 plus 38.6% of the excess over $9,350

Like other taxable entities, trusts are entitled to deductions from income. Unique to trusts is the distribution deduction, which a trust receives for paying out income to beneficiaries. It pays taxes only on such income as it is deemed to have retained, and the beneficiaries are taxed according to the type and amount of income they are deemed to have received. Because of their tax brackets and rates of tax, most trusts don't retain income if they can distribute and deduct it. Other deductions are similar to those available to individuals, but there are differences that will be explained.

A trust has a personal exemption, but the amount depends upon the requirements for the distribution of income. Trusts are treated differently for several purposes depending upon whether they are "simple" or "complex." A simple trust is one where the trust instrument requires the trust to distribute all of its income currently and prohibits it from setting aside, paying, or using amounts in the tax year for charitable purposes, and the trust itself makes no distributions from principal during the year.

A complex trust is any other trust. A simple trust could become a complex trust in a particular year, as it would if the trustee exercised a discretionary power to invade principal, or if the trust terminated and made distributions to remaindermen. Conversely, in a year in which a complex trust met all the criteria for a simple trust, it could be classified as a simple trust.

We should point out a possible problem that might arise if a state's adoption of The Uniform Principal and Income Act of 1997 gives a trustee the right to make adjustments between income and principal. Under certain circumstances this might cause a trust that would otherwise be classified as "simple" to be classified as "complex." If you think this is an issue that might apply to your trust, you should review it with your attorney or accountant.

The parallel income tax system of an alternative minimum tax (AMT) for individual taxpayers also applies to trusts. AMT rules were designed to exact at least a minimum amount of tax from tax entities who have large incomes but who shield substantial amounts of it with certain available deductions and exemptions called "preference" items. The AMT system recaptures a degree of sheltered income, which is then taxed according to AMT rates. The taxpayer is liable for any excess of AMT over his regular tax. You must deal with AMT for trusts that have preference items or make distributions to beneficiaries, and you must consider it in calculating estimated tax payments.

You are free to use an accounting method of your choice for tax purposes, but it must be used consistently and it must reflect income clearly. One exception is that the accrual method must be used if the production, purchase or sale of merchandise is a material part of trust income. Most trustees account on a cash basis. Trusts must use a calendar year for filing purposes.

The tax life of a trust begins when the trust has been funded, except for revocable trusts and most grantor trusts, which we discuss in the next chapter. At this point, or at the filing of the first Form 1041, you should file Form 56, which notifies the Internal Revenue Service of your fiduciary relationship. This gives the Internal Revenue Service your address so that it can send all correspondence to you, including notices of deficiency. You would also file a Form 56 if you replaced a prior trustee. If you fail to file Form 56, you could end up forfeiting a right to appeal a deficiency notice and having to pay the deficiency. For example, this could happen if a prior trustee received a deficiency notice and didn't forward it to you, unless you had notified the Internal Revenue Service with a Form 56. You would then be violating your duty to protect trust property.

As taxable private trusts must file on a calendar year basis, you would file the first Form 1041 after the end of the first calendar year.

The trust's tax life ends when all of the assets have been distributed, except for reasonable amounts kept in reserve for unascertained or contingent expenses or liabilities. You would file the final Form 1041 for the trust's last calendar year, and you would file a new Form 56 to notify the Internal Revenue Service that the trust relationship has ended. This does not relieve you of personal liability for taxes owed by the trust, nor does your discharge by a state court. You would also file Form 56 if your relationship as trustee ended before the termination of the trust.

Multiple trusts are taxed as one trust if the primary beneficiaries of each trust are substantially the same, the grantors of each are substantially the same, and a principal purpose for their creation was the avoidance of income tax. For this purpose, a husband and wife are treated as one person. Irrevocable trusts created before March 1, 1984, are not affected by this multiple trust rule, but a subsequent contribution of corpus to such a trust would trigger its application.

As we proceed, it might be helpful to keep in mind the following general outline of how taxable trust income is arrived at:

Total Income
less
<u>Deductions from Total Income</u>
= Adjusted Total Income
less
Income Distribution Deduction
and
Certain Federal Transfer Taxes
and
<u>Personal Exemption</u>
= <u>Taxable Income</u>

To arrive at a result called Adjusted Gross Income (AGI) used in certain calculations (such as the 2% limit on certain deductions), the following items are subtracted from Total Income:

- administration expenses
- the income distribution deduction
- deductions arising from operating a business or trade or from the production of income, if they were not allowed for in calculating Gross Income
- the personal exemption

B. Trust Accounting vs. Tax Accounting

Trust financial accounting and tax accounting are not the same. The purpose of trust financial accounting is to provide information to parties of interest to the trust about your administration, and is based upon the allocation of receipts and disbursements to income and principal. The purpose of tax accounting is to determine the trust's tax liability by identifying what income items are taxable and what expenses are deductible. However, tax accounting accepts many concepts of trust financial accounting. For instance, the trust instrument's determination of what items constitute income will also determine income for tax accounting, unless it makes fundamental departures from state law concepts, such as labeling long-term capital gains as income to be distributed to an income beneficiary.

An Extended List of Federal Tax Reporting Forms

Form 56: An information form as explained above.

Form 1041: Essentially the trust-equivalent of Form 1040. Among other things, it identifies the trust by name and type, carries out the steps necessary to arrive at taxable income, and declares any tax liability or claim for refund. It's the assembly line for the results taken from supporting schedules and other forms.

Form 1041, Schedule A: This is included on Form 1041, and is for the purpose of calculating any charitable deduction for a complex trust.

Form 1041, Schedule B: Also included on Form 1041, this is where you first determine the trust's distributable net income and then the deduction for distributions to beneficiaries. Interest and dividend income isn't detailed on this form.

Form 1040, Schedule B: This is the schedule you file with your personal Form 1040 to report interest and dividend income in detail, item by item. You aren't required to file one with Form 1041, but you should consider doing this anyway. You can use your copy to substantiate this detail as a very formal-looking tax document for anyone who subsequently inquires.

Form 1040, Schedule C: This schedule is required to report profit or losses if the trust is operating a proprietorship.

Form 1041, Schedule D: Specialized for trusts, this is like your Form 1040 Schedule D for reporting gains or losses from capital transactions. The major difference is that it allows for the fact that gains can be allocated to beneficiaries, but losses must remain in the trust.

Form 1040, Schedule E: This form is filed with Form 1041 to report income from rental real estate, but see Form 4835 below if farm lands are rented out.

Form 1040, Schedule F: This is the equivalent of Schedule C, but for reporting of profit or loss from farming activity.

Form 1041, Schedule G: Included on Form 1041, this is where the tax liability, if any, is computed.

Form 1041, Schedule I: This schedule must be filed for any trust claiming an income distribution deduction.

Form 1041, Schedule J: You must file this form for a trust with accumulated income if the total distribution exceeds trust accounting income.

Form 1041, Schedule K-1: This is an information return you must file with Form 1041 and also use to report to each beneficiary separately his amounts and classes of income, deductions and credits. The responsibility with respect to the beneficiaries is both a tax requirement and a fiduciary duty.
As trustee, you may also be the recipient of Forms K-1 from other pass-through entities, which include partnerships, S corporations, other trusts and real estate mortgage investment conduits.

Form 1045: This "Application for Tentative Refund" is used for carry-back of Net Operating Losses.

Form 1099: This form, in its varieties, is used by payors of income to report such income both to recipients and to the IRS. For example, you might receive Form 1099-OID from the issuer of original issue discount bonds. Another example: you would provide yourself and the IRS with a Form 1099-Misc to report trustee fees paid to you by the trust.

Form 4562: For reporting depreciation and amortization.

Form 4797: For reporting ordinary gains and losses from sales or exchanges of business-use property.

Form 4835: If the trust is involved in renting out farmland or in sharecropping operations, this form must be used to report profit or loss.

Chapter V
Taxation—Selected Details

A. Your Tax Compliance Responsibilities

You don't have to file tax returns for some trusts, so let's deal with them first. If a trust has no taxable income, less than $600 of gross income, and no nonresident aliens as beneficiaries, no Form 1041 is required.

If you are trustee or co-trustee of your own trust which you created as grantor, and you are treated as the owner of all of the trust assets because you can revoke the trust, you don't have to file form 1041. This also holds for a trust where a husband and wife are sole grantors, with one or both as trustee(s), and they file joint tax returns. Furthermore, this also applies to most grantor trusts (described in Exhibit I, A Variety of Trusts, in the Appendix) with a third-party trustee where the grantor or other person is considered to be the owner of all income and principal (after December 31, 1995). Personal residence trusts (described in Exhibit I) are grantor trusts. In these cases, the trustee has two options.

1. One is to furnish the address of the trust and the Social Security number of the grantor or other person to payors of income, such as dividend-paying corporations, who will then send you copies of Form 1099 that they have filed with the Internal Revenue Service. You then furnish the grantor or other person with a statement of all income items, deductions and credits to report on his or her Form 1040 in lieu of any Forms 1099.
2. The other is to furnish the name, address and tax identification number of the trust to the income payors, and when they send you Form 1099s, to then file your own Form 1099s with the IRS. Here the trust is considered to be the payor to the grantor or other payee. As above, you furnish the grantor or other person with a statement of tax items.

However these procedures are optional. You can choose to file a Form 1041 with the trust's own tax identification number, attaching a statement of items of income, deduction and credit. You would then furnish a copy of the statement of tax items to the grantor or other person so that he can report these items on his Form 1040. The primary advantage of doing it this way is that you avoid the necessity of sending information to each new income payor for Form 1099 purposes. If you change investments frequently, filing a Form 1041 might result in less paper work, on the whole.

Where a grantor or other party is considered to be the owner of only a portion of the trust, such as just the income, just the principal, or just some part of each, a Form 1041 must be filed for the trust with respect to its share of tax items. Also there are certain types of grantor trusts that must file Form 1041 even if they are owners of all trust income and principal. Of these, the ones you might be trustee for are qualified Subchapter S trusts, foreign trusts, trusts with a sole grantor filing with a fiscal year end, or trusts with a grantor who is not a United States citizen.

For other trusts, you would have to file a return for any year in which the trust has:

- taxable income
- gross income of $600 or more irrespective of taxable income
- a nonresident alien beneficiary

It isn't appropriate for us to go into all of the tax rules that apply to ordinary income, capital gain and loss, deductions and credits and the rest in a book of this nature. What we'll do here is highlight those rules that we think that you should be sensitive to and comment on certain potential problems.

B. Income

On the trust's tax return, a preliminary sum called "Total Income" is arrived at by adding amounts for the following classifications of income:

- interest income
- dividends
- business income
- capital gain or loss
- farm income or loss
- ordinary gain or loss
- other income

However, because most trusts are not involved in businesses or farms, we'll divide theses classes of income into two broad categories, investment income and business income (including farm income), and disregard "other income," which is a catch-all category. If you have no business or farm activities, you won't have to read about the business income category.

1. Investment Income

Tax-Exempt Income

Some investment income is tax-exempt and is not included in gross income (it doesn't constitute "other income" on the tax return). Therefore it must be taken into account in calculating a trust's deductions. For example: without a provision in the trust instrument to the contrary, a trust's contribution to a charity is considered to have been made ratably from taxable and tax-exempt income, and the portion consisting of the latter is a non-deductible charitable contribution. It also has an effect on a trust's deduction for income distributions to beneficiaries, which will be discussed further on.

Dividends

Dividends, more often than not, are payments of corporate income, and they are therefore normally allocated to trust income. Suppose that a simple trust received extraordinary dividends and that they were required by the trust instrument, in a direction that doesn't differ fundamentally from state law, to be allocated to principal. In this case, these dividends wouldn't be trust accounting income and wouldn't be distributable, and therefore wouldn't be included in the distribution deduction. They would be taxable to the trust, however, because for tax purposes, they are still income.

Dividend income earned by mutual fund shares that are a trust asset is taxable income, to the extent the underlying securities are taxable, whether such income is distributed or reinvested. Dividends declared and payable within one tax year are taxable for that year, even if not paid by January 31 of the following year.

Interest

When fixed income securities, other than tax-exempt bonds, United States Treasury bills and Series E and EE United States Savings Bonds, are purchased at a discount or premium, the same rules that apply to individual investors apply to trusts. So do the rules for bonds purchased with accrued interest. You would have to deal with amortization and allocations of income and capital gain accordingly. Because of the characteristics of deferred income, the tax treatment of interest on United States savings bonds, zero coupon bonds and other deferred interest obligations, and the elections concerning them may also be troublesome. You would have a present tax on income that won't be received until the future. How you deal with this will depend upon what authority you have been given by the trust instrument or state law.

Capital Gains and Losses

We assume that you have a general understanding of how cost basis is established in order to determine gain and loss for tax purposes. Trusts follow rules similar to those for individuals in determining gain and loss. You shouldn't have any trouble establishing cost basis for assets that you purchase or acquire subsequently as a result of a purchase, but assets will most likely come into your hands in other ways, too, unless the funding of the trust was solely with cash.

You should understand how cost basis is established for gifts to a trust if the settlor transfers non-cash assets to the trust. Transfers by gift generally carry over the donor's original cost basis, with adjustments for gift tax paid at the time of transfer. However, for the purpose of determining loss on the sale of gift property, the basis would be the fair market value at the time the gift was made, if this value is lower. There could be neither gain nor loss if the proceeds from sale were less than the basis for gain or more than the basis for loss. These rules would apply to any gifts to the trust.

Property received from the settlor's estate generally has as its basis the value it had on the decedent's date of death or on the estate's elected alternate valuation date six months later. There would be adjustments for amortization, depreciation, *etc.*, during the estate's holding period. No gain or loss is realized on property distributed in kind unless the executor elects to recognize it, or unless the distribution substitutes for a fixed-dollar amount. The executor might wish to recognize gain or loss at the time of transfer to the trust to provide you with a step-up in basis or to aid you in balancing gains and losses upon subsequent disposition of the assets. You should obtain a copy of the federal estate tax return Form 706 for your records to verify cost basis information on assets transferred from an estate.

The basis of assets "poured" into a trust from a different trust would depend upon the circumstances. For example, assets transferred from a marital deduction trust at the surviving spouse's death would have a basis established in a manner similar to that used to establish the basis for assets received from a settlor's estate. Assets received from such a trust during the spouse's lifetime according to her direction would be subject to the basis rules for gifts. If assets were poured over from another trust in default of the execution of a limited power of appointment (such as that a surviving spouse might have over a non-marital deduction trust), the basis for the assets in the prior trust would be carried over, but without application of the gift tax rules.

The "Two Year Rule" is now repealed, but you may have to deal with it for tax returns filed for years prior to 1998. If appreciated property was transferred to a trust, that rule required the property, if sold within two years of the transfer, to be taxed as if the transferor had sold it. The trust paid the tax. You were authorized by the Code to inspect the transferor's income tax return to the extent necessary to calculate the tax based on the transferor's tax rates for the year of sale. This rule was intended to prevent the application of the trust's possibly lower tax rate, but it became generally irrelevant after tax brackets for trusts were compressed. The rule never applied to charitable lead or charitable remainder trusts.

Capital gains realized by a mutual fund are taxable income, whether distributed or reinvested, and whether the underlying securities are taxable or tax-exempt. Dividends, including capital gains, declared and payable within one tax year are taxable for that year, even if not paid by January 31 of the following year. Some mutual funds elect not to distribute long-term capital gains, retaining them and paying tax on them. In this case your basis on the fund shares is increased by the gain and reduced by the tax. You would report the gain and the tax with information provided by the fund.

Be careful about selling shares in a mutual fund where dividends are reinvested. Unless you sell the entire mutual fund holding, dividends might be reinvested within thirty days before or after the sale, triggering the "Wash Sale Rule." This rule disallows losses for securities that are sold if substantially identical securities are purchased within that time frame, and the losses then decrease the basis of the newly purchased securities.

You should also consider your relationship with grantors, beneficiaries and other trusts when executing capital transactions. Losses are disallowed on sales or exchanges between related parties, whether direct or indirect. As a trustee, you are a related party to a grantor, a beneficiary, the trustee or a beneficiary of another trust having the same grantor as yours, and any corporation where the trust or the grantor owns more than 50% of its stock.

The recently changed rules for separating and taxing capital gains according to how long the assets were held before they were sold apply to trusts as well as individuals. One additional wrinkle for complex trusts and charitable remainder trusts is that where such gains are distributed, those in the highest-taxed category must precede the others in descending order. In other words, you can't distribute the gains subject to the lowest rate of tax until you have used up the others.

Rents, Royalties, Partnerships, Estates, Other Trusts, Etc.

Income or loss from these entities, including real estate mortgage investment conduits, is passed through them to the trust, as are certain deductions, credits, and capital gains and losses.

2. Business Income

There is always a potential danger for trusts carrying on a business or a farm. Such a trust could be taxed as an "association" (a corporation) and lose its distribution deduction, if it has more corporate than non-corporate characteristics. A trust can have:

- continuity of life
- centralization of management
- limited liability
- free transferability of interests

These are four common characteristics it can share with a corporation without having the problem.

However, if the trust also has:

- an objective to carry on a business and divide profits that could as easily be attained within a corporate structure
- associates

It could be considered to have corporate status for tax purposes. Beware of a trust holding a business interest if the trust's objectives go beyond protecting and conserving trust property. Beware of parties to the trust who are associated with a business interest held by the trust, such as a beneficiary who manages the business.

Rental activity could be construed as operation of a business rather than a passive activity. If you actively engage in buying real estate, improving and managing it , you might be doing more than protecting and conserving the trust property, and the trust could be considered an association for tax purposes for the years in which this activity takes place.

Business-use property, such as machinery that has been subject to depreciation deductions, or a gravel pit that has been subject to depletion deductions, can result in ordinary gains and losses upon disposal. Any recapture gain (ordinary gain), is reported on Form 4797, while any capital gain is transferred to Schedule D.

If the trust engages in farming or fishing activities and distributes the income to an individual beneficiary, this income should be properly described when you disclose it to the beneficiary. If he or she meets an applicable gross income test, he or she can take advantage of special rules pertaining to income from farming or fishing sources.

Businesses often have unprofitable years. A trust can have net operating losses, but a deduction for them can't be passed out to the beneficiaries until the trust terminates. Also, where trust financial accounting requires a net operating loss to be charged against principal, the loss can't be carried forward to another accounting period to determine trust accounting income. Consequently the remaindermen bear the loss.

3. Income in Respect of a Decedent

A testamentary trust, or a trust under an agreement that serves as a substitute for a will, may be a recipient of Income in Respect of a Decedent (IRD). This is income earned by a decedent or attributable to his or her actions before his or her death that wasn't paid to him or her before he or she died. It can fall into any of the classes that constitute income on Form 1041. It can be taxed for federal estate tax purposes as an asset of the decedent's estate; if the estate is large enough, it can be taxed for generation skipping transfer tax purposes, and it is taxed as income when received by the trust or the trust's beneficiaries. For example, an installment note could be an IRD-producing asset, but the IRD would be taxed only as the installments carrying out this income were actually paid. For income tax purposes, there is a deduction for any estate tax paid. This is taken as a miscellaneous deduction that is not subject to the 2% of adjusted gross income limit. However, tax-exempt income is not IRD and there is no deduction for federal estate tax paid on such income included in an estate.

IRD can arise from many types of activity, including investing, business and farming enterprises, compensation, installment sales and distributions from retirement plans. As an asset of the decedent, it is generally not classed as trust accounting income. If you receive an IRD-producing asset from an estate before its income is paid, you won't have received any distributable net income from the estate. If you collect the income from the IRD asset subsequently, the income is taxable to the trust. Distributions you make to a beneficiary after you have collected this income are subject to the normal rules for determining a distribution deduction.

C. Deductions - Other than the Deduction for Distributions

A major deduction for most trusts is the one for distributions to beneficiaries, but before you can determine this deduction, you must first take into account a number of other deductions as a separate group. The sum of this group is deducted from Total Income.

No expenses relating to tax-exempt income are deductible. Expenses are either direct or indirect. An expense directly related to tax-exempt income, such as fees for collecting interest of tax-exempt bonds, would not be deductible. An indirect expense, such as the total fees for collecting the dividends and interest of mixed portfolio of taxable and tax-exempt securities, would have to be allocated on a "reasonable" basis. In this case, "reasonable" is easy to determine; the fees would be multiplied by the fraction of taxable income divided by total income to arrive at a deductible expense. If it were very difficult to collect taxable income, a disproportionate allocation of expense to this income would be justified.

1. Interest Expense

The rules for the deduction of interest expenses are the same for trusts as they are for individuals. Investment interest deductions can't exceed investment income for any one year, but an excess expense can be carried forward. You can also increase investment income in a tax year by electing to include investment capital gains as ordinary income, if you are willing to forego the benefit of the special rates that apply to capital gains. An example of one situation where this election could be beneficial is where a carry-forward loss would otherwise be wasted at termination of the trust. Here the investment income could be offset by the loss carried forward.

Mortgage interest is deductible for a residence owned by a trust that is the residence of a beneficiary with a current or residuary interest in the trust. Interest incurred for carrying on a trade or business is fully deductible. Personal interest expense of a trust, such as that paid on income tax deficiencies, is not deductible.

2. Taxes

Deductible taxes include state, local and foreign taxes on income, excess profits and real estate, state and local taxes on personal property, and the generation-skipping transfer tax on distributions of income.

3. Administration Expenses

Certain administration expenses of a trust are deductible in full without the limitation of 2% of adjusted gross income that might otherwise apply to certain expenses of individuals. These include your trustee fees, fees of attorneys, accountants and preparers of tax returns, and other expenses that would not have been incurred but for the existence of the trust. Fees paid to you and co-trustees are deductible regardless of their allocation between income or principal, provided they are reasonable. This includes additional fees for extraordinary services.

Fees payable to you because of the termination of the trust might not be fully deductible from income for the final year. You would have to employ a "reasonable" method of allocation. This could mean taking into account tax-exempt income, taxable income, net realized gains and net unrealized appreciation for the entire term of the trust.

Some expenses may be subject to the 2%-of-adjusted-gross-income limitation. It isn't clear if investment advisor fees are fully deductible, for example. The Sixth Circuit Court of Appeals and the IRS are at odds on this issue. The Sixth Circuit finding was that the assistance of an investment advisor is essential to an inexperienced trustee in preserving the assets of a trust, because such a trustee could be subjected to liability for losses arising from his inexperience. However, in view of the Internal Revenue Service's opposite view, you must have a strong case for fully deducting the expense of investment advisory services.

4. Charitable Contributions

Simple trusts may not make charitable contributions. Complex trusts may make charitable contributions if the trust instrument so provides, but only to the extent that they are made from gross income (no deduction is allowed for tax-exempt income, which is not included in gross income). The deduction is unlike that available to individuals in that it is unlimited, and it also applies to contributions made to foreign charities. Generally the recipients must exist for a charitable, religious, literary, scientific or educational purpose, as defined in the Code.

One exception to the unlimited deduction rule is that contributions from net income from a trade or business or debt-financed property are subject to the percentage limits of adjusted gross income that apply to individuals. Where a trust has such unrelated business income, an allocation of the contribution must be made between it and investment income, unless the trust instrument has restricted contributions to investment income. The charitable contribution attributable to unrelated business income isn't deductible.

You can offset income in the current year with charitable deductions available in the following year by electing to do this by the due date of the return for the current year. This applies to the due date for an extended filing.

Where a complex trust makes contributions that include either principal or tax-exempt income, you have to make adjustments to arrive at the deductible amount. For instance, to find the deductible amount for a contribution consisting of both taxable and tax-exempt income, you would use the formula:

$$\frac{\textit{Taxable Income}}{\textit{Total Income}} \times \textit{Charitable Distribution} = \textit{Includible Taxable Income}$$

If the trust instrument for a trust with tax-exempt income required that charitable contributions are to be made out of gross income in order to make the entire contribution deductible, there could be an opportunity to allocate more tax-exempt income to a non-charitable beneficiary's distribution. Accordingly, the Internal Revenue Service requires that there must be an economic effect arising from the allocation provided for in the trust instrument. There probably would not be an economic effect if the amount a charity receives is unaffected by the allocation of taxable and tax-exempt income. However, if the amount the charity receives is increased by allocating more tax-exempt income to the non-charitable beneficiary, an economic effect would exist.

Unlike individuals, who can carry forward an unused charitable deduction for five years, no such benefit is available for trusts. Where this might be a problem is if charitable contributions were made out of accumulated income and the charitable deduction exceeded gross income. In this case the excess contribution would be lost as a future deduction.

A trust created on or before October 9, 1969 is allowed an unlimited deduction for amounts that it sets permanently aside for charitable purposes. To qualify for this deduction, the trust must provide that the amount set aside be an irrevocable remainder interest to a charity or one that can't be revoked by the settlor on account of mental disability, death or contractual arrangement. The accounting records would need to show that the amounts were excluded from income and included in principal. If you were a successor trustee for such a trust, you would want to be assured that the prior trustee had done this.

5. Other Deductions Not Limited to 2% of Adjusted Gross Income

Other deductions that can be taken in full include the following.

Casualty Losses and Theft Losses

The rules for deductions for casualty and theft losses for trusts are the same as those for individuals, except that the reduction by 10% of Adjusted Gross Income (AGI) that applies to personal-use property is based upon the different definition of AGI that applies to trusts.

Deductions in Respect of a Decedent

Deductions in respect of a decedent arise from liabilities of a decedent at the time of his death. These items are limited to expenses for interest, business, taxes, investments and depletion. They are generally deductible at the time they are paid. They offset IRD in computing the deduction for estate tax.

Amortization of Bond Premiums

You can deduct amortization for taxable bonds acquired before October 23, 1986.

6. Deductions Limited to 2% of Adjusted Gross income

A trust can deduct certain expenses it pays that are subject to a ceiling of 2% of the trust's AGI. A trust might also receive miscellaneous deductions subject to the 2% limitation that are passed through from a partnership, Subchapter S corporation, or other conduit-like entity. There are two problems with deducting these expenses.

First, it isn't clear what some of these expenses are. The identity problem is that you must determine if they were incurred because of the trust's unique purposes that separate it from an individual as a tax entity. For example, are the fees of a custodian necessary because you need one to preserve trust assets and protect you as trustee from liability? The findings of the Sixth Circuit would seem to make them so, but these fees, and such items as the following expenses, should be heavily substantiated in this respect if you intend to disregard the 2% ceiling limitation in deducting them:

- clerical assistance
- safe deposit box rents
- equipment depreciation and rent allocated to investment management
- investment publication or on-line investment service fees
- travel expenses related to investment management
- costs of managing property held for appreciation

Secondly, you will encounter a circular mathematical problem involving two unknowns in trying to determine what 2% of AGI amounts to. In the previous chapter we explained that one of the steps you must take in order to determine AGI was to subtract Distributable Net Income (DNI) from Total Income. But a factor in determining DNI is the sum of itemized miscellaneous expenses after the 2% ceiling limitation is applied. The determination of these expenses depends on what DNI amounts to, and DNI depends on what the expenses amount to. This problem is solvable, but an explanation of it goes beyond the purpose of this overview. (By now, however, you may have grasped why tax work for trusts is best left to specialists.)

7. Depreciation and Depletion

Certain deductions are taken indirectly on Form 1041. They may be taken on supporting schedules attached to the trust's tax return, before income or loss is netted out and transferred from them to the return. Among these are depreciation and depletion.

You are allowed deductions for depreciation and depletion only to the extent not allowed to the current income beneficiaries. These deductions are apportioned on the basis of trust income allocated between the beneficiaries and the trust. However if you maintain reserves, the deduction is first allocated to the trust to the extent that cash is transferred to the reserve; then the excess deduction is apportioned between beneficiary and trust.

You would have to consult the trust instrument, or if it is silent, then state law to determine if reserves are required or permitted. If state law were the determinant, you would have to check further to see if the expense for trust accounting purposes differs from its allowance for tax purposes. An excess tax expense would be apportioned between trust and beneficiary.

Individual taxpayers may elect to expense a certain amount of tangible personal property purchased to use in a trade or business. This election is not available to a trust.

8. Net Operating Losses

The rules for deducting a net operating loss (NOL) are similar to those for individuals, except that a trust's allowed charitable contribution deductions and allowed distribution deductions are taken into account in adjusting taxable income for the NOL computation.

NOL can be carried back three years. Beneficiaries affected positively by this rule may be entitled to a refund. Where income reported to them in prior years has been reduced, you should notify them.

You might wish to elect not to carry back NOL for a number of reasons. You might expect tax rates to increase over the fifteen-year carryforward period. If carryback completely offsets income for a prior year, tax credits that are carried forward may be lost. Other tax benefits, such as miscellaneous itemized deductions may be lost. Subsequent adjustments for the three prior years may minimize the effect of a NOL. There could be no benefit to a beneficiary if his deductions from other sources had offset his distributed income. In any event, the election not to carry back NOL would also apply to Alternative Minimum Tax NOL.

9. Additional Deductions

From Total Income, you would subtract the above deductions for interest, taxes, fees paid to trustees, attorneys, accountants and return-preparer fees, and other deductions either subject to or not subject to the 2% of AGI requirement to arrive at Adjusted Total Income (or Loss). At this point, three more deductions are available to finally determine the Taxable Income for the trust. One is a deduction for estate and generation skipping transfer taxes. Another is the personal exemption. The third (second in order on the tax return) is the Income Distribution Deduction.

An estate tax deduction can arise where the trust is entitled to a deduction for estate taxes paid on items that were included in an estate as income in respect of a decedent. Certain events, such as a distribution to a beneficiary in two or lower generations beneath that of the settlor, can trigger a generation-skipping transfer tax, for which a deduction would also be available.

A trust required to distribute all of its income currently is entitled to a personal exemption of $300. Such a trust doesn't have to meet the other requirements for being a simple trust. This exemption is useful only when the trust has income that isn't included in trust accounting income, such as capital gains or extraordinary dividends allocated to principal (and therefore not required to be distributed). The exemption must be pro-rated for the inception year, or for any year in which there is a change in accounting period. All other trusts are entitled to a $100 personal exemption. Pro-ration is required if there is a change in the accounting period, but not for the inception year. No trust is entitled to an exemption in its year of termination.

This leaves the Income Distribution Deduction to deal with.

D. The Income Distribution Deduction

Distributions of cash and distributions of property are treated differently for tax purposes. For either type of distribution, you are required to provide each beneficiary with the information Schedule K-1, and you would be subject to a penalty of $50 for each failure to do so, unless you could establish reasonable cause for failure.

1. Distributions from Simple Trusts

Most distributions are treated as distributions of current income for which the trust is entitled to the Income Distribution Deduction (IDD). The term "income" unless modified, means trust accounting income, as defined by the trust instrument or otherwise by local law. To arrive at IDD, you must first determine a reference point, Distributable Net Income (DNI). This is the maximum amount you can claim as the IDD, and the maximum amount that a beneficiary must include in his gross income.

To determine DNI, you would start with Adjusted Total Income - and adjust it further. First you would increase it by any tax-exempt income, adjusted downward for allocations to charitable contributions and allocable income-producing and interest expenses. This is because such income is part of the total available to beneficiaries.

Next you would deal with capital gains and losses, which are ordinarily excluded from DNI. However if they are required to be allocated to income, or allocated to corpus but actually distributed, or required to be used to determine the amount that is actually distributed or required to be, you would combine them with Adjusted Total Income. For a complex trust, this includes capital gains that are required to be distributed, or are actually paid or credited to a beneficiary or paid to, used or set aside for a charity. Capital losses are excluded except to the extent of their use in determining capital gain. For a simple trust, extraordinary dividends and taxable stock dividends would be excluded if you made a good-faith allocation of them to principal.

Example–Income Distribution Deduction for a Simple Trust

Assume the following receipts and disbursements within a tax year for a simple trust, where capital gains are required to be allocated to principal, and the trustee makes a good faith allocation of all extraordinary dividends to principal.

1. Cash, sale of stock (basis $25,000)	*$100,000*
2. Stock dividend	*50,000*
3. Extraordinary dividend	*1,000*
4. Ordinary dividend	*30,000*
5. Tax-exempt bond interest	*3,000*
6. Legal fee to protect principal	*(5,000)*
7. Trustee fee Allocable to income	*(2,000)*
8. Trustee fee allocable to principal	*(2,000)*
Total transactions	*$175,000*

First you must calculate trust accounting income, which consists of the following:

Dividends	*$30,000*
Tax-exempt bond interest	*3,000*
Trustee fee allocable to income	*(2,000)*
Trust accounting income	*$31,000*

This amount is what would actually be distributed to the beneficiary.

The trust's Taxable Income is computed as follows, with trustee fees adjusted for an allocation of 10% to the tax-exempt bonds and their interest:

1. Capital gain, sale of stock (basis $25,000)	*$75,000*
2. Stock dividend	*50,000*
3. Extraordinary dividends	*1,000*
4. Ordinary dividends	*30,000*
6. Legal fee to protect principal	*(5,000)*
7. Trustee fee Allocable to income (approx.)	*(1,800)*
8. Trustee fee allocable to principal (approx.)	*(1,800)*
9. Personal exemption	*(300)*
Taxable Income before Distributions:	*$152,100*

Next adjustments are made to arrive at DNI

Exclude capital gain	*($75,000)*	
Exclude stock dividend	*(50,000)*	
Exclude extraordinary dividend	*(1,000)*	
Include net tax-exempt interest	*2,600*	
Include personal exemption	*300*	*(123,100)*

DNI	*$29,000*

To follow through on this example for a simple trust, DNI would be adjusted to arrive at the trust's IDD.

DNI	*$29,000*
Less: tax-exempt interest	*3,600*
IDD	*$25,400*

Now the IDD is deducted from the trust's Taxable Income Before Distributions to arrive at its taxable income of $126,700.

In the above example, all distributions were in cash. If distributions had been made in property, special rules would apply. A simple trust does not lose its classification if it distributes property instead of cash in distributing all current income. However, the trust would recognize gain or loss if the property had a lower or higher value than the market value on the distribution date. This market value then would become the beneficiary's cost basis. You should advise the beneficiary of the cost basis and the trust's holding period for the property, so that he can determine long or short term gains and losses if he disposes of it.

2. Distributions from Complex Trusts

Now we move on to distributions from complex trusts, and you will find out how appropriate the term "complex" is. These are trusts that distribute principal, can accumulate income, and/or are allowed a charitable deduction.

The distributions from a complex trust are divided into two tiers. Tier One consists of income required to be distributed currently. It corresponds to the distributions required of simple trusts. It's a deductible amount only to the extent of the taxable portion of DNI, exclusive of any charitable deduction. Tier Two is made up of all other amounts paid, credited or required to be distributed during the tax year, such as discretionary payments of principal, accumulated income, or an amount required to be paid from principal to a beneficiary upon attaining a certain age. Tier Two distributions are deductible only to the extent of the excess of taxable DNI over Tier One distributions and deductible charitable distributions.

The first step in determining the distribution deduction for a complex trust is to determine trust accounting income, on which the Tier One distributions are based. The second step is to determine Tier Two distributions, which consist of any other amounts paid, credited, or required to be distributed. The third step is to calculate DNI. Finally you compute the distribution deduction, which is done by adding the first two steps, subject to the DNI limitation of the third step, adjusted for tax-exempt income and expenses allocable to it.

Example –Distribution Deduction for a Complex Trust

Step #1

The trust has the following income and expenses for the current tax year (depreciation reserves are mandated by the trust instrument):

Dividends	*$20,000*
Interest	*10,000*
Tax-exempt interest	*20,000*
Rent	*10,000*
Trustee fees	*(6,000)*
Rental property depreciation	*(1,000)*
Rental property repairs	*(3,000)*
Combining these amounts results in trust accounting income of:	$50,000

Total income, for the purpose of allocating trustee fees and charitable transfers to tax-exempt income, is $60,000.

Step #2

The trust is required to distribute $20,000 of its current income to one David Jones. It is required to transfer $3,000 to The Salvation Army. It can accumulate any excess income or apply it for the use of Alfred Smith. The trustee applies $8,000 of the excess income for Alfred Smith and accumulates the rest. David Jones is a Tier One beneficiary to the extent of $20,000. The Salvation Army is not considered a beneficiary for tax purposes. Alfred Smith is a Tier Two beneficiary to the extent of $8,000, the entire Tier Two distribution.

Step #3

DNI is calculated as follows:

Dividends		*$20,000*
Interest		*10,000*
Tax-exempt interest	*$20,000*	
Trustee fee allocated to tax-exempt interest	*(2,000)*	
Charitable deduction allocated to tax-exempt interest	*(1,000)*	*17,000*
Rent		*10,000*
Rental property depreciation		*(1,000)*
Rental property repairs		*(3,000)*
Trustee fees allocated to taxable income		*(4,000)*
Charitable contribution allocated to taxable income		*(2,000)*
DNI		*$47,000*

Step #4

Taxable DNI is $30,000 ($47,000 less adjusted tax-exempt interest). The trust can't deduct all of this because the Tier One and Tier Two distributions amount only to $28,000. David Jones' distribution is 43% of the $47,000 DNI, so the Distribution Deduction for his distribution is his $20,000 less 43% of the $17,000 adjusted tax-exempt interest (approximately $7,300), or $12,700. Alfred Smith's distribution is 17% of DNI. His $8,000 is reduced by 17% of $17,000 (approximately $1,200) to arrive at a Distribution Deduction of $6,800. The total Distribution Deduction for the trust is therefore only $19,500.

A distribution of property to a Tier One beneficiary in lieu of cash is treated as it would be if made from a simple trust, with the trust realizing gains or losses. In a distribution to a Tier Two beneficiary, the property value for purposes of calculating the Distribution Deduction and the beneficiary's income is the lesser of the market values on the distribution date and its adjusted cost basis, and the trust realizes no gain or loss. However the trust can elect to recognize gain or loss, in which case the distribution date market value sets the amount for the Distribution Deduction, the beneficiary's income, and his cost basis.

A distribution of property from a complex trust could consist of a gift or bequest of specific property. Subject to exceptions, such a distribution isn't a deduction for the trust and isn't taxable to the beneficiary.

3. Accumulated Income and the Throwback Rules

Prior to the Taxpayers Relief Act of 1998, most trusts that accumulated income were subject to the complex "throwback" rules. They now apply only to:

- certain trusts created before March 1, 1984 that have to be treated as multiple trusts;
- foreign trusts;
- domestic trusts that were once treated as foreign trusts.

However you might have to deal with these rules if you have to re-open tax returns filed for years prior to 1998 on behalf of any non-charitable remainder trust that accumulated income. If none of this applies to you, feel free to disregard the following explanation–unless you want yet another demonstration of why the proponents of a flat tax may not have a bad idea.

Without some kind of mechanism to level the playing field, you could use a trust to accumulate income for a beneficiary while he or she is in a high tax bracket and then pay it out to him or her when the top tax bracket is lower. This would make a trust an excellent retirement planning device, if it were not taxed so heavily itself. However, several years ago trust income wasn't taxed severely, and the throwback rules were enacted to prevent abuses growing out of the differences between the tax brackets for individuals and those for trusts. The rules applied to all trusts for years after 1968, except charitable remainder trusts. Trusts that accumulated income for a beneficiary under age twenty-one were also exempt, unless they fell into the multiple trust category.

According to these rules, a beneficiary is taxed on a distribution of accumulated income in the year he or she receives it, but his or her tax is calculated according to a formula that throws back the income to prior years and taxes it as if it had been received in those years. The beneficiary receives a credit for taxes paid in prior years by the trust on the accumulation distributions.

An accumulation distribution is the excess of Tier 2 distributions ("other amounts properly paid, credited or required to be distributed") over DNI reduced by the total amount of Tier 1 distributions (income required to be distributed). However if trust accounting income exceeds the sum of Tier 1 and Tier 2 distributions, no accumulation distribution takes place.

When making distributions of property, you could unintentionally make an accumulation distribution. If you made an election to recognize gain, a step-up to fair market value could increase Tier 2 distributions to an amount that exceeds DNI or exceeds trust accounting income when added to Tier 1 distributions.

The throwback rules don't apply to a trust making an accumulation distribution if there is no undistributed net income (UNI) in any prior year. UNI exists for any year in which DNI exceeds the sum of Tier 1 and Tier 2 distributions together with taxes to which the trust is subject because of the undistributed DNI. As a trust can be taxed on income not included in DNI, to arrive at the taxes attributable to undistributable DNI, you have to allocate the tax between the items not included and the retained DNI.

The throwback rules don't throw back the accumulation distribution income into each of the beneficiary's years in which it was accumulated. This is fortunate, because the tax calculations could be even more unreasonably complicated.

Instead, the excess distribution is thrown back to the earliest of the years it is attributable to and then to the subsequent years in order. The beneficiary is then considered to have received an amount equal to the average annual amount of accumulated income deemed to have been distributed in each of the beneficiary's previous five years, disregarding the highest and lowest taxable income years. The beneficiary's tax is then recomputed for each of these years and the average increase in tax is multiplied by the number of years to which the throwback rules apply. The taxes paid by the trust for those years is subtracted to arrive at the additional tax payable by the beneficiary.

Example - Application of the Throwback Rules

Step #1

	UNI	Taxes Attributable to UNI	Tax-exempt Income
1990	$ 5,000	$ 500	$ 0
1991	4,000	1,000	500
1993	5,000	1,000	500
	$14,000	$2,500	$1,000

Step #2

UNI	$14,000
Attributable Taxes	2,500
Accumulated income amount	$16,500

Step #3

$16,500/3 = $5,500

Step #4
Beneficiary's Taxable Income (beginning with year 1998)
Highest and Lowest Years Eliminated

	1998	1997	1996	1995	1994
Taxable Income	~~$40,000~~	$30,000	$24,000	~~$10,000~~	$26,000
Average annual accumulation		5,500	5,500		5,500
Recomputed taxable Income		$35,500	$29,500		$31,500

Step #5
The taxes for the years (1997, 1996 and 1994 in this example) are recalculated using the tax rate tables or schedules then in effect. Then the taxes paid in those years are subtracted from each result to arrive at a net increase in tax for each of those years. Assume that the net combined increase for the three years is $4,000.

Step #6

Increase in tax	$4,000
Taxes Paid by Trust	2,500
Beneficiary's Additional Tax	$1,500

When UNI deemed distributed for a preceding year is less than 25% of the average annual accumulation distribution, that year is disregarded in counting the number of throwback years by which the average annual accumulated income is divided.

Under the multiple trust rules, when accumulation distributions are made from three or more trusts to the same beneficiary with a throwback to the same year, the taxes paid by the third and subsequent trusts can be used by the beneficiary only as a deduction and not as a credit against his additional tax. The beneficiary can determine the order of the trusts. It doesn't matter if the trusts had different grantors; you might therefore want to determine for distribution planning purposes if the beneficiaries of your trust are also the beneficiaries of other trusts.

While the throwback rules generally don't apply to income accumulated while a beneficiary is under age twenty-one, they do apply if distributions are subject to the multiple trust rules. However if the UNI for a trust for a preceding year is less than $1,000, or if an accumulation distribution thrown back to the preceding year is less than $1,000, the multiple trust rules do not apply to any beneficiary.

E. Credits

The tax credits that apply to trusts are essentially the same as those to which individual taxpayers are entitled. These are the foreign tax credit, the regulated investment company credit, the non-conventional source fuels credit, the credit for minimum tax for the previous year, the credits which make up the business credit, and various refund credits, such as for withheld federal income tax on wages. The credits must be apportioned between the trust and the beneficiaries according to how the income is allocated. This allocation rule is also applied to the $25,000 amount used in determining the limitations on the general business tax credit.

F. Split Interest Charitable Trusts

These trusts are more fully described in Exhibit I, A Variety of Trusts in the Appendix. One of the most important features of a Charitable Remainder Trust (CRT) is the income tax deduction available to the settlor for establishing it. The amount of the deduction depends upon the value of assets transferred to the trust, the amount and timing of distributions, and the term of the trust, which could be a specific period or based upon life expectancies. However it isn't normally your duty to calculate this deduction. The calculation should be made by the settlor's advisors, preferably his attorney or his CPA, and therefore we don't address this issue here.

For charitable remainder trusts, as with complex trusts, you exist in a vale of tiers. In this case, the tiers refer to the classification of distributions from CRTs as ordinary income, capital gains, tax-exempt income and principal. If there is any current or accumulated ordinary income available it is carried out first in the distribution. If the distribution exceeds available ordinary income, net short-term gains followed by net long-term gains are next in order from current and accumulated gain. If there is still an excess, current and accumulated tax-exempt income is then deemed distributed. Finally, any excess over the first three tiers is considered to be principal.

A charitable remainder trust (CRT) is generally exempt from tax because to the extent that its income is not distributed and taxed to the beneficiary, it is accumulated for charity. You would file Form 1041-A in lieu of Form 1041 for a CRT.

An exception would be where the trust has unrelated business taxable income, which consists of net income from carrying on a trade or business. This income could also come from the trust's participation in a partnership, or from debt-financed property. In this case a CRT is taxed as a complex trust, and you would file Form 1041 in addition to the other forms required for a charitable remainder trust. It would be subject to tax on its undistributed taxable income. Because courts have ruled that unrelated business taxable income invalidates the trust's tax-exempt status for the year in which it is received, an asset that produces it is a poor investment for a CRT.

You must also file Form 5227–Split Interest Trust Information Return. There are certain excise taxes that can be levied upon CRTs. They arise from transactions involving self-dealing, excess business holdings, jeopardy investments, or taxable expenditures. Form 5227 reports the financial activities of the trust and determines if it is subject to excise taxes for any of the prohibited transactions.

A charitable lead trust (CLT) is a CRT in reverse, making distributions to a charity during its existence and ultimately distributing what is left in the trust at termination to non-charitable beneficiaries. Unlike a CRT, there is no income tax deduction available to the settlor, because he or she isn't the owner of the income interest –unless the trust meets the definition of a grantor trust.

The CLT is a complex trust for tax purposes and requires the filing of Form 1041. It receives a charitable contribution deduction for required annual distributions to charity, and any taxable income in excess of these distributions is taxed to the trust. A Form 1041-A is also required for a CLT that isn't required to distribute all of its income annually because it may be required to distribute accumulated income to charity in a future year if current income in that year is insufficient.

As with the CRT, you would also be required to file Form 5227 for a CLT.

G. The Documentation of Tax Decisions

If you manage tax decisions properly, you benefit both the trust and its beneficiaries in terms of their tax burdens. However this may also mean, as it can with investment management, that you sometimes have to make compromises unpleasing to beneficiaries, especially unsophisticated ones who can't grasp complex issues. You shouldn't have to explain all of your tax decisions to them, as you have no duty to do this unless asked. However, you should document the reasons for your decisions, and it is advisable to warn beneficiaries when they are likely to be adversely affected.

Tax returns provide a good record of asset transactions and the taxes paid on them. They won't always easily reveal a tax strategy, however. For instance, you might decide to take an action that intentionally increases the trust's tax liability because it helps a beneficiary in some way. It would be unfortunate if you were subsequently criticized for doing this many years later and could no longer recall why you did it. Therefore, you should keep notes on why you made certain decisions, and file them with your copies of the tax returns. If you delegate tax work to a professional, you should require the same procedures of him or her.

This concludes our two chapters on taxation, which we suspect are the most difficult ones to digest in this entire book. We congratulate you for finishing it (if, in fact, you did), and we give you the rest of the day off.

H. Ongoing Changes in the Tax Laws

Changes in the tax laws are frequent and it takes time to publish a book after the writers have finished their work. Some of the information on taxation, such as the federal fiduciary income tax rates, may already be out-of-date. The reader is urged not to rely on it and to seek out the most current information available.

Chapter VI
Intermediate And Final Accountings

A. The Purpose of Accountings

An accounting could be characterized as a long-term trust statement on steroids, but with an important distinction: it can provide the trustee with relief. The main purpose of an accounting is to discharge you of your responsibilities as trustee for the period of time covered by it. It is a record of your transactions, which you provide to the parties in interest at the close of your administration, or at some intermediate point within it, so that they can review it and release you from liability for what it discloses to them. Accountings are most often required when a trust terminates, but they may also be called for when important events take place during the life of the trust, such as a change of trustees, the death of a beneficiary or a court-scheduled date.

If an accounting is informal, where the beneficiaries are asked to review your accounting and release you from liability without a court-supervised procedure, it can take any form acceptable to the beneficiaries, as long as you remember that you can't be released from actions that you haven't disclosed. However the trust instrument or the court having jurisdiction may require a formal accounting, or you or the beneficiaries may want the protections afforded by this procedure. A formal accounting provides an opportunity for an independent party with authority–the court–to review the accounting and represent the parties to the trust. Where a court-approved accounting is required, you must follow the format prescribed by the state or the individual court. These formats vary.

B. The Construction of an Accounting

Most states have adopted the Uniform Principles on Fiduciary Accounting as one method of accounting, which are as follows:

- Accounts should be stated in a manner that is understandable by persons who are not familiar with practices and terminology peculiar to the administration of estates and trusts.
- A fiduciary account shall begin with a concise summary of its purpose and content.
- A fiduciary account shall contain sufficient information to put the interested parties on notice as to all significant transactions affecting administration during the accounting period.
- A fiduciary account shall include both carrying values - representing the value of assets at acquisition by the fiduciary - and current values at the beginning and end of the accounting period.
- Gains and losses incurred during the accounting period shall be shown separately in the same schedule.
- The account shall show significant transactions that do not affect the amount for which the fiduciary is accountable.

We ask you to keep these principles in mind as you review the following elements of a Model Account that is finding acceptance in some states and is being used in jurisdictions where formalities aren't rigid.

Outline–Model Trustee's Account

I. Description of the Account

Name of the trust
Date of settlor's death (if relevant)
Date of trustee's receipt of funds
Statement of purpose of the account

2. Summary of Account

Proposed distribution to beneficiaries at current and trustee's acquisition values.

Principal

Summary of principal receipts.

Plus gain (or less loss) on sales or other disposition.

Total of above.

General disbursements.

Fees.

Total of above subtracted from principal receipts and gain/loss to arrive at a principal balance before distributions.

Less distributions to beneficiaries subtracted to arrive at a balance on hand.

For information: investments made and changes in investment holdings.

Income

Summary of income receipts.

Less disbursements.

Leaving a balance before distributions.

Less distributions to beneficiaries to arrive at an income balance on hand.

The principal balance on hand and the income balance on hand are added to arrive at a combined balance on hand.

3. Receipts of Principal

Original assets of trust are listed at trustee's acquisition value.

Subsequently received assets are listed chronologically at acquisition value.

4. Gains and Losses on Sales or Other Dispositions

Describes gains and losses chronologically.

5. Disbursements of Principal

Describes general disbursements chronologically.

Describes fees paid chronologically.

Shows total.

6. Distributions of Principal to Beneficiaries

Describes distributions chronologically by asset type to each beneficiary.

7. Principal Balance on Hand

Describes each remaining principal assets at current value and trustee's acquisition value, with the values totaled.

8. Information Schedule

Shows any significant information, although it does not affect the amount for which you are accountable, such as:

Investments made, and

Changes in investment holdings through stock splits, *etc.*

9. Receipts of Income

Recites any waiver of income accounting for the period beginning with the inception of the period covered by the accounting to the date of the last income statement.

Shows the balance at inception, or the balance per last statement rendered if there has been an income accounting waiver.

Describes each income receipt in chronological order.

Shows total income receipts.

10. Disbursements of Income

Describes each payment of expenses and fees in chronological order.

Shows total disbursements.

11. Distributions of Income to Beneficiaries

Shows distributions to each beneficiary.

Shows total distributions.

12. Balance of Income on Hand

Describes remaining income assets at current value and trustee's acquisition value.

13. Proposed Distributions to Beneficiaries

Recites the reason for the distributions.

Separately lists the principal and income assets to be distributed to each beneficiary.

There follows a statement to be signed by the trustee, sworn before a notary, or under penalty of perjury, depending upon the jurisdiction, that:

- the trustee has fully and faithfully discharged the duties of his or her office,
- the foregoing account is true and correct, and fully discloses all significant transactions occurring during the accounting period,
- all known claims against the trust have been paid-in-full,
- to the trustee's knowledge, there are no claims outstanding against the trust, and
- all taxes presently due from the trust have been paid.

Possibly you could prepare an accounting without assistance, if you followed the required format and have an accounting background. There are companies such as Trust Tax Services of America, in Worcester, Massachusetts, who sell automated accounting system software for IBM-compatible computers, if you want to use this approach. However, we recommend delegating this work to an independent accountant who could question details of your transactions and record keeping. Unlike corporate trustees, individual trustees don't have a system of examination and audits to uncover their errors, and this step would at least provide some professional oversight. Also, the professional accountant will probably do a better job describing and categorizing the more complex or arcane transactions.

Chapter VII
Termination of Your Responsibilities

At some point, there will be an end to your duties as trustee. This could come about in a variety of ways, but there are two main causes. Either your involvement with the trust will be cut short before its natural termination, or the trust itself will end by its very terms.

A. Your Resignation, Removal or Death

Your duties might end before the trust does, if you resign, are removed or die.

1. Resignation

Generally you can resign if the trust instrument provides for this. You can also resign with the consent of the beneficiaries, if all of them have the capacity to give it. Otherwise, you would have to petition the proper court to obtain permission for your resignation.

If your resignation won't be detrimental to the trust, your chances of obtaining court permission are good. Normally a court wouldn't want a trust to be administered by a reluctant trustee. However, it would help your case if you could demonstrate that it would be burdensome for you to continue. Ill health, or an involuntary, permanent increase in your other responsibilities, are common reasons why trustees resign. Sometimes the fee structure becomes a money-losing proposition for the trustee, too, and there may be no practical way to remedy this. If this is your situation, the burden will be upon you to convince the court that a once-acceptable fee arrangement (to which you agreed) is no longer acceptable, due to changes in inflation, or increases in your trustee duties or expenses.

In resigning, you should notify all of the beneficiaries, being careful to follow the instructions stated in the trust instrument, an agreement with the beneficiaries, or a court directive for this process. For instance, you should be sure to provide written notice as far in advance of the effective date of your resignation as the trust instrument calls for. Otherwise you risk an ineffective resignation, leaving you exposed to whatever potential liabilities lurk in an extended administration.

2. Removal

In modern wills and trust agreements, there is frequently a provision enabling removal of the trustee by a person or persons authorized to do so. A majority of the beneficiaries could have this power, or another party sometimes called "The Trust Protector," who has no other association with the trust, might hold it. Removal provisions frequently don't require the person holding the power to give reasons for exercising it. Where a reason is most often required, it is in the event that a trustee becomes incapacitated. In this situation, there are usually methods stated in the trust instrument for determining the lack of capacity, such as certification by two physicians.

The court may remove a trustee if it finds that his or her continuing administration will be detrimental to the trust. It can do so if it determines that the trustee lacks the necessary capacity to continue. It can remove a trustee if he or she has committed a serious breach of trust or a crime, especially a crime involving dishonesty. For example, if you have refused to give bond, refused to account, favored one beneficiary over another, were unreasonably uncooperative with a co-trustee, or were convicted of fraud (even though the fraudulent activity was unrelated to the trust), a court would most probably remove you, if petitioned to do so.

Beneficiaries have frequently tried to remove an unpopular trustee, claiming that there is too much friction between them. They usually fail for lack of sufficient proof that their interests have been harmed. It is unlikely that a court will remove you merely because you and the beneficiaries don't get along, unless this interferes with carrying out the purpose of the trust.

A trustee who becomes bankrupt might seem to be a risk to a trust, but a court might not necessarily remove him or her, although it might require the trustee to give security to cover the trust assets.

A court is somewhat less likely to remove a trustee who was named by the settlor, than one who was appointed by someone else, such as a third person authorized by the trust instrument to do so, or the court itself. There is a strong inclination on the court's part to adhere to the wishes of the settlor, in the absence of compelling reasons to the contrary.

3. Death or Loss of Capacity

Obviously your death would terminate your responsibilities as a trustee. Title to the trust property would pass to a surviving co-trustee or to a named successor trustee, if there were such. Otherwise common law or state statutes would determine how the replacement of a deceased trustee takes place. This will hardly be a concern of yours at that point.

There might be implications for your estate, however. You should be concerned that whoever is in charge of your estate will have some involvement with the new trustee who assumes control. To the extent possible, you want to make this involvement as trouble-free as possible. For this reason you might want to prepare a memorandum that gives the executor of your estate the location of assets, files, safe deposit keys, and other pertinent information. It should be filed with the original copy of your will.

Another trustee would also have to take over for you if you were incapacitated by a sudden disability. In this event, there might be arrangements for your removal and replacement in the trust instrument, or a court might have to remove you, but the effect wouldn't be greatly different than if you had died, because you wouldn't be able to personally assist in a transition of the trust's control. In such an event, you would want your guardian to be able to understand where you were with the trust. The copy of the memorandum intended for your executor could be kept in your personal safe-deposit box for this purpose, if your will is located somewhere else. A legal guardian would have access to your safe-deposit box.

We don't suggest that you should administer a trust as if each day will be your last. We do recommend that, in addition to preparing memorandums for your executor or a guardian, you maintain your records in such a state that a successor trustee can step into your shoes and carry on without much head-scratching. Your files should be accessible, even if it means summoning a locksmith to open them (it probably should mean summoning a locksmith). Information concerning the beneficiaries and your accounting records should be current. The investment policy statement should provide your successor with a clear explanation of the trust's investment direction.

B. Your Responsibilities When You Resign or Are Removed

Unless you are removed because you are no longer capable of administering the trust, you'll have certain responsibilities if you resign or are removed. If you resign, you'll have the duty to transfer the trust property to a successor trustee with proper credentials. A successor trustee should be identified in the trust agreement or by authorized parties, and you should have written proof of acceptance of his or her appointment. If you don't know him or her, you should also ask for personal identification, a detail that can be curiously overlooked at times.

It would be a breach of trust to transfer trust assets to a successor trustee before your resignation or removal is effective, and before the effective succession of the new trustee. If your resignation calls for a written direction of your removal, don't make any transfers until it is executed by the appropriate parties–settlor, beneficiaries, successor trustee, or the court, depending upon the requirements - and in your hands. Don't make any transfers until you have possession of an acceptance of his or her appointment by the successor trustee.

You should account for the period of your administration from the date of the last accounting or the inception of your administration to the date of the transfer of assets. Whether the accounting is formal or informal will depend upon circumstances, but if you are being removed by the court it will be formal. You should provide the successor trustee with the following records:

- a copy of your resignation
- all data concerning the beneficiaries

- a tax log for the current year
- copies of tax returns for the past three years
- a list of assets, with tax costs and carrying costs
- a copy of your resignation or removal document
- the original trust agreement or certified copy of the will
- a copy of your accounting

The successor trustee should supply you with:

- transfer instructions for the trust assets
- a receipt for assets transferred
- receipts for all documents
- a copy of his or her appointment and acceptance of the trust as successor trustee

C. The Trust Terminates by Its Own Provisions

Personal trusts have to end sometime, although there are increasing exceptions to the rule against perpetuities in the statutes of governmental entities here and abroad. Relatively few trusts last long enough to run up against a legal term limit, and there is a good chance that you'll see the administration of a trust through to its conclusion. Here are the ways your trust could end.

1. Expiration of the Term of the Trust

Eventually, the period for which a trust was created expires. A revocable trust created by the settlor for his or her own benefit may provide that the trust shall end when he or she does, so that the remaining corpus can be distributed under the terms of his or her will. At his or her death, the period for which the trust was designed has ended. Or you might have a trust designed to last for several generations. Such a trust would normally be subject to the rule against perpetuities that limits it to a period not longer than that measured by lives in being at the creation of the trust, plus twenty-one years. In all probability it would end before the extremity established by this rule because some other condition has been fulfilled, such as the death of a beneficiary.

2. Revocation

Another common cause of termination is revocation. A trust could be revoked by the settlor of an *inter-vivos* trust, if he or she reserved this right to him or herself. The right to revoke a trust should be clearly stated in the trust agreement. It would be appropriate for such a provision to state that the revocation must be made in writing to the trustee. The details in the provision concerning the method of revocation must be adhered to. For example, if a trust agreement provides that the settlor can revoke the trust only during his or her lifetime, it can't be revoked after his or her death by a direction in the will.

However, a power to revoke that doesn't set forth a specific method for its exercise is still valid. The settlor would have to take a definitive action, such as giving notice to the trustee. Notice only to the beneficiaries might not be sufficient. In a poorly drafted instrument, the intention of the settlor to reserve a power to revoke might be ambiguous, in which case it would be necessary to determine in court if the circumstances under which the trust had been created would permit a revocation. If a trust is clearly a complete expression of the settlor's intentions, and there is no stated power to revoke it, the trust can't be revoked.

It may be that the settlor can't exercise his or her power to revoke without the consent of another party, such as a trustee, beneficiary or third party. If a party other than you must provide consent, you have a duty to make a reasonable effort to ensure that the party is competent when he or she gives consent, and that the consent is given in an appropriate manner.

If the settlor required your consent as trustee to revoke, you would have to determine if it is your duty to consent. You would do this by reviewing your responsibilities with respect to the trust. In some cases, this may be clear-cut. For example, you may have the expressed duty to consent to a revocation if the settlor is in need, in which case you could not consent if you can clearly determine that he or she isn't in need. In other cases, there may be no restrictions on your power to consent, unless it could be found that you somehow abused your power because of an improper motive, such as a bribe. If you refused to consent only because you didn't want to lose your trustee's fees, this would be another abuse of your power. A proper test to apply in these situations is to ask yourself if a revocation would be a reasonable act on behalf of all of the beneficiaries, or would it be counter to the purpose of the trust.

The creditors of a settlor may be able to reach assets of a trust over which he or she holds a power of revocation to the extent necessary to satisfy their claims; this depends upon local law. They have no power to revoke the trust, however. It is a different matter where such a settlor becomes bankrupt, because then the trustee in bankruptcy has the same powers that the bankrupt settlor might have held for his or her own benefit, and can exercise the settlor's power to revoke.

Whenever an attempt is made to revoke a trust, it's your duty to see that the revocation is proper before assisting in the revocation. If you think the revocation is improper, it's your duty to resist the revocation by all legal means.

D. Other Causes of Termination

1. Rescission

A trust can be rescinded, which is a less common event. Rescinding a trust is something like annulling a marriage. It's a remedy only for terminating a trust that never should have been created in the first place. The settlor is restored as nearly as possible to the situation he or she occupied before the trust was created. This can happen when there was no consideration paid to the settlor for creating the trust and there are grounds of mistake, undue influence, duress or fraud.

You should avoid becoming involved in trusts that are likely to be rescinded. If you think the settlor has been misled about the advantages of creating a trust, such as by being offered a doubtful tax benefit, or if he or she appears to be incompetent, or is susceptible to undue pressure from self-serving relatives or salespeople, decline to serve.

2. Impossibility or Illegality of Trust Purpose

As said at the beginning of this book, a trust must have a purpose. This may be expressed in the trust instrument, but if it isn't, extrinsic evidence, such as the settlor's demonstrated desire through his or her lifetime actions to protect a beneficiary, may determine a purpose. Extrinsic evidence can't overrule a stated purpose in the trust instrument, however.

If the original purpose of a trust became impossible or illegal, the trust would have to be terminated for those reasons. For example, a trust, intended to provide for an impoverished beneficiary "until such time as his annual income exceeds $25,000," would have to end when a winning lottery ticket provides him or her with $250,000 per year for the next twenty years. It probably would be your duty to verify this change in circumstances, but in any event, when the news reached you, you would have to inform the poor wretch that the annual stream of $1,200 he or she had been receiving has been turned off. If tobacco were to become an illegal crop, a trust for the purpose of promoting the use of tobacco would have to be terminated.

However, if an impossible or illegal purpose of a trust were not the trust's sole purpose, and its other purposes were still attainable, the trust would be terminated only with respect to the part dedicated to the unattainable purpose. The trust would continue, while the funds intended for the unattainable purpose would either have to be directed to a different purpose or distributed. This would depend upon the terms of the trust instrument or court direction.

3. Emergency

There could be circumstances where, although not impossible or illegal for the trustee to continue to administer all or a part of the trust, it becomes impractical for him or her to do so. It may be that carrying out a purpose of the trust becomes a money-losing proposition, for instance, such as the continuation of a business interest for a fixed number of years. In this case a court might authorize the sale of the business and a distribution of the proceeds, if no other purpose for continuing the trust exists.

4. By Consent of the Beneficiaries

If continuation of the trust is unnecessary in terms of carrying out a purpose of the trust, the beneficiaries can compel its termination, provided that none of them is under an incapacity. You would have to obtain the consent of each beneficiary.

A trust may be designed to give one beneficiary an income interest for some period of time before another receives distribution of the trust assets. However this isn't necessarily indicative of a material purpose to deprive the income beneficiary of legal ownership of trust assets. It may be that the only purpose of such a trust is to preserve assets for the second beneficiary. In this case, if the income beneficiary is willing to forego the benefits of the trust, the trust can be terminated with the consent of both beneficiaries.

In a situation like this, you need to be careful of fraudulent consents. For example, suppose that you administer a trust for an income beneficiary whose children will receive the trust assets at his or her death as remaindermen. The trust's purposes are to provide protection for the income beneficiary, who is a spendthrift, and assure that all of the assets will pass to his or her children. The income beneficiary asks you to terminate the trust so that the assets will be distributed to his or her children now. The children, who will consent to the termination, have an agreement with their father to make gifts of some of the trust property back to him or her if the trust is terminated. The income beneficiary's justification for this plan is that his or her children won't have to wait for him or her to die in order to have possession of some of the trust assets, and he or she can bequeath to them at his or her death the trust assets he or she received from them. The consents would be fraudulent in this case, as they would defeat the purposes of the trust, because the spendthrift would not have the protection of the trust and his or her children would have no assurance that he or she would not squander assets intended for them at his or her death.

What should you do in a situation like this? Even if you didn't know of their plan, could you insist on indemnification from all parties for terminating the trust and require the children to agree not to transfer trust assets to their father? Despite taking such steps, you would nevertheless be contributing to the defeat of the trust's purposes, in our view. We think that you should refuse to terminate a trust under these circumstances.

A beneficiary can always withdraw a previously issued consent prior to the termination of a trust. If he or she does so, other beneficiaries can't compel a termination, unless he or she had previously entered into a contract with the other beneficiaries to provide his or her consent.

E. Your Responsibilities at the Termination of a Trust

When a trust ends, you must wind matters up and transfer the trust property, with marketable title, to those entitled to it as expeditiously as possible. With some trusts, however, this doesn't necessarily mean "quickly," as we shall illustrate below, and you are not liable for breach of trust if there are good reasons for a prolonged termination. You remain trustee as long as you have duties with respect to the trust, even after the time for its termination has come and gone.

1. Identifying the Remaindermen

One of your most important duties is to ascertain the correct identities of the parties to whom the trust assets are to be distributed. This is always easier if you have already done this so far as possible at the time you assumed administration of the trust. At that time, there may have been remaindermen who were not ascertainable, such as unborn children, or those who can only be identified by reference to the last will of a decedent. However even an incomplete list may point the way to discovery, if it contains the names and addresses of family members or others who may be called upon to help you when the trust ends.

In most instances, the remaindermen will be identifiable because they are direct descendants of income beneficiaries, but this is not always so. Not long ago, one of the authors was involved in the termination of a trust established for herself by the widow of a well-known entrepreneur. The widow, a Kentucky resident, who died in her late 80s, had eight brothers and sisters, and in her will she had divided her estate into eight separate portions for each of the siblings or their descendents. Some of these had already died, and were represented by surviving issue (children, grandchildren, and members of still lower generations). The trust, which terminated at the settlor's death, was required to distribute directly to the same entities whom the settlor had named in her will, in the same proportions. All distributions were *per stirpes*.

Methods of Distribution: *Per Stirpes* and *Per Capita*

Let's begin with the easier of the two definitions. If you leave your estate to your issue, *per capita* (by the head), it will be divided equally among all of your surviving issue. A share that you left to your sister, *per capita*, would pass to her descendents in a similar manner, if she had predeceased you.

Per Capita Distribution

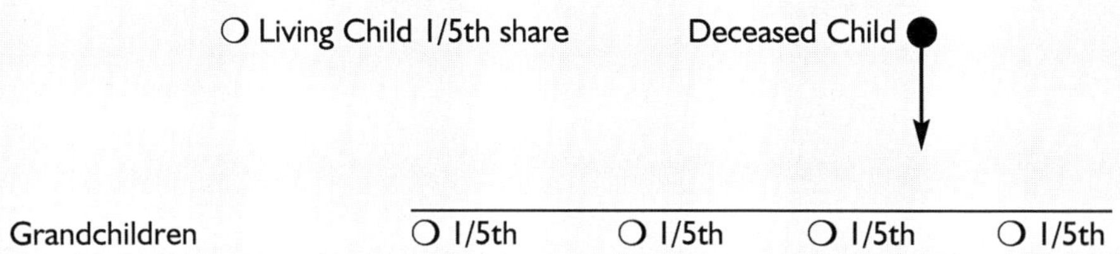

A distribution to your issue, *per stirpes* (by the root), would first divide your estate into as many shares as you had living children, and dead children leaving surviving issue. It would give each of your living children one of these shares. The share for a deceased child survived by living issue would flow to the issue, and be divided according to the lines of descent.

Per Stirpes Distribution

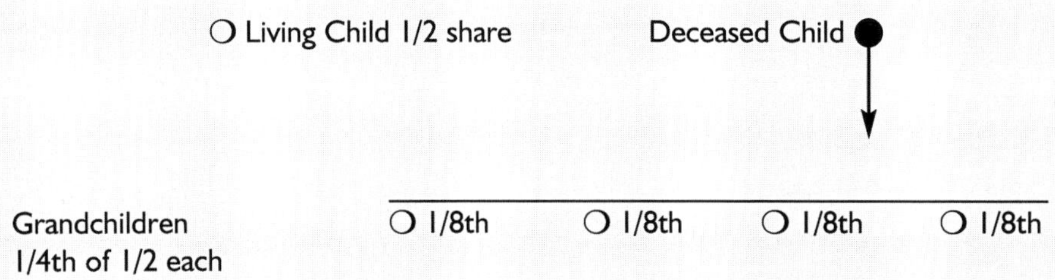

Two siblings survived to receive their shares. Most of the sisters and brothers of the settlor had predeceased her, and their shares had to be distributed to their issue in equal shares, *per stirpes*. One sister survived the settlor, but then died prior to distribution as a resident of a mid-western state, leaving no survivors, no assets and no will. The share of another sister, who had predeceased the settlor without issue, was to be divided between two small colleges, one of which had already ceased to exist at the time the settlor died.

Needless to say, the ascertainment of the beneficiaries was challenging work. The descendents of some deceased brothers and sisters entitled to *per stirpes* distributions were traced down to the great-niece, great-nephew level of the settlor. The estate of the impoverished sister, who had died *intestate* after the settlor, was entitled to a share, but there had been no settlement of the estate. The share that would have gone to the defunct college was claimed by the other college under the (mistaken, in this case) presumption that the share set aside for the two colleges should have gone to the surviving institution.

The corporate trustee determined who the surviving family members were by first obtaining a family tree from the executor of the settlor's estate, and then verifying it by consulting as many of the remaindermen as possible. Just obtaining the correct addresses of the far-flung recipients to do this much was a major undertaking. It turned out that the original family tree was unreliable with respect to some of the more remote remaindermen.

The will had to be interpreted to determine that the defunct college's share should be distributed not to the extant college but to the family members in accordance with a *per stirpes* distribution. An estate had to be opened for one sister who died without any assets or a will after the settlor, so that the trustee could distribute her share to her estate's appointed administrator. (That estate was eventually distributed in many small shares to family members according to state laws governing *intestate* estates.)

In this case, there was a temptation to settle on a receipt-and-release basis, because everyone was eager to see an end to the matter. However, there were too many remaindermen and too many opportunities for someone to dispute the accuracy with which his or her share had been calculated. Additionally, substantial legal fees were divided between the settlor's estate and the trust because legal services for the estate benefited remaindermen of the trust, and the estate's funds were insufficient to cover the costs. The trustee required a formal accounting for its own protection, and fended off impatient remaindermen for the many months the whole termination process took. The remaining trust assets were finally distributed to forty-two separate remaindermen.

It would have been much easier for the trustee if the trust agreement had simply directed a transfer of the assets to the executor of the settlor's estate. Then all of the assets would have been concentrated in one place for payment of expenses and distribution. One of the settlor's objectives had been to by-pass the estate settlement process, but it is doubtful that direct distribution from the trust saved either time or expense.

This rather long example points out the need to verify information and to seek court protection, when it appears desirable, in identifying and making distributions at the termination of a trust. You should crosscheck as much as possible in order to identify all of the remaindermen and determine how much they are entitled to. Where many different fractional share distributions are to be made, it goes without saying that you should run a proof that makes sure that you are distributing no more and no less than 100% of the total trust assets.

You should periodically update your original list of all possible beneficiaries during the term of your administration. We recommend annual checks on the accuracy of addresses and on additions or losses of family members. A standard questionnaire is adequate for this purpose, and copies of it in your files will attest to your diligence at this important record-keeping task.

2. Preparing an Account

At the termination of your services, you'll have to account for your period of administration. This responsibility has already been discussed at length in Part Three, Chapter VI. We recommend here that you begin the work of preparing an accounting, whether it be formal or informal, as early as possible. Although they can't force an untimely distribution, impatient remaindermen are troublesome to deal with. If you have forewarning that your administration is drawing to an end, you can do most of the work early, and update the accounting at final termination.

You can also help your cause with a communication that tells them:

- how the termination process works (accounting, *etc.*)
- when they are likely to receive their distributions
- what approximate expenses remain to be paid
- how much their shares are likely to be

Advance Distributions

Where the resources of the trust permit, it is appropriate to make advance distributions to remaindermen before final distributions are made, as long as the term of the trust has been completed. It isn't reasonable to keep a remainderman waiting unnecessarily for his or her entire share, if some of it can be paid out early. However, you can't be compelled to transfer trust property until you are paid or secured for compensation to which you are entitled, and until you are paid or secured for expenses you have properly incurred. If advance distributions are to be made, it's important to create appropriate reserves for anticipated expenses (including your fees), and taxes.

Advance distributions weren't made to the forty-two remaindermen in the above example for a number of reasons. The trustee wasn't certain that all of the remaindermen had been accounted for until the time of final distribution. The extent of the trust's share of legal fees couldn't be ascertained until late in the termination process. The amount of potential total distributions to each remainderman was in most cases quite small, a fact that the trustee weighed against the impracticality and potential for error of making two separately timed distributions to forty-two different entities.

3. Making Distributions in Cash or in Kind

It is usually more convenient for a trustee to make distributions in cash proceeds from the sale of trust property, rather than distributions in kind of the property itself (when we refer to cash, we are talking about checks, not currency). However the convenience of the trustee shouldn't be a factor in determining the method of distribution. The most important consideration is the instruction in the trust instrument or in other sources of legal authority if the instrument is silent. But the rights and best interests of the beneficiaries are also important factors. The instrument could require a distribution in cash, but the beneficiaries might be able to compel the trustee to make distribution in kind. A court could also direct a distribution in kind if it found this to be in the best interests of those entitled to the property.

Cash proceeds may be the only appropriate distribution where some assets or beneficiaries are involved. Division of some assets may be impractical, as is the case with municipal bonds, where small denominations can be difficult and expensive to sell. A majority share in a business entity becomes much less valuable if divided into minority shares among unrelated parties. It may be illegal for a beneficiary who is a resident citizen of a foreign country to possess certain types of non-cash assets. Works of art are frequently sold because they can't be divided. While a set of silverware could be divided, a single fork would probably be worth less by itself than the cash proceeds realized from selling it as part of the set.

There could be adverse tax consequences for a beneficiary if he or she received a distribution in kind of property with a low-cost basis. If the beneficiary had to sell the property and sustain a substantial capital gains tax, it might be better for the trust to sell the property and offset the resulting gains with available losses. Some beneficiaries may not have the sophistication to deal with complex assets, and would prefer to have you sell them prior to distribution. You should do what is reasonable, and what is best for the beneficiaries, where you have the leeway to do so and have the proper consents.

A beneficiary can compel a trustee to pay him or her trust funds instead of using them to purchase some other form of property, such as an annuity, despite a direction in the trust instrument to do so.

Where there is more than one beneficiary, the possible methods of distribution are selling the property and distributing cash, dividing the property into separate shares and distributing the shares, and transferring the property to the beneficiaries as tenants in common. You should generally follow a direction in the trust instrument to use only one of these methods, subject to the exceptions noted above. Without a specific direction, you should do what is reasonable. Certain factors should be taken into account:

- implied direction in the trust instrument
- the purpose of the trust
- the nature of the trust property
- the number of beneficiaries
- the value of their shares

In our example of the forty-two remaindermen, the trustee distributed in cash. It had the power to distribute in kind under the trust instrument, but most distributions were modest in amount. None of the recipients had requested an in-kind distribution. The tax consequences of reducing the trust assets to cash were negligible to all concerned. So the trustee sold the assets and distributed in cash. It did what was reasonable under the circumstances. There was no land in the trust, which consisted entirely of marketable securities and cash. If there had been land, the trustee would have had to consider a duty under normal circumstances to convey the land to the beneficiaries as tenants in common according to their respective shares. But it would not have been in the best interests of so many beneficiaries, distantly related and widely scattered in many cases, for the trustee to make this type of distribution.

While a beneficiary has certain rights with respect to taking his or her share in kind rather than in cash, these rights don't necessarily apply if other beneficiaries could be harmed. This could be the case if the beneficiary insists on receiving a piece of a real estate holding, but distribution of his or her share in kind would seriously jeopardize a profitable sale of the total holding. If you made an exception for this beneficiary, and then distributed the proceeds of a sale from the remaining property to the others, you would not have obtained the best obtainable price.

You should cancel your insurance policies for assets you have insured as soon as they have been sold or transferred. It would be appropriate to notify the recipients of in-kind distributions in advance that this is your intention, so that they may make their own arrangements for insurance coverage.

4. Completing the Tax Work

There are opportunities for coordinating the taxation of a trust with that of beneficiaries when the trust terminates. Part Three, Chapter V discusses final tax returns and provides some insights into the coordination of tax management between trust and beneficiary. Additionally it might be helpful to keep in mind at a termination that:

- There may be some benefit to the trust in selling assets and realizing taxable gain or loss rather than having this occur in the hands of a beneficiary, as mentioned above.
- If deductions can be concentrated in the final year of a trust, the excess of them over the trust's gross income can be carried out to the beneficiaries.
- The same is true of net operating loss carryovers and capital loss carryovers.
- So far as it is possible, the creation of a short tax year by extending or shortening the termination process may benefit the trust, the beneficiaries or both.

Obviously you won't make final distributions until you're sure that all tax liabilities are accounted for and paid. Yet it would be unreasonable to withhold distribution until the three-year period of limitations for a normal income tax audit has passed. Therefore you should make every effort to see that all returns for the final year and the three prior years have been filed accurately and that you have paid the proper taxes. It is also advisable to obtain indemnity agreements from the distributees to indemnify you against any tax deficiencies not caused by your negligence.

In addition to the normal tax reporting information for the trust's tax year, you should provide each beneficiary with the cost basis and dates of acquisition for each asset distributed in kind.

5. Documentation for Final Distributions

If your final account is adjudicated by the court having jurisdiction, your documentation will be that court's formal approval and direction to distribute the assets shown to be remaining in the account.

You may, however, be willing to terminate the trust on an informal basis, if

- your administration of the trust has been uneventful
- there have been continuous good relationships with the other parties to the trust and their representatives
- there are no questions as to the identities of the beneficiaries or their respective distributive shares
- there are no concerns raised by elections on your part or theirs to distribute shares in cash or in kind
- all of the beneficiaries or their representatives are willing and able to settle on this basis

In this case, your attorney should prepare a receipt and release agreement (frequently called simply a "receipt and release," as is the process itself). The form of the document will vary, depending upon the number and type of trustees and beneficiaries, the shares being distributed, the type of account (intermediate or final) and other details. Each beneficiary should execute a copy of this document and provide you with it, retaining a copy for his or her own records. When you have received an executed receipt and release agreement from all beneficiaries entitled to a final distribution, then–and only then–you make the distribution.

Example: Receipt and Release Agreement

Trust under Will Dated ____________
Of ____________________, Deceased
____________________, Trustee

Approval of Administration
Receipt, Release and Indemnity Agreement

I, ________________, have requested ________________, Trustee, to distribute to me all of the principal (valued at $ __________ as of ____________, ____) upon my having attained age _____ on ___________, ____, pursuant to Paragraph ______ of the Trust for my benefit under the Will dated ________, ____, of my late ___________; and in consideration of the avoidance of the expense and time incident to a final accounting, do hereby:

(a) Declare that the attached Account of administration of the Trust has been examined; that it has been found true and correct in all particulars; and that it is acceptable and approved, as if it had been duly filed, audited, adjudicated and confirmed absolutely by the Court having jurisdiction over the Trust and as if the amount shown as distributable to me has been duly awarded to the undersigned as beneficiary.
(b) Waive an Account of income prior to ___________, ____, all income prior to that date having been accounted for and paid over to the income beneficiary entitled thereto.
(c) Waive the filing and auditing of the Account of the administration of the Trust in the court having jurisdiction over the Trust and agree that the court having jurisdiction may by its decree confirm the Account.
(d) Request the Trustee to make distribution of the principal and income of the Trust and effective upon delivery to me of the amount shown as distributable, acknowledge receipt of such property.
(e) Agree to refund to the Trustee any amount which may at any time be determined to have been an erroneous distribution to me regardless of the cause of such distribution. Agree that any period for the limitation of actions for the collection of any erroneous distribution to the undersigned shall commence only at such time as the Trustee shall obtain actual knowledge of such erroneous distribution and that in no event shall the period for collection of any erroneous distribution be less than two years after the actual discovery thereof by the Trustee.
(f) Absolutely and irrevocably remise, release, quitclaim and forever discharge the Trustee, in his capacity as Trustee of the Trust and in his individual capacity from any and all actions, suits, payments, accounts, reckonings, liabilities and demands relating in any way to the administration of the Trust.
(g) Agree to indemnify and hold harmless, to the extent of the funds received by me hereunder, the Trustee, in his capacity as Trustee of the Trust and in his individual capacity against any and all claims, loss, liability or damage (including legal fees and costs in connection therewith) which he may suffer or to which he may be subjected by reason of his administration of the Trust, settlement of his account and the distribution of the assets of the Trust without having the formal approval of the court having jurisdiction over the Trust.
(h) Declare it to be the undersigned's intention that this instrument shall be governed by the law of ___________, and it shall be legally binding as an agreement under seal upon the undersigned, the undersigned's heirs, executors, administrators and assigns.

IN WITNESS WHEREOF, I have hereunto set my hand an seal this ___ day of _____________, ____.

Witness:

________________ ____________________ (Seal)

Address _____________

____

Social Security # ___________

(An acknowledgement by a notary public would be attached to this document.)

6. Retaining Records

When termination has been completed, you can now store records that you should retain permanently or for a certain number of years, as discussed in Part Two, Chapter I. If space is a problem, you might want to convert selected records to a reliable long-term media, such as microfiche. This would be at your own expense, if you have not already done so during the term of the trust as an expense of administration.

Undoubtedly you will eventually receive an inquiry concerning the trust from a beneficiary, or some relative of a beneficiary or his or her representative. "Was all of the money distributed?" "Do you know where Uncle Charles is living?" "What happened to the Hummel collection that my mother thought was part of the trust?" Even if you don't have to respond to such inquiries, you may want to be helpful. For this reason, we suggest that you keep handy a list of the names and addresses of the beneficiaries living at the time of termination, a copy of the trust instrument and a copy of the final accounting.

You'll be required to respond if tax authorities inquire after the trust has closed. We assume that you will take every step to be sure that there are no tax liabilities before you make a final distribution, but you should have ready availability of all tax records in case there are questions.

Your duties as a trustee would now finally be concluded, and you could say to yourself with relief and satisfaction the words that General Douglas MacArthur once intoned.

"These proceedings are now closed."

APPENDIX

Exhibit I

A Variety of Trusts

Probably you are concerned with only one type of trust, or at most a few related types, which you have investigated in depth. For example, you might presently be a trustee of a living trust or an irrevocable life insurance trust, and in the future you may become trustee of a marital trust and a credit shelter trust, all created by a single settlor. Here we give you a brief explanation of different types of trusts that you might want to know something about, even if you don't have to deal with all of them.

This Exhibit won't cover many types of trusts that are either similar to those reviewed here or so specialized that they would rarely be encountered. The descriptions are limited, because a full treatment of the tax considerations for some of the trusts described would require whole chapters in themselves, and this is not a tax book. In keeping with our book's role as a guide, we try to point out the practicalities of dealing with these trusts from the trustee's point of view and encourage you to consult other sources for in-depth tax treatment of a particular type of trust. We will begin with trusts where the settlor is living and the trustee is likely to have either an active or passive relationship with him.

A. The Revocable Living Trust

This trust is of real value to senior citizens or someone with a serious health problem, but it frequently has been oversold to individuals who have either misunderstood its benefits or have been misled about them. A Living Trust is simply a revocable trust that someone creates under a trust agreement for his or her own benefit, and perhaps for a spouse as well, where he or she is both the settlor and the beneficiary, and possibly also the trustee. Where an outsider is the trustee, he or she has the responsibility of managing the assets, but as long as the settlor is alive and competent, the settlor is in control, and he or she can amend or revoke the trust at any time.

If the settlor becomes incapacitated, the trustee (or a successor trustee, if the settlor were the original trustee) continues to manage the assets and use them for his or her welfare according to the directions in the trust agreement. The trust can end if and when a competent settlor decides to revoke it, or it can end at his or her death so that the assets can be distributed directly to his survivors. A third alternative is for it continue for the benefit of his or her spouse or other survivors, providing them with the same financial protection and management it afforded the settlor.

The trust is frequently created by someone in his or her sixties or older who may have no close relatives or friends nearby who could be relied (or imposed) upon to manage his or her affairs if he or she became incapacitated. This individual may prefer to make his or her own investment decisions, but is willing to delegate that responsibility if the day comes when he or she has to. The settlor may also want to benefit and protect a spouse, who may not have his or her financial management abilities, if he or she can no longer exercise them. The settlor may be motivated by a desire to avoid the costs and procedures of having assets pass under his or her will. However, some glib professionals, seeking new clients through seminars and publications, often overstate the benefits of avoiding probate. Most states don't make estate settlement an unreasonably complicated process, and the legal costs of dealing with a revocable trust as part of the taxable estate are not usually a great deal less than if the assets had merely passed under the will.

A Living Trust can be funded as soon as the trust agreement is executed, but sometimes funding is deferred. Some settlors give another individual a power-of-attorney which can be used to fund the trust if the settlor becomes incapacitated and unable to fund it him or herself.

You might be asked to be a trustee of a Living Trust at its beginning if the settlor is ready then to have someone else manage his or her investments. In this case, you could find yourself holding investments that may not be of good quality or suitable for the beneficiary, but this is not a major problem for you if you are directed by the settlor to hold them. The assets are still his or hers, because the settlor can revoke the trust. You serve only at the settlor's convenience.

Nevertheless, you should review the assets at inception, make recommendations that are prudent, and document what you do–in other words behave like a trustee. Your objections to holding questionable investments should be on file. There should be a prior understanding that this is what you intend to do and that you will be paid for acting like a true trustee. You should avoid any appearance of a passive trustee, and that you went along with poor investing in a trust for which you may have exclusive decision-making later.

You can, of course, clean out dubious investments if and when you assume full investment responsibility, but by then you may have the dilemma of having to trigger capital gains taxes because some of these investments actually performed well. A step-up in the investments' cost basis resulting from the settlor's death might solve your problem, and some trustees, with this in mind, retain assets they otherwise would have sold. But waiting for the settlor's death to resolve a tax problem can be an imprudent gamble in many situations.

More likely you will be appointed as a successor trustee of a Living Trust. Frequently a settlor/trustee becomes incapacitated or dies, and you replace him or her as sole trustee or as co-trustee with a remaining trustee, such as his or her spouse. As a co-trustee with the settlor's spouse, you may have to deal with a loyalty problem if the spouse wants to continue past investment practices, ("my husband always said that Palm Fronds International would come back someday"). You will simply have to do what you think is right.

Another problem for trustees taking over trust management from a settlor is poor record keeping and lack of follow-through, particularly if the settlor is of advanced age or in poor health. Frequently there are missing details about cost basis and dates of acquisition. Assets intended for the trust may not have been transferred to it. Federal, state and local income tax returns may need to be amended. It would be helpful if you could review the trust periodically while the settlor is still in charge, even if you are not yet a trustee, so that such problems could be uncovered and addressed. Unfortunately this is usually difficult to arrange.

B. Grantor Trusts

The Living Trust belongs to a group of trusts called grantor trusts because the grantor (we will call the settlor the grantor here for the sake of consistency) reserves to him or herself or his or her spouse important powers over the trust. The income from all of these trusts is taxable at the federal level to the settlor or his or her spouse with certain exceptions. The main difference between a living trust and other grantor trusts is that the living trust is for the settlor's own benefit, although any spouse is often also a beneficiary. Other grantor trusts benefit someone other than the settlor, usually with the purpose of transferring income benefits to others while keeping a measure of control over the principal and/or certain aspects of the trust's administration.

The federal tax rules define a grantor trust as one in which:

1. There is a reversionary interest to the grantor in either the principal or income that exceeds five percent. There is an exception for reversion at the death of a minor lineal descendant;
2. There is a power to control beneficial enjoyment, such as by changing beneficiaries or either directly or indirectly changing the benefits bestowed upon a beneficiary;
3. There is a retention of administrative powers which would enable the grantor to obtain benefits from the trust, such as a loan, without dealing with the trust on an arm's length basis;
4. There is a power to revoke the trust resulting in a reversionary interest to the grantor;
5. The income may be accumulated, distributed, or used to pay premiums on life insurance policies (except policies payable irrevocably to charities) in any way that benefits the grantor; and
6. Any of the above powers or conditions apply to the grantor's spouse.

The income of a grantor trust may be taxable to someone other than the grantor if that individual can vest the income or principal in him or herself. For example, if a mother created a trust for her child, giving her husband the right to take the trust assets at any time, the income would be taxed to the husband.

While grantor trusts don't relieve the grantor of income tax liability, they can be used in some ways to reduce federal estate taxes, and they are created with some frequency where sophisticated estate planning is employed. Without the benefit of large estate tax savings, it is doubtful if they would be created at all. Usually family members, such as children of the grantor are the beneficiaries. A review of the above rules suggests that you are likely to be associated with a grantor who is a strong-control personality, who will have his or her own ideas about how the trust is to be managed. He or she may have little regard for the finer points of your fiduciary responsibility. Accordingly if you are asked to accept an appointment as trustee, you should have a frank discussion with the grantor about the extension of his or her authority. This authority should not exceed the limitations of the trust agreement.

C. The Grantor Retained-Interest Trust

The federal tax laws have been revised many times to prevent abuses. One abuse occurred when a grantor placed property in an irrevocable trust for family members while retaining an income interest in it. The grantor paid federal gift taxes only on the remaining value of the property transferred after the grantor's life interest was subtracted from it. In many cases, the value subtracted was more than realistic. The Internal Revenue Code now provides that the retained interest in such a case is zero, making the entire transfer subject to the gift tax rules, subject to an exception. The exception is if the retained interest is a "qualified" one, the value of which can be ascertained by consulting government tables and periodically revised lists of federal interest rates. This resulted in the grantor retained-interest trust, commonly referred to as a GRIT.

A qualified interest can be of three types:

1. A qualified "unitrust" interest - the right to receive at least annually a fixed percentage of the fair market value of the trust as determined each year (the trust is called a GRUT); the advantage is that the distributions can increase if the trust property grows in value;
2. A qualified annuity interest - the right to receive a fixed amount annually, which can be either a predetermined number or a fixed percentage of the initial trust property (the trust is called a GRAT); the advantage is that the distributions are certain, and they do not decrease if the trust property decreases;
3. A qualified remainder interest–a non-contingent remainder interest if other interests in the trust consist only of the other two types of qualified interest.

GRUTs and GRATs must be irrevocable. They can be for the life of the grantor, a term of years, or the shorter of the two. If the grantor survives the term of years, which ends his or her interest in the trust, the remainder interest is not included in the estate, a major objective for creating a GRIT. Transfers to either type of trust are gifts of future interest, not subject to the annual gift tax exclusion. Additions after the initial transfer can be made to a GRUT, but not to a GRAT. Settlors who prefer an annuity payout may therefore create more than one GRAT with identical provisions.

As a trustee of a GRUT, you should be careful to value the assets accurately, as the amount of the distributions depends upon the annual revaluation. The trust instrument is required to provide that if you make an incorrect valuation, a correcting payment will be made by or to the beneficiary, but you don't want to be in a position where you must rely on a beneficiary to repay. Also, if you make incorrect payments, you would have to calculate interest at varying federal rates for every outstanding incorrect payment and collect or pay it. You can select any consistent date for valuation, but the first day of the year is usually preferred. You must adjust for a short year (such as when the trust is created, added to, or terminated, if these events don't happen on January 1).

As trustee of a GRAT, the same rules for correcting incorrect distributions and adjusting for short years apply, but there is only one valuation at the inception of the trust to be concerned with.

D. The Qualified Personal Residence Trust

There are two GRITs that can hold personal residences, and they are unique in that the retained interest is not a periodic payment but a residence. With other GRITs, the retention of an interest in non-income-producing property would result in an overvaluation of the remainder interest.

Both trusts allow a grantor to retain the use of a principal residence, one other residence, or a fractional interest in either, while giving a remainder interest to others. Both are established for a term of years, with the expectation that the grantor will survive the term, so that remainder interest will be excluded from his estate. The Personal Residence Trust (PRT) is the simpler of the two, but it is less flexible than the more complex Qualified Personal Residence Trust (QPRT). The latter can cope better with such significant matters as the trust's need to hold cash for payment of taxes, repairs, or other expenses, a relocation by the grantor, a sale of the residence, or a loss of the residence by fire or other calamity. Consequently the QPRT is normally the trust of choice.

If the grantor were still alive when the term of the trust ended, he or she could lease the residence from the remaindermen. However, if there were any expressed or implied agreement concerning a leasing arrangement when the residence was transferred to the trust, the residence would be included in the grantor's estate for tax purposes.

Because an individual is reluctant to give up control over his or her residence, it is likely that the grantor will also be the trustee during the QPRT term, unless he or she is in poor health, or unless applicable state law prohibits this. However, if the trust continues for other purposes beyond this term, and he or she continues as trustee with any discretionary power to affect the enjoyment of income or principal, that would result in the trust property being taxed as part of the estate. His or her replacement with a successor trustee at the end of the QPRT term would avoid this risk. Therefore you could become involved as a successor trustee if not as the primary trustee.

As a trustee of any trust with a residence as all or part of the trust property, you may encounter the problems we discussed in Part One, Chapter IV, concerning such property under Real Estate. Grantors of such trusts are likely to be elderly and may decline in physical or mental capacity, with family members at remote locations. You may be dealing with a beneficiary who still regards the residence as belonging to him or her, and resistant to your administrative duties with respect to it as trust property. It is best to have clear understandings in advance of acceptance of your appointment about how you must act as a trustee, and what you probably would do if certain events happen.

E. Charitable Remainder Trusts

In order to obtain a charitable deduction for a remainder interest that passes to a qualified charity from a trust, the trust must meet several requirements. As you read about them, you will immediately note similarities to GRUTs and GRATs, except that now we are dealing with charitable remainder trusts (CRTs), which consist of charitable remainder unitrusts (CRUTs) and charitable remainder annuity trusts (CRATs).

These trusts are popular with wealthy individuals because in addition to serving a donor's charitable purposes, they can also provide him or her with an immediate charitable deduction for the remainder interest, and with a retained income as beneficiary of the trust. They also provide a way for him or her to convert low-basis assets without directly incurring capital gains taxes, and reinvest the proceeds to better advantage. This is because the assets transferred to the trust eventually will pass to charitable organizations, and the trustee can sell them without tax consequences–or at least with lesser ones.

With a CRUT, the annual distribution to the non-charitable beneficiary is a percentage of the annual value of the trust assets. If the trust assets increase in value over time, so too will the CRUT distributions, providing a good hedge against inflation for beneficiaries with a long life expectancy. The percentage must be at least 5%. There is some flexibility in making distributions. The trustee could distribute just the net income, if it were less than the percentage amount, and the beneficiary could defer receiving the difference to later years when income exceeded the percentage amount (assuming the trust property grows in value). A beneficiary with little current need for income could, in this manner, defer a higher annual distribution to a time of greater need, such as retirement. This variation is called a Net Income Makeup Charitable Remainder Unitrust, or NIMCRUT.

As to the CRAT, the annual distribution is an amount fixed at a dollar value or at a percentage of the trust property at the trust's inception. It can't be less than 5% of the trust property. There is no potential for increased distributions, as with a CRUT, but neither will the annual distribution decline, if the trust assets last. If there were a greater than 5% chance when the trust is created that the assets will be exhausted, the remainder interest would not qualify for a charitable deduction. No additions can be made to a CRAT.

Both types of trust distribute in four tiers. Taxable income is considered distributed first, to the extent available in the trust. This is then followed by available capital gains. Next follows available tax-free income. Last in succession are non-taxable distributions of principal. Both types of trust are subject to the same rules concerning valuations and short years as GRITs.

As a trustee of a charitable remainder trust, you may find yourself dealing with agents of the settlor, if not the settlor him or herself, asking you to use their services and buy their products. The reason is that, in many cases, these agents have originated the idea of creating the trust. For example, securities brokers may recommend a charitable remainder trust to their clients, pointing out a way to dispose of low-basis assets without serious tax consequences. Life insurance agents also often promote such trusts as a form of "asset replacement" trust. They demonstrate to the settlor the merits of replacing the remainder interest lost to his or her family with life insurance, recommending that he or she finance the purchase with the new funds generated by the charitable deduction and the possibly higher yields from the conversion of low-cost basis assets.

Let us make it clear that we aren't in any way disparaging useful ideas just because they are advanced by brokers or insurance agents. It may well be that the family broker is someone you can work with to advantage, assuming that his or her commissions are reasonable and that he or she can execute your trades as well as anyone else. It may also be helpful that he or she is managing other accounts for the family, as he or she may be able to combine purchases and sales from more than one account to reduce transaction costs. Our only observation is that you, as trustee, must assure yourself that the broker's rates, services and expertise measure up to the standards you should be applying.

The same observation applies to buying insurance policies through a family life insurance agent. You should insist on an impartial search for appropriate policies, even if he or she represents only one insurance company or a few companies. Keep in mind when dealing with any agents that your only duty is to the beneficiary. If a settlor wants to repay an agent for a good idea or good service by having you do business with that agent, see to it that the settlor gives you a valid direction and exoneration for doing so.

Ultimately the CRT assets will pass to one or more charitable organizations, and these organizations have proven time and again that they can be uncharitable with respect to a trustee if they believe that the trust he or she managed is distributing to them less than they deserve. It is not likely that they will investigate while you are administering the trust. When the trust terminates, however, they will carefully review your past administration, not only with respect to investments, but also to your fees and other expenses charged to the trust. You can't be faulted if the trust property is diminished or exhausted because of a high distribution requirement, but you will be accountable in all other respects.

F. Charitable Lead Trusts

The Charitable Lead Trust (CLT) is essentially the reverse of a charitable remainder trust. The charity receives an annuity from a Charitable Lead Annuity Trust (CLAT), or unitrust payments from a Charitable Lead Unitrust (CLUT) for a fixed term, and the remaining principal is distributed to non-charity remaindermen, normally members of the settlor's family. It is more likely that a corporate trustee would be selected, because individual trustees tend to be favored more when a trustee is administering a trust for family members; a CLT distributes to them only when it terminates.

G. Trusts for Minors

Many trusts have minors as beneficiaries. Two types that are used for minors are encouraged by Sections 2503(b) and 2503(c) of the Code, which are found in Code, Chapter 12–Gift Tax. Transfers to these two types of trust are afforded relief from federal gift tax in that they can qualify as gifts of a present interest. A gift of a present interest is one where the beneficiary has immediate enjoyment of the gift, as opposed to having to wait for it until some time in the future. For such gifts there is currently an annual gift tax exclusion of $11,000 - or $22,000 if the spouse of the donor joins in the gift. An exclusion not available for gifts of a future interest.

The requirement for a 2503(b) trust is that it payout all income currently to the beneficiary. This constitutes a gift of a present interest. The principal can be paid to the beneficiary or his estate at any time in the future without reference to his attaining the age of majority, but this is not a requirement. The difference between the value of the property transferred to the trust and the beneficiary's life interest in the income doesn't qualify for the exclusion, but this may be of little consequence for a very young beneficiary unless the transferred assets are extremely large. This trust isn't specifically a trust for minors, but as a practical matter, that is its most frequent application.

The 2503(c) trust is minor-specific. The rules under this section state that no gift to a minor in trust shall be considered a gift of future interest, even if the income is not currently paid out to him or her, if:

- The transferred property and income from it may used by or for the minor before attaining age twenty-one (without reference to a state's laws concerning the attainment of majority), and
- The property will pass to the beneficiary at age twenty-one, or be paid to his or her estate or paid according to his or her general power of appointment if he or she dies before attaining that age.

This trust permits accumulations, which can result in complex record keeping and also high taxes for the trust if the income is large.

Both trusts are frequently used to accumulate funds for an education. In the case of the former, the income is paid into a custodianship under a statutory transfers-to-minors act, or to a guardian, or possibly placed in a deposit account in the name of the minor. The latter type trust is used in lieu of a custodianship, as the trustee him or herself can accumulate or use funds for the beneficiary as the trust instrument directs. These trust are inclined to have small beginnings in order to stay under the $11,000 or $22,000 annual gift tax exclusions for yearly transfers to them.

As a trustee of trusts for minors, you have the potential problem of investing limited assets in an effective manner. A trust that is likely to be small should provide, for that reason, that the trustee should have the flexibility to disregard any requirement for diversification and to invest in vehicles that are appropriate to the size of the trust, such as certificates of deposit or a single mutual fund.

You may also have to resist pressure from parents who may want more control over investments and use of funds than they are entitled to. Such parents may want funds to be used for purposes not authorized for the child's benefit. The trust instrument may relieve you of the duty to inquire into the use of funds distributed to the child's representative, but otherwise you may have a responsibility to make a reasonable effort to see that payments from the trust are used appropriately. One way to discharge this responsibility is to require that bills be sent to you directly for approval and payment.

If there is one trust for a minor child or children, there are likely to be others as well. Separate trusts are often created for each child in a family. A child may be the beneficiary of more than one trust created by family members. How closely the trusts are related depends upon how they were created, under one instrument or several, and how separate instruments relate to each other. You have read earlier about how related trusts must be managed in terms of keeping assets segregated, but parents may regard separate trusts as all belonging in one pot.

With settlors, parents and third parties, take the initiative, making it clear at the outset what you can and can't do, and what actions you would be obliged to take if you disagree with outside directions. You may have other relationships with these parties, but your first loyalty is to the beneficiaries. If you forget this, you may have to answer to the minor beneficiaries when they become adults.

You will also need to have a fair compensation arrangement in place, as the settlor may equate the size of your fee to the size of the trust. The settlor may not recognize that your responsibility and the work you have to perform for a small trust are probably not much less than what you would have for administering a much larger one. Banks and trust companies charge minimum fees to discourage small trusts. However they often waive a minimum fee where other related business makes up for an unprofitable trust, and this might apply to you. Otherwise you might consider an arrangement that provides a reduced fee while the trust is below a certain size but with the difference to be made up in years when the trust is larger, or you could require a substantial fee when your duties terminate.

Much of what we have said here applies to any small trust, whether it be for minor or adult beneficiaries. We also recognize that trusts for minors can be large.

H. The Special Needs Trust

In an earlier day when there was less attention paid to the sensitivities of unfortunate individuals and their families, there was a large stone building in Philadelphia with the legend "Philadelphia Home for Incurable Persons" over the front entrance. It is not difficult to imagine how a patient entering such a place for the first, and presumably last time might have felt upon seeing this. "Special needs" is a decent way to describe the purpose of a trust for individuals who are mentally or physically challenged.

This type of trust may be created voluntarily by a parent of the challenged beneficiary, but it could also be one created by agreement with a third party, such as an insurance company or a court. When a parent creates it, his or her intention is to provide for a child who will be unable to manage for him or herself after the parent is no longer able to care for him or her. In other instances, it may be a receptacle for money paid as compensation by or on behalf of some other party who caused the beneficiary's disability. Insurance companies often structure settlements that provide for a relatively large front-end payment, followed by a stream of smaller payments for an extended term of years, with perhaps a final payment when the term ends. A special needs trust is a good long-term device for structured settlements.

Where a parent or some other concerned individual creates a special needs trust; the trust instrument has to be drafted carefully. The trust shouldn't disqualify the beneficiary from receiving governmental benefits. It should also protect the trust assets against the claims of a state or other agency that wants to be reimbursed for providing the beneficiary with services or financial aid. Accordingly the trust instrument often employs two defenses. First the trustee is given complete discretion over distributions, so that the beneficiary has no claim upon them, as this would normally prevent most creditors from reaching them. Secondly, other beneficiaries are named to whom the trustee could make distributions, so that the trust is not exclusively for the handicapped beneficiary.

This can put you in a difficult position, if the trust instrument is not artfully crafted. You may know that the handicapped beneficiary is intended as the only beneficiary, and the other beneficiaries may understand this as well. However, you must balance these facts with your duty to treat all beneficiaries impartially, and it may be that another beneficiary also develops serious support needs from the trust.

You should also be aware that the law pertaining to the rights of others to assets in this type of trust isn't always clear, and that you may have to defend the trust despite the best efforts of the trust instrument's draftsman. See Exhibit IV for a special needs trust provision.

I. The Spendthrift Trust

The label "spendthrift trust" doesn't adequately describe either the purpose or the beneficiary of this type of trust. It can be established to protect a beneficiary who is a true spendthrift (the one who tells you that, "Father would have wanted me to have a Ferrari"). But it can also provide for someone who is truly incapacitated, such as an infant, or an adult suffering from Alzheimer's disease. It is a trust that is usually established by a parent or grandparent for a child or grandchild (minor or adult). You are typically given the discretion "to pay over to, or apply for the benefit of the beneficiary so much of the income and so much of the principal as you determine is advisable for his or her support and maintenance." The trust might also give you the right to terminate the trust and pay over to the beneficiary all of the principal and accumulated income upon the beneficiary reaching a particular age or upon another event or condition, such as regaining capacity.

This broad discretionary power is frequently coupled with a provision that you must consider the beneficiary's other income and resources. The trust instrument also prohibits the beneficiary from pledging or assigning his interest in the trust to a third party. Thus the beneficiary theoretically would receive funds only for what he or she actually needs, and his or her creditors could reach only what was actually paid out to him or her, or less. The term "need" would be defined by some combination of provisions in the trust instrument, the trustee's discretion, and the resources of the trust.

The spendthrift trust is not necessarily foolproof. According to Restatement Second, Trusts, a beneficiary's interest in a spendthrift trust may be reached for necessary services rendered to the beneficiary, for services or materials which preserve or benefit the beneficiary's interest, for claims of alimony or child support, or for claims of the federal or state government against the beneficiary. Georgia and Louisiana have statutory exceptions for tort creditors of a beneficiary, and Mississippi's Supreme Court has held that a spendthrift trust is against public policy if it shields a beneficiary from torts arising from his or her gross negligence or intention to do harm. Kentucky, Rhode Island and New Hampshire have found spendthrift trusts to be invalid, although Kentucky recognizes certain protective trusts as valid. In Pennsylvania, a settlor can not establish a spendthrift trust "to enable the beneficiary to live criminally or riotously."

Although it is rare that they do, a settlor can create a spendthrift trust for him or herself, as one admitted spendthrift we knew did. Later this individual changed his mind and wanted to revoke it. He was enraged to find out that this was impossible, and that, what was worse, his creditors could still reach the funds even though now he could not. See Exhibit IV for a spendthrift trust provision.

J. The Asset Protection Trust

While a spendthrift trust is an attempt to protect a beneficiary against him or herself as well as his or her creditors, the purpose of an Asset Protection Trust (APT) is merely to protect him or her against creditors, and the beneficiary is usually also the settlor. The objective is to make it either illegal or extremely impractical for a creditor to reach assets transferred to the trust.

As with the spendthrift trust, creditors have certain legal rights to trust property, and those rights are strongest where the settlor and beneficiary are the same. Therefore it is difficult in many cases to protect assets from legal claims of creditors. One way is to select a jurisdiction whose laws are unfavorable to creditors. While there is a variety of protection for trusts against creditors within the United States, other countries provide much wider opportunities for jurisdiction shopping. In some other countries the standards of proof required and statutes of limitation for fraudulent conveyances is often less severe, and laws of secrecy may prevent disclosure of the provisions of the trust instrument. Many countries refuse to enforce a judgement rendered here, or refuse to enforce an order of a United States Bankruptcy Court.

A refusal to enforce by a foreign country would require the creditor to travel to it and pursue his claim under that country's legal system. This is hardly practical in some cases, especially if the location is so remote as the Cook Islands, which are approximately halfway to New Zealand from Hawaii. The assets of an APT can remain in the United States, but they would be held in the name of the trust and no major actions could be taken without the signature of the foreign trustee. Assets could also be transferred to a foreign account, and they could be invested in foreign investments not available in this country.

Tax compliance for an APT is that of a grantor trust. If the APT had substantial foreign activity, it would then have reporting requirements under federal law concerning its creation and any transfers to and from the trust, and it would have to file annual returns with respect to its activities and income.

Normally there would be a domestic trustee, but you probably wouldn't serve in this capacity unless you were the settlor or his or her successor. The domestic trustee would be able to act on routine matters without the consent of the foreign trustee. The domestic trustee would also serve in a capacity called "the protector," having the right to change trustees or beneficiaries. If you do serve as trustee of an APT, it is reasonable to expect forays by creditors of the settlor, because that is what he or she anticipated when he or she created it. See Exhibit XIII for discussion of the trust protector.

K. The Irrevocable Life Insurance Trust

Sometimes your job won't be as simple as it might be described to you. Such is often the case with the irrevocable life insurance trust (ILIT). In its most common form, professionals call it a "Crummey" trust. Back in 1968, a certain Mr. Crummey, or more probably his attorneys, discovered a way to make an irrevocable life insurance trust more effective, and he succeeded in his battle with the Internal Revenue Service to legitimize it. As comets are named after their discoverers, some trusts also bear the names of those who made them known.

These trusts generally have two distinct lives. At inception, while the insured is living, the ILIT leads a relatively inactive life, as the assets consist only of life insurance policies and cash, and any duties you perform for beneficiaries are minimal. The second life begins when the insured dies. If the insurance proceeds are then invested instead of being distributed, the trust continues on to provide for beneficiaries like any active trust. Individual trustees are frequently appointed to administer these trusts, at least during their first life.

There are two reasons for this. The duties of the trustee during the "quiet" stage may seem to be negligible to a settlor who doesn't want to pay what a corporate trustee might charge to manage the trust at this time. A relative or friend of the settlor can often be convinced to act as trustee during this stage for a modest annual fee or no fee at all.

A second reason is that the settlor may not be able to find a corporate trustee who is willing to manage an ILIT that holds only policies and cash. Some corporate trustees don't want to manage a trust that they view as troublesome and liability-prone (something that should make you think). Alternatively, many corporate trustees will charge a high fee as a disincentive unless they are named as executor of the settlor's will and/or have other present or future benefits from their relationship with the settlor. Also, corporate trustees will be unenthusiastic about acting as trustee of an ILIT if it is to terminate shortly after the death of the insured and distribute proceeds from matured policies, because they will not be able to collect full fees on an ongoing trust.

Therefore individuals are frequently asked to serve, with the assurance that they "won't have much to do." An individual trustee may be appropriate, but there are definite responsibilities, and they have to be understood and taken seriously. Before we discuss these responsibilities, however, we need to explain more about the nature of the irrevocable life insurance trust in terms of its purpose and the tax laws.

The ILIT Is a Solution. What Are the Problems?

Problem #1. Life insurance can increase the tax liability of an estate. The proceeds are generally taxed in the estate of the person having the "incidents of ownership." An individual buys life insurance to offset tax erosion or provide liquidity at his death, but then the proceeds themselves are included in his taxable estate. If a spouse buys the insurance on the other spouse's life, the policy's unmatured value will be taxed in that spouse's estate and the proceeds will likely be taxed in the surviving spouse's estate. A last-to-die policy on the lives of both spouses will also be taxed as part of the survivor's estate.

The solution: Arrange to have the policies transferred to, or purchased by an irrevocable life insurance trust over which neither the insured nor the insured's spouse has either ownership or meaningful control. The beneficiaries of the trust are the surviving spouse, children or other individuals. Proceeds can also be available for estate liquidity needs or to restore tax erosion. Done properly, this removes the insurance policies and proceeds from the estates of both spouses (but policies transferred by the owner/insured can be included in the owner's estate if death occurs within three years of transfer).

Problem #2. Premiums paid directly to an insurance company or indirectly to the trustee are gifts of future interest to the beneficiaries, if they receive no current benefits from the trust. As such, they don't qualify for the annual federal gift-tax exclusion, and they eat into the donor's available unified gift & estate tax credit. The payment of premiums might exhaust this credit eventually, requiring the payment of tax on subsequent gifts.

If the trust is funded with a paid-up policy or a group life policy, there are no premium payments, and this problem won't exist. The settlor could also make arrangements so that the payment of premiums is a gift of present interest. The settlor could give the beneficiaries an opportunity to take the money out of the trust when he or she puts it in to pay the insurance premiums. The annual federal gift tax exclusion per beneficiary with such a withdrawal right would now be available. Because the gift to a beneficiary is considered to be from the settlor, not the trust, the exclusion can be doubled if the settlor's spouse consents to split the gift on a joint gift tax return. The opportunity to take the money can be limited to a short interval, but most practitioners recommend no shorter than thirty days to assure that beneficiaries have adequate time to be informed of this right and respond. Minor beneficiaries are treated as having same present interest rights as adults, but we recommend that they be represented by an independent guardian who can exercise their withdrawal rights.

Problem #3. The beneficiaries can exercise their rights and scoop out the money, because the settlor is prohibited from controlling their actions. This can wreck the trust, if the premiums on the policies are not paid.

There is no legal way to prevent a beneficiary from exercising a right of withdrawal, but there can be a provision in the trust agreement to the effect that any beneficiary who exercises his or her right shall lose it for the future. This may have other adverse effects on the premium payment process, however. The elimination of a withdrawal right could result in the contributor of the premium money having greater exposure to gift tax.

In most cases, this provision isn't needed. The actual danger of beneficiaries making withdrawals is slight, if they understand the purpose of the trust and why they have rights of withdrawal. They are usually the ultimate beneficiaries of the trust when the insurance proceeds are collected, and therefore it would be counter-productive for them to interfere with the premium payment process. Also, they undoubtedly understand that a thwarted and furious settlor would probably find ways to avenge him or herself.

Problem #4. A beneficiary can't withdraw more than the greater of (a) $5,000 or (b) 5% of the available funds from the trust each year. If he or she is allowed to withdraw more than this, he is considered to have a general power of appointment over the funds he or she can withdraw. Anyone who holds a general power of appointment with respect to an asset, and who fails to exercise that power by allowing it to lapse, is considered to have made a reverse gift back to the holder of the asset. In the case of an ILIT, a beneficiary who allows a lapse of his or her right to withdraw assets makes a reverse gift back to the trust. And because the gift is not a gift of present interest (the benefits to other beneficiaries of the trust are in the future), it is taxable.

To avoid having taxable gifts attributed to the beneficiary, the trust instrument can provide him or her with two things in tandem. It can provide for a limited power of appointment to withdraw the larger of $5,000 or 5% of his or her share of a premium payment within a limited amount of time. It can then give him or her a separate general power of appointment over any balance of his or her share of premium money without any limits on withdrawal time. The continuing right to withdraw the balance is called a "hanging" power. Later, in years when possibly no premiums have to be paid, or when 5% of the current value of the trust is greater than the current transfer of premium money, the hanging power with respect to the annual excess balances can be allowed to lapse. This approach is not perfect. The beneficiary's temptation to withdraw might grow as the available sum subject to the hanging power increases. Also, if the beneficiary dies, any amount subject to the unexercised power will be included in his or her estate.

The concept of how a hanging power works is not easy to understand, but the example below may help.

Hanging Power Applied to a Policy with Limited Premium Payments

Premiums are used to purchase paid-up additions in the early years, and to reduce premiums in later years when the paid-up additions can pay any balance of future premiums. The insured dies in the tenth year.

Year	Total Gift to Trust	Beneficiary's Share of Gift	Trust Fair Market Value	Greater of $5,000 or 5% of Additions to the Trust	Cumulative Hanging Amount
1	$50,000	$20,000	$50,000	$5,000	$15,000
2	$50,000	$20,000	$54,000	$5,000	$30,000
3	$50,000	$20,000	$88,000	$5,000	$45,000
4	$50,000	$20,000	$125,000	$6,250	$58,750
5	$50,000	$20,000	$169,000	$8,450	$70,300
6	$50,000	$20,000	$213,000	$10,650	$79,650
7	$50,000	$20,000	$275,000	$13,750	$85,900
8	-0-	-0-	$310,000	$15,500	$70,400
9	-0-	-0-	$338,000	$16,900	$53,500
10	-0-	-0-	$1,650,000	$82,500	-0-

What You Really Need to Know.

Here is what is important to understand, if you have been asked to assume the "modest" duties of an ILIT trustee. In the phase before the policies are surrendered for collection of benefits, this trust is sometimes referred to as "dormant." This is entirely misleading. The trust is not some kind of sleeping creature that will awaken when the insured dies. It is already awake. The life insurance policies are real assets. There is probably money flowing in and out of the trust, and there are beneficiaries who have current rights to it. The trust is a taxable entity, whether or not it has any actual tax liability, and it should have a tax identification number; therefore the Internal Revenue Service knows that it is awake.

As the insurance policies are trust assets, you have responsibilities with respect to them. If the policies are to be purchased by the trust, you must perform due diligence in selecting them in terms of quality of the issuer, type, annual premium cost, and a number of other factors that would depend upon the type of policy. This can be a diplomatic problem for you, because the settlor may have been urged to create the trust by an insurance agent acquaintance who wants to sell a particular policy. If you are going to act in the best interests of the trust, however, the policy selection process should be done independently, and you should work with a cooperative insurance counselor. We are intentionally repeating advice we gave you earlier.

You should review the policies at least once a year for the credit-worthiness of the company behind them, and you should record any increases in cash value. Any offers by the company to enhance the policy at the expense of other features should be carefully weighed. If you hold a policy issued by a mutual insurance company that wants to convert to a stock company (a recent trend), you may have to take whatever steps are available to see that the value of the policy is not adversely affected. You should give consideration to replacing questionable policies, if possible or practical. Many supposedly astute professionals are still wringing their hands over losses they incurred because they were caught off guard when The Executive Life Insurance Company failed. You should document reviews and any actions taken, so that, if necessary, you can prove that you acted responsibly. Additional information on managing life insurance policies as an asset is presented in Part One, Chapter IV.

You should take special care in notifying the beneficiaries concerning their rights of withdrawal, a responsibility that some trustees take lightly. Improper notice or lack of notice can result in serious tax consequences, such as inclusion of the trust assets in the settlor's taxable estate. You should follow the instructions in the trust agreement, but be sure that you complete the following steps.

- At any time a contribution is made to the trust, give a written, timely notice to each beneficiary who has a withdrawal right. Some trustees attempt to minimize the chore of giving notice by providing only one "blanket" notice at the trust's inception. In this type of notice the beneficiary is advised, in so many words, that it is up to him or her to remember that he has withdrawal rights that he or she can exercise. The Internal Revenue Service holds this inadequate. You must advise a beneficiary of a withdrawal right each time new funding provides him or her with an opportunity to exercise it.
- Send each notice by certified mail or other evidentiary means, and keep the receipt verifying that the beneficiary received notice. We suggest that you keep a complete, accessible file of all correspondence relating to the trust, particularly the notices. Some advisors recommend that the beneficiary sign an original or copy of the notice to acknowledge his or her receipt and return it to the trustee. If the beneficiary is a minor, you should send the notice to the minor's parent or guardian. Some attorneys recommend sending notice to the minor, as well.
- Give the beneficiary at least thirty days after the receipt to exercise withdrawal rights, even if the trust allows a shorter time.

Here is a suggested form of notice (for a trust with no hanging power provision):

JOHN H. DOE, TRUSTEE
410 HIGHRISE TOWER
YOURTOWN, XY 99999
VIA CERTIFIED MAIL NO Z 309 436 565
RETURN RECEIPT REQUESTED

November 15, ______

Dear Beneficiary

Under the terms of that certain Irrevocable Trust between George H. Roe as Settlor and myself as Trustee, dated June 1, ______, you have a non-cumulative power to withdraw from the principal of the Trust in each calendar year an amount equal to the lesser of either (i) the portion you would receive if all additions to the Trust during such calendar year were divided equally among all withdrawal beneficiaries; or (ii) such amount as to which the Settlor and/or the Settlor's spouse could claim as a gift tax exclusion under Section 2503(b) of the Internal Revenue Code if the property were given outright to the beneficiaries.

You have a thirty (30) day period commencing on the date you receive notice that property is transferred to the Trust in which to exercise such power. In order for you to effectively exercise such power, I must receive within thirty-five (35) days after your receipt of this notice, your written election requesting such withdrawal.

On November 15, ______, a transfer of $10,000 was made into the trust. If you have not signified in writing to me within thirty-five (35) days after the receipt of this notice that you desire to withdraw a portion of this contribution, your power so to do will lapse. If you do not intend to make such a withdrawal, please sign the enclosed copy of this letter in the lower left-hand corner and return the copy to me in the envelope I have enclosed for your convenience.

Very truly yours,
John Doe, Trustee

____
Beneficiary

____
Date

Where a hanging power of appointment is provided for, you will have the additional duty of keeping track of the accumulative amount over which each beneficiary has a continuing right of withdrawal. Normally you won't have a duty to inform a beneficiary of this increasing amount unless he asks, which is probably just as well. As we mentioned above, this amount can become temptingly large.

The form of your notice will depend upon the provisions for it in the trust agreement and also on the actual amount and timing of a particular premium payment.

Needless to say, premiums have to be paid on time. As trustee, you should have a good tickler system for making sure that they will be. You shouldn't rely heavily on a grace period for paying premiums after their due date. Permitting an insurance policy to lapse could subject you to serious liability for violating your duty to preserve trust property.

Not infrequently, an irrevocable trust outlives its purpose, as in the case where the settlor's spouse, who may be the primary beneficiary, files for a divorce. Then suddenly the settlor wishes to undo what he or she has done irrevocably. The settlor may be able to accomplish this him or herself, by ceasing to make premium payments or taking other actions, but it is often more practical for the trustee to take whatever steps are available. Sometimes there aren't any, but the settlor may pressure you to terminate the trust.

If the attorney who drafted the trust agreement was provident, he may have included provisions that enable someone to shut the trust down. A beneficiary might have a special power, subordinate to any beneficiary's power to withdraw funds, to appoint the trust assets to designated beneficiaries. Then, stripped of assets, the trust becomes ineffective. This approach relieves the trustee of responsibility for the trust's effective termination. Or you might have the right to make discretionary distributions of the trust assets to the beneficiaries for certain purposes, such as for their maintenance and support, another way of emptying the trust and making it useless. Or you might have the right to reform the trust by amendment or restatement, so that the trust can continue for some other purpose than its original one.

You might also be asked by a settlor to terminate the trust by bending the rules. Settlors who create these trusts are wealthy people, but that doesn't mean that they are sophisticated when it comes to complex legal creations. They may think that a request to terminate a trust that has become an expensive nuisance is perfectly reasonable. However you can't terminate a trust without legal authority.

The best approach, if a trust of any type is to be terminated, even if there are provisions that appear to facilitate this, is to review the matter with competent counsel. It is a major enough event to warrant this action. You want to make sure that you are acting in the best interests of the beneficiaries, and you also want to protect yourself. Resignation may be the wisest course to follow (your successor may not have read this book).

L. Marital Deduction Trusts

There are a number of trusts created for a surviving spouse that qualify for a marital deduction. All of these trusts are for the exclusive benefit of the survivor, so that the trustee is acting on behalf of only one beneficiary during the survivor's lifetime. However these trusts might provide that, if the assets are not disposed of by the survivor, they will continue in further trust for others. The trustee's primary duty is to the surviving spouse, nevertheless.

The trust assets remaining at the surviving spouse's death are taxed as part of that spouse's estate. The estate of the predeceasing spouse therefore obtains a federal estate tax marital deduction for assets transferred to the trust. Assets donated during his life to such a trust by the transferring spouse qualify for the federal gift tax marital deduction. Because the assets will be taxed in the survivor's estate, a marital trust may often be invested more for income than for growth, while a related trust for the entire family may be invested in the opposite manner. The trustee may also be directed to use up principal of the marital trust for the surviving spouse's benefit before invading any other trusts for her. But this will depend upon such circumstances as the relative size of each spouse's estate.

Income with General Power of Appointment Trust.

The spouse must receive the income for life and can appoint the remaining trust property to whomever he or she wishes at his or her death, including the estate or his or her creditors. This is a general power of appointment that results in the trust property being included in his or her estate for tax purposes. The spouse might also be given a limited or unlimited right to withdraw principal. The trustee might be given the power to invade principal for his or her benefit.

Estate Trust.

Income is accumulated, and at the spouse's death the accumulations and trust property are subject to his or her general power of appointment. When taxes on accumulated trust income were relatively low, this strategy was used more frequently if the surviving spouse didn't need marital trust income. The progressive tax rate schedule currently in effect for trusts makes this an unrewarding strategy.

Qualified Terminable Interest Property Trust.

A husband and wife may not share the same objectives for the disposition of their estates after the death of the survivor. This is frequently a concern in a second marriage situation where one or both spouses have children by a prior marriage. Each may want the surviving spouse to live comfortably, but each wants his or her own descendants to eventually receive estate assets. However, concern about the disposition of the assets of one spouse at the death of the survivor is not limited to second marriage situations. Any husband and wife can disagree about the disposition of their separate estates.

The qualified terminable interest property trust, or "Q TIP" trust is ideal in this situation, because the settlor can control where his or her assets go at the surviving spouse's death and still obtain a marital deduction for his or her estate. The assets are said to be terminable interest property because the surviving spouse's interest in them terminates at his or her death. This trust can qualify for a marital deduction, but only if the settlor's executor makes an election to have it do so.

One spouse leaves assets in trust for the surviving spouse. The trust provides the surviving spouse with all of the income. Availability of principal for the spouse can range from none at all to very broad access by the spouse, or by the trustee for the spouse's benefit. No principal is available to others, and the spouse is not given a general power of appointment over it. The surviving spouse may have withdrawal rights, but they are limited so as not to defeat the purpose of the trust. At the survivor's death, the remaining principal passes to beneficiaries selected by the settlor.

Qualified Domestic Trust.

The marital deduction is intended as only a tax deferral device, not as a tax avoidance one. For federal estate tax purposes, assets that qualify for a marital deduction at the death of the first spouse will theoretically be taxed in the estate of the surviving spouse. Congress didn't want to provide a marital deduction for gifts or bequests by a settlor to a non-United States citizen spouse because that spouse could then avoid federal estate tax at his or her death by leaving the country. Consequently transfers to a non-citizen spouse that qualify for a marital deduction have been limited. Such transfers by gift are limited to annual gifts of $100,000.

Deductible transfers at death are limited to the benefits of a qualified domestic trust (QDOT), which looks something like a Q-TIP. An outright bequest to a non-citizen spouse doesn't qualify.

The trust will qualify for a marital deduction if the following conditions are met:

- the settlor's executor makes an election to have the trust qualify
- the surviving spouse receives all of the income at least annually for life
- any distributions during the spouse's life are taxed as the distributions are made, and the entire trust is taxed if the trust becomes disqualified or the spouse dies
- the trustee is required by the trust instrument to be a United States citizen or a domestic corporation

There is no requirement concerning principal distributions to the spouse, but to the extent that distributions are permitted and made, they are taxed. The tax on them is at estate and gift tax rates and is cumulative and incremental, and the value of the deceased settlor's estate is the starting point. As trustee of such a trust, you would therefore have to keep a running record of any distributions and file federal estate tax returns each year you made one or more. Because you are personally liable for the tax, you would want to be careful that it is calculated properly and that reserves are created to pay it. This work would be an extra burden for you, and an extra potential source of liability, which should be should be taken into account in your fees, whether you perform the work yourself or have it performed by others.

M. The Credit Shelter Trust

The credit shelter trust is another creature spawned by the federal estate and gift tax rules. It exists in conjunction with the marital share of the estate of a decedent who dies leaving a surviving spouse. It is sometimes called a family trust, because, unlike a marital trust, it can benefit a surviving spouse and other family members concurrently. It might also be called the "B Trust" if there is a marital "A" trust.

Anyone who transfers assets has a credit ($345,800 for 2002 and 2003) that can be applied against federal gift taxes and/or federal estate taxes. To the extent that this credit isn't used up against taxes on lifetime gifts, it is available to offset any federal estate taxes on estate assets at death. Applied against either tax, it eliminates the tax on a certain amount of assets ($1,000,000 for 2002 and 2003), starting with the lowest level of taxable assets. Therefore an individual or his estate can transfer substantial amounts during life or at death before incurring federal gift or estate taxes. The Economic Growth and Tax Relief Reconciliation Act of 2001 (2001 Act) has increased the applicable exclusion amount as follows:

Year of Death or Gift	Estate Tax Exclusion Amount	Gift Tax Exclusion Amount
2002 and 2003	$1,000,000	$1,000,000
2004 and 2005	$1,500,000	$1,000,000
2006, 2007 and 2008	$2,000,000	$1,000,000
2009	$3,500,000	$1,000,000

The federal estate tax is repealed in 2010, but in 2011 a sunset provision exists that automatically restores the federal estate and gift taxes to a level that existed under the law in effect prior to the 2001 act. Unless Congress changes the existing law, beginning in 2011 the federal estate and gift exclusion amount will be $1,000,000.

As we have explained in the section on marital trusts, the federal gift and estate tax rules also allow an unlimited marital deduction for assets transferred between husbands and wives during their lifetimes or at the death of the first spouse. An individual can therefore give or bequeath his or her entire estate to a spouse free of federal tax, without needing to use his or her tax credit. However, if his or her spouse survives him or her, at the spouse's later death there will be a tax on everything he or she owns, except for the amount sheltered by his or her own tax credit. In other words, the predeceasing spouse has wasted his or her credit.

To avoid this waste, an individual can arrange to transfer an amount equivalent to the amount sheltered by his or her tax credit to a trust, and give or bequeath only the remainder of the estate to his or her spouse. The transfer to the trust is taxable, but the tax is offset by the credit (so it is essentially tax-free), while the remainder of the settlor's estate is sheltered by the marital deduction. The trust can be primarily for the spouse's benefit, but with just enough restrictions built into it so that the Internal Revenue Services can't claim that it is part of his or her taxable estate. In this way the taxable estate of a surviving spouse is reduced by the amount of the predeceasing spouse's credit, but he or she benefits from the entire estate.

A credit shelter trust doesn't have to benefit a surviving spouse at all; it can benefit anyone. In fact, there doesn't even have to be a transfer to a trust to make use of the credit, as the credit can be used up with outright gifts or bequests. In many cases, however, it is used in situations where one spouse wants the other to benefit from his or her entire estate after his or her death. In its most liberal form in this case, the trust can:

- pay the survivor all of the income
- give a trustee the right to invade liberally for his or her benefit according to an ascertainable standard (not for an objective, such as "happiness," which would be unascertainable); an independent trustee who has no beneficial interest can use a more liberal standard
- give the spouse a limited power to appoint to others
- give the spouse the right to withdraw annually the greater of $5,000 or 5% of the principal

At the death of the surviving spouse, any remaining principal not appointed by that spouse is disposed of according to the terms of the trust.

The trust can be more restrictive, with respect to a surviving spouse, such as one that gives a trustee the discretionary power to allocate ("sprinkle" or "spray") income among spouse and other family members and/or to use principal for their health, education, maintenance and support. There are many variations.

With a credit shelter trust, you have to know whether your duty to treat beneficiaries impartially must be observed, or whether you are to favor a particular beneficiary (in most cases the surviving spouse). The trust instrument can make this clear with a direction or precatory statement, but sometimes it is only implied through discretionary powers and other related provisions. The credit shelter trust is a classic type of trust where current and future beneficiaries, related or not, may have opposing interests.

As an investment consideration, it could be a good strategy, under certain circumstances, to invest a credit shelter trust more for growth than for income, as the trust property won't be taxed in the estate of a surviving spouse beneficiary.

N. Generation Skipping Transfer Trusts.

Here are trusts, which, like the ILIT, require a lengthier explanation. There is a federal transfer tax on property that passes from individuals in one generation to others in two or more generations below. The intent is to tax assets that would otherwise escape federal estate or gift taxes if the estate of someone in the next generation is by-passed. It is a separate tax, with a chapter all its own in the Internal Revenue Code (ominously, Chapter 13). It is called the generation skipping transfer tax (GSTT). The tax rules that apply to generation skipping transfers are highly complex, and while we have done our best here to give you an overview, we encourage you to read more comprehensive explanations.

For 2002, the tax is applied at a flat rate of 50%. It will be adjusted for succeeding years.

It applies to transfers, as indicated above, that by-pass a generation between the transferor and the transferee, such as one that passes from grandfather to granddaughter, but the tax is not restricted to transfers between relatives. A key word is "transfer." It applies to both lifetime gifts and transfers occurring because of death, such as a bequest under a will or receipt of proceeds from a life insurance policy.

The tax is triggered when a "taxable distribution" or a "taxable termination" occurs for a trust that benefits members of certain generations below the settlor's called "skip persons." A distribution of principal to a grandchild of the settlor while the settlor's child is an income beneficiary would be one example of a taxable distribution. The replacement of the child by the grandchild as income beneficiary would be one example of a taxable termination.

There is an exemption for all generation skipping transfers. For 2002 the exemption is now $1,100,000. It will be increased for inflation for 2003. Beginning in 2004, the increases in the GST exemption will match the estate tax exemption increases described earlier: $1,500,000 for 2004 and 2005, $2,000,000 for 2006 through 2008, and $3,500,000 for 2009. For 2010 the GST is repealed, but as with the estate tax, without the intervention of Congress it is restored in 2011 with an exemption of $1,000,000 (indexed for inflation). This exemption applies to all of the transfers made by one individual. It can be used up entirely on either lifetime gifts or transfers made at death or it can be allocated against each. It applies cumulatively to more than one transfer.

Examples of the GSTT on Transfers.

1. Samuel leaves his estate to his son, Samuel II, who in turn leaves his estate to his son, Samuel III. There is no generation skip. Any of Samuel's assets left in Samuel II's estate at the latter's death would be subject to federal estate tax, but not to a GSTT. There would be a similar result at Samuel II's death: no skip, no GSTT.

2. Samuel leaves his estate directly to his grandson, Samuel III. A generation skip takes place, and there would be a GSTT if the estate exceeded the exemption amount. However, because of a special rule, there would be no GSTT if Samuel II had predeceased his son before the transfer took place.

3. Samuel leaves his estate in trust for his son's lifetime, with the trust distributing to Samuel III at Samuel II's death. Samuel III receives no benefits from the trust until his father dies. When Samuel II dies, there is a "taxable termination" which triggers a GSTT, assuming the trust is not taxed as part Samuel II's estate. A generation skip takes place because the trust bypasses Samuel II's estate. The tax is paid from the trust on whatever part is not attributable to the exemption amount.

4. Assume the same arrangement, except that the trust assets can be used for Samuel III while his father is still a beneficiary of the trust. The trustee does pay funds out of the principal for Samuel III's education. This amounts to a "taxable distribution" which triggers the GSTT. The amount of the distribution is taxed, and Samuel III must pay the tax, presumably from the distribution. Additional tax will be due at Samuel II's death when the trust ends and a "taxable termination" takes place.

How the GSTT Exemption Works.

1. Assume a direct transfer of $2,200,000, by gift or will, from Samuel to Samuel III. The exemption of $1,100,000 reduces the taxable transfer to $1,100,000, which would then be subject to a tax that is based on the highest estate tax rate (50% for 2002, with present law providing for staged reductions). Thus the tax on the total of $2,200,000 is $550,000 in 2002, disregarding any other gift or estate taxes paid by Samuel or his estate.

2. A transfer in trust becomes more complex because every dollar that is paid out of the trust to a skip person is subject to GST tax (the first $1,100,000 is not exempt). Rather, every dollar distributed to a skip person is taxed based upon an "inclusion ratio", a complicated formula that takes the exemption into consideration. Assume that the trust in example 3 above grows to $6,000,000 from an original $2,200,000 before Samuel II dies. Assume further that Samuel did not make any other transfers subject to the GST. The trust will have an inclusion ratio of .50 (the calculation of the inclusion ratio is beyond the scope of this text). The taxable amount of the transfer is then multiplied by the "applicable rate." The applicable rate is calculated by taking the highest estate tax rate in effect at the time of the transfer (50%) multiplied by the inclusion ratio (.50), for a result of .25. The taxable amount of the transfer, $6,000,000, is then multiplied by the applicable rate of .25 to arrive at the total GST of $1,500,000.

Basic Estate Planning.

1. For the settlor and his or her spouse: Consideration should be given to transferring property from the "rich" spouse to the "poor" spouse so that each can make use of a $1,100,000 exemption if both intend to make transfers to third generation beneficiaries.

2. For the settlor's descendants: The settlor should consider the estate and gift tax brackets of the intended beneficiaries of his or her gifts or his or her estate. While the GSTT is a flat 50% rate at this writing, the estate and gift tax rates are graduated, and there is a unified estate and gift tax credit that shelters substantial assets. Where children and grandchildren are concerned, it may reduce total taxes to have assets pass through

the children's taxable estates and be subjected to estate tax than to by-pass these estates and have the assets subjected to the GSTT.

This can be accomplished most simply by transferring the assets outright to a child, if the transferor is reasonably certain that his child will in turn transfer them to his or her children.

A generation skipping trust that will be subjected to estate tax provides a more certain method of assuring that the assets will pass to more remote descendants. The settlor could place the assets in trust for the child's lifetime, designing the trust in such a way that its assets would be included in the child's estate for federal estate tax purposes before they pass to grandchildren. One way to arrange this result would be for the settlor to give his or her child the right to appoint the trust assets to his or her creditors. This constitutes a general power of appointment, and while neither the settlor nor his or her child has any expectation that it will be exercised, it causes the assets to be included in the child's estate for federal tax purposes.

If a settlor wanted to create a trust for a child that will eventually distribute the assets to the settlor's grandchildren, he or she might create two trusts instead of one: Trust A for the exemption amount (identified as such), and Trust B for the rest of his or her estate. Trust A would be for the exclusive benefit of the grandchildren and could be invested purely for capital appreciation. Trust B would provide the child with income and any necessary principal, and would be invested for high-income yields. Both trusts could terminate at the death of the child and distribute to the grandchildren. Trust A might grow substantially while Trust B might not grow at all. The GSTT would be levied only on Trust B, and only when it terminated.

Problems to Anticipate.

A generation skipping trust that is not sheltered by the exemption has special tax compliance requirements. Certain occurrences will trigger taxable distributions or taxable terminations as the benefits of the trust extend to individuals in generations lower than the one below the settlor's. These tax events would require that you file special returns on which you must report taxable amounts and pay taxes on them. Moreover, this tax reporting is on a cumulative basis, so that you would have to calculate tax liability based upon prior reports.

It is possible to not recognize an event that triggers the GSTT when it occurs, unless you understand its nature and have information that tells you when the event is to take place. You should therefore acquire a sound understanding of the rules concerning taxable distributions and taxable terminations and be able to anticipate when they might happen. With a generation skipping trust you have work and potential liability which should be reflected in your fee schedule.

Exhibit II

Typical Trustee Provisions

These provisions, or similar ones, are adequate for most trusts that do not contain complex assets. The provision for investment in common trust funds accommodates a corporate co-trustee or corporate successor trustee.

Section A. Acceptance by Trustee. The trustee, by execution of this trust, agrees to hold all Trust Property placed in trust pursuant to this trust, whether by will or otherwise, and to manage, invest and reinvest this Trust Property in accordance with the terms and conditions of this trust. If more than one trustee shall serve together from time to time, the signature of one trustee may be accepted by any interested party as representing the will of, and as binding upon, all trustees.

Section B. Bond. The trustee shall not be required to furnish any bond or other security in any jurisdiction. If a bond is required by authority, however, the trustee shall not be required to furnish any sureties on it.

Section C. Powers. In addition to any other powers, duties and discretions conferred upon the trustee now or hereafter by law, the trustee shall have the following powers and authority, without authorization by any court:

1. Receipt of Property. To receive additional property, real or personal, from any person at any time by gift, devise or bequest, by designation of the trustee to receive insurance proceeds, or otherwise.
2. Retention of Property. To retain, without liability for loss or depreciation resulting from said retention, any property, real or personal, for such time as the trustee shall deem advisable, although said property may not be of the character prescribed by law for the investment of trust assets and although it represents a large percentage of this trust.
3. Sales. To sell, grant options to purchase, exchange and alter assets of any trust at any price which the trustee, acting in good faith, shall consider represents an adequate consideration in money or money's worth, and upon any terms which the trustee shall deem proper.
4. Investments. To invest and reinvest, from time to time, all or any part of any trust in such stocks, common or preferred, bonds, debentures, notes, securities, life insurance and annuity contracts, or other real or personal property, including property located outside the situs of the trust, either of the class or kind now or hereafter ordinarily approved or held to be lawful for the investment of trust funds or not, as the trustee may select, and to make and change such investments from time to time as the trustee shall consider advisable.
5. Common Trust Funds. To invest any or all of the trust property in any common trust fund, including any common trust fund which may be established and operated by and under the control of the trustee.
6. Name of Registered Owner. To cause any of the investments which may be delivered to or acquired by the trustee to be issued, held or registered in the name of the trustee, in negotiable form, in the name of a nominee, or in any form in which title was passed by delivery; and any corporation or its transfer agent may presume conclusively that said nominee is the actual owner of securities submitted for transfer.
7. Stock Rights. To exercise, in person or by proxy, all voting, option, subscription, reorganization, consolidation, merger and liquidation rights, and all other rights and privileges of whatever nature, incident, appurtenant or pertaining to securities in any covenant or agreement binding any trust; and to purchase any new securities issued as a result of, or in connection with, any such act.
8. Residential Property. To purchase, maintain and sell residential properties. To hold for occupancy, rent free, for the settlor, the settlor's spouse, or minor children of the settlor, including supporting and contributing to the purchase, addition and maintenance of the residential property of the guardian or other person with whom any minor child or minor issue of a deceased child resides; and to pay all taxes and assessments, expenses of maintaining the properties and premiums of insurance on such residences, including insurance to cover liability for accidents to persons on such properties; and to make such purchases or payments out of principal or income as the trustee shall determine.
9. Reserves. To maintain reasonable reserves for depreciation and depletion and for amortization and obsolescence.
10. Leases. To lease property on any terms and conditions and for any term of years, although extending

beyond the period of any trust.

11. Property Improvements. To insure, improve, repair, alter, develop, partition or abandon real estate; to erect or raze improvements; to grant easements; and to subdivide and dedicate to public use.

12. Borrowing. To borrow money, assume indebtedness, extend mortgages and encumber by mortgage or pledge, although extending beyond the period of any trust.

13. Settlement of Claim. To settle, compromise, contest or abandon claims or demands in favor of or against any trust, including claims arising out of any life insurance policy included in any trust, as the trustee shall so decide.

14. Determination of Principal and Income. To determine whether any money or other property coming into its hands is part of the principal of the trust or the gross income therefrom or the net income available for distribution thereunder, and to apportion between principal and income any loss or expenditures which, in the trustee's opinion, should be apportioned and which may seem just and equitable; and any such determination as between principal and income so made by the trustee in good faith shall be conclusive and binding upon all beneficiaries or other persons interested in any trust.

15. Taxes. To pay all lawful taxes, including income taxes, all charges and other expenses properly incident to the management of the trust out of the principal or income as the trustee shall determine; to make returns for all federal and state taxes and to settle and compromise any and all claims which may, from time to time, arise in connection therewith; and to pay estate and other taxes in installments and request extensions of time to file the same if it deems any or all of the aforesaid actions to be in the best interests of the beneficiaries. To make any elections as the trustee shall deem proper for tax purposes with respect to a business or investment interest.

16. Life Insurance. To purchase and maintain life insurance, health and accident, long term care, or annuity contracts on the lives of any of the beneficiaries or their spouses or any person in whom a beneficiary shall have an insurable interest; and to pay the premiums thereon out of such beneficiary's portion of the principal or income as the trustee shall determine.

17. Payment to Minors or Incapacitated Beneficiaries. To pay any sum or sums due to any minor or incapacitated beneficiary directly to such person, or to his or her parent or parents on his or her behalf, or to such other person or persons in such manner as the trustee may deem for such minor's or incapacitated beneficiary's benefit, including payment to the custodian of the minor under any state's Uniform Gifts to Minors Act or Uniform Transfers to Minors Act (and to appoint such custodian if none is then serving), and such payment shall be a full and complete discharge.

18. Determination of Values. To determine the market value of any investment of any trust for any purpose on the basis of such quotation, evidence, data or information as the trustee may deem pertinent and reliable; and to distribute in cash or in kind upon partial or final distribution.

19. Consolidated Funds. To hold the principal of two or more trusts in one or more consolidated funds in which the separate shares shall have undivided interests.

20. Employment of Agents. To engage the services of legal, accounting and investment counsel, including members of a firm of which any trustee may be a member, to assist and advise in the administration of any trust, and to pay for such services out of the principal or income as the trustee shall determine.

21. Merger of Trusts. To merge any trust created hereunder with any other trust or trusts created by the settlor or the settlor's spouse if the terms of any such trusts are substantially similar and held for the primary benefit of the same persons.

22. Loans. To make loans, secured or unsecured, with or without interest and without responsibility or liability therefor, to the settlor's estate for the preservation of legacies, to the settlor's spouse, to the settlor's spouse's estate or any estate, including their own, or trust in which the beneficiaries of this trust have an interest. The trustee shall not incur any liability for any loss resulting to the trust from the exercise of this power.

23. Appointment of Ancillary Trustee. To appoint another trustee to act on behalf of this Agreement in any jurisdiction, without limitation, in which the named trustee or any successor shall, for any reason, be unable to act.

24. Investment Managers. To appoint one or more outside investment managers to provide discretionary investment management of all or part of the Trust Property, and to delegate investment authority to such managers with respect to the Trust Property committed to such managers' discretion. The trustees may compensate any such investment manager for its services without reduction of the trustee's compensation. Any

such delegation shall be evidenced by an investment advisory agreement or similar document.

Section D. Discretion. The trustee may exercise every power and discretion in the management of any trust in the same manner as if the trustee were the absolute owner thereof, and this general power shall not be limited in any way by the specific powers set forth in Section C, except that no beneficiary-trustee may participate in any decision regarding any payment to any person whom he is legally obligated to support if such payment discharges such legal obligation of support.

Section E. Compensation. The trustee shall be entitled to reasonable compensation for its services.

Exhibit III

Amplified Trustee Provisions

The following provisions, taken as a group, are more extensive than those in Exhibit II, and better enable a trustee to deal with complex assets, such as real estate and business interests.

Section A. Trustees' Powers The trustees are granted all of the following rights and discretions to administer all trusts created under this Agreement, each of which is described in this section as "the Trust." In addition to those granted elsewhere in this Agreement and by applicable law, these rights and discretions are to be exercised only in a fiduciary capacity at any time or times, within the limits of the rule against perpetuities, including during the period after the termination of the Trust prior to the final distribution of assets, as the trustees may determine, in the trustees' absolute discretion to be advisable, without authorization of any court. The exercise of all rights and discretions shall bind, and be conclusive against all persons who are interested in, or who claim an interest in, the Trust.

1. Retention. To retain assets for any period in the same form in which they are received, regardless of whether they are authorized as trust investments, and regardless of any requirement that they be diversified, with no liability for loss due to depreciation in value.

2. Investments. To invest and reinvest assets in other assets, regardless of their location, regardless of whether they are acquired from a beneficiary, the estate of a deceased beneficiary, a trust or estate in which a beneficiary has an interest, or any other person; regardless of whether they are acquired for cash or wholly or partly for a series of installment payments or on credit for a period; regardless of the proportion that any asset bears to the type or character of the other assets in the Trust; and regardless of any requirement that they be diversified; even though any asset is or becomes speculative or unproductive of income; with no liability for loss due to depreciation in value.

3. Dispositions.

a. Sales. To sell assets to any person, at public or private sale, without notice, for cash or wholly or partly on credit for any period, regardless of any law limiting that period, with or without security, and upon any terms and conditions; to make short sales of assets, even if those assets are not in the Trust, and to borrow assets from any person with which to make short sales.

b. Exchanges. To exchange assets with any person for other assets of equivalent fair market value, regardless of whether they are of a similar kind or used for a similar purpose.

c. Options. To grant options to any person to purchase assets, upon any terms and conditions, for any period, regardless of any law limiting that period, and regardless of whether any consideration is received for that grant.

4. Securities.

a. Voting. To exercise all rights and discretions over securities in the Trust as a person who is the absolute owner of those securities may exercise, including the power to vote at any meeting of security holders for any purpose, including electing any trustee, any employee, partner or officer of any corporation, or any other person as a director or officer of a corporation, the securities of which are in the Trust; to grant discretionary proxies to any person, to vote at any security holders meeting, with or without power of substitution.

b. Reorganizations. To consent to, join in, become a party to, or oppose any reorganization, readjustment, recapitalization, foreclosure, merger, voting trust, dissolution, consolidation, exchange, sale, redemption, encumbrance or lease of assets, or other corporate action, and to deposit securities with a protective reorganization or similar committee, depository or trustees.

c. Options. To exercise warrants, options, conversion rights, subscription rights and other rights, to sell any rights, or refrain from exercising any rights, permitting them to expire.

d. Deposits. To deposit securities with a clearing corporation, and to permit them to be merged with securities owned by others, and held in bulk in the name of the clearing corporation's nominee, regardless of whether any trustee owns capital stock of the clearing corporation; to deposit securities payable

by, or guaranteed by, the United States or any of its departments, agencies or instrumentalities, with a Federal Reserve Bank; to permit ownership of, and other interests in deposited securities to be transferred by entries on the books of the clearing corporation or Federal Reserve Bank, without physical delivery of any securities.
e. Miscellaneous. To give investment letters and other assurances in connection with the acquisition or disposition of any securities; to rely upon advice of counsel in disposing of securities subject to investment letters or other restrictions

5. Management.
a. Title. To hold assets in a nominee's name with no indication of their fiduciary character, or in a form permitting title to pass by delivery.
b. Operations. To possess, manage, operate, develop, subdivide, dedicate to public use, make or obtain the vacation of public plats, adjust boundaries, demolish, construct, reconstruct, exchange, re-exchange, partition, make ordinary and extra-ordinary repairs, alter, improve and change, structurally or otherwise, any assets in the Trust; to grant or release easements or other charges of any kind, upon any terms or conditions, including credit, for any period, regardless of any law limiting that period, and regardless of whether any consideration is received for that grant.
c. Mortgages. To mortgage assets to any person, and to modify, renew, extend, refinance, recast, reduce, continue beyond maturity, pay off and satisfy mortgages on any asset, and any installments of principal or interest due on any mortgage; to waive any default; to foreclose any mortgage; to purchase any mortgaged property, or to accept a deed from a mortgagor in lieu of foreclosure.
d. Abandonment. To permit any asset to be lost by tax sale, foreclosure or similar proceeding; to abandon, destroy or convey for nominal or no consideration any asset which is, or becomes, worthless, hazardous, subject to confiscatory taxation or of insufficient value to justify keeping or protecting, and thereafter to have no further responsibility to keep informed of its status.
e. Insurance. To insure assets or any Trustee personally against any risks, hazards or liabilities.
f. Leases. To lease assets upon any terms and conditions for any period, regardless of any law limiting that period; to renew, modify or extend leases; to grant options to lease, and options to renew leases, for any period, regardless of whether any consideration is received for that grant.

6. Businesses.
a. Retention. To retain business interests in the Trust for any period, and to acquire additional business interests from any person, upon any terms and conditions; the term "business interests" includes equity and debt interests in any business including an association or corporation, partnership, limited partnership, joint venture, proprietorship, or other entity engaged in any business activity.
b. Participation. To form one or more corporations or limited liability companies, alone or with any other person in any jurisdiction, and to transfer assets in the trust to any such entity in exchange for its securities; to form one or more partnerships; with any other person in any jurisdiction, to determine whether the Trust shall be a general or limited partner, and to transfer assets of the Trust to any partnership as a capital contribution; to enter into one or more joint ventures or associations with any other person in any jurisdiction, and to commit assets to the purposes of those joint ventures or associations; to obtain insurance coverage for officers' and directors' liability, and to pay the premiums out of the Trust; to obtain capital through private or public offerings of securities and to pay the costs and expenses of underwriting and registration from the Trust.
c. Agreements. To enter into, modify, renegotiate or terminate agreements governing voting rights, management, operation, retention or disposition of interests in corporations, partnerships, joint ventures, associations or other businesses in the Trust; to continue to operate any business in which the settlor owns an interest, and to dispose of any business interest to any person, on any terms and conditions. Because of the speculative nature of a business, no trustee shall be liable for loss due to depreciation in value, unless that loss is due to that trustee's own actual fraud, gross negligence or willful misconduct.
d. Subchapter S. To consent to the election by any corporation, the securities of which are in the trust, to be taxed pursuant to Subchapter S of the Internal Revenue Code of 1986, or pursuant to any amendatory or supplemental federal legislation or any corresponding state tax law; to consent to making that

election, even though doing so increases the income taxes payable by the Trust.

7. Lending. To lend any asset of the Trust to any person, including any beneficiary of the Trust, the estate of any deceased beneficiary, or any estate or other trust in which any beneficiary has an interest, upon any reasonable terms and conditions, for any period, with or without security, for any purpose which will benefit the Trust or any beneficiary of the Trust.

8. Borrowing. To borrow assets on behalf of the trust from any person, including any trustee, any beneficiary of the Trust, the estate of any deceased beneficiary, or any estate or other trust in which any beneficiary has an interest, upon any terms or conditions, for any purpose connected with protecting, preserving or improving any assets of the Trust (including for the purposes of making optional and questionable investments), exercising options or other rights, making distributions to beneficiaries, and paying taxes and expenses; to renew, modify or extend existing loans on similar or different terms and conditions; to mortgage or pledge any asset in the Trust as security for the repayment of any borrowings.

9. Banking. To retain cash uninvested, and to open and maintain one or more savings or checking accounts with any bank, including any corporate trustee, or with a savings bank, savings and loan association or building and loan association; to deposit assets to the credit of any of those accounts, and to permit those assets to remain on deposit in those accounts; to lease one or more safety deposit boxes for the safekeeping of assets.

10. Allocation. To reasonably determine, when there is reasonable doubt or uncertainty as to the applicable law or the relevant facts, which receipts of money or other assets should be credited to income or principal, and which disbursements, commissions, costs, expenses, assessments, calls, fees, taxes and other charges should be debited to income or to principal; to reasonably apportion receipts or charges between income and principal; but no beneficiary who is a trustee of any trust shall participate in the exercise of this power to allocate.

11. Distributions. To make distributions wholly or partly in kind, regardless of whether each resulting share contains identical property; regardless of whether any resulting share contains undivided interests in assets; for that purpose, to the extent permitted by law, and whether or not otherwise directed in this Agreement, to reasonably determine the fair market value of each asset which is distributed in kind; to distribute assets with a higher income tax basis to one beneficiary, and other assets with a lower income tax basis to another beneficiary, without making any adjustment between those beneficiaries; except where otherwise directed in this Agreement, to sell assets for the specific purpose of minimizing the income taxes estimated to be payable by a beneficiary on sale of those assets, even though doing so increases the income tax payable to the Trust.

12. Consolidated Holdings. To hold and invest separate funds held for disabled persons and separate trusts, if there is more than one, in one or more consolidated accounts, and to allocate undivided or fractional interests in one or more assets to each fund or trust; but the trustees shall maintain separate records of the assets of each of those funds or trusts.

13. Claims. To litigate, enforce, abandon, adjust, compromise, compound, settle, collect, pay, prepay, defer or discharge any obligation, debt, tax, premium, dividend, insurance policy, death benefit, claim, controversy or suit at law or in equity, which exists or arises against or in favor of any trustee or the Trust, upon any terms and conditions; to submit any claim to arbitration, and to agree to be bound by the terms of that arbitration; to extend the time of payment for any claim, for any period, with or without security; but if the assets of the Trust are insufficient, the trustees need not maintain any litigation without being indemnified to the trustees' satisfaction against all reasonable expenses and liability arising because of that litigation.

14. Removal of Assets. To remove all or any part of the assets of the Trust from the jurisdiction which is that trust's sites, and to take and keep those assets outside that jurisdiction and in any other place or places in the world, during the term of the Trust or for any lesser period; to move the tax situs of the Trust.

15. Agents. To employ brokers, realtors, accountants, lawyers, custodians, appraisers, investment counselors, private investigators and other agents, employees and advisors, including any trustee, any employee, partner or officer of any trustee, or any other person; to pay all disbursements, costs, expense, fees and other charges from the Trust, without diminution of any trustee's commissions; to act or refrain from acting upon advice received from any of those sources, with no liability for acting or failing to act in good faith reliance upon that advice.

16. Delegation. To delegate any ministerial duties in connection with the rights and discretions granted in this Agreement to any suitable and appropriate person; to delegate to any other trustee, if there is such, any rights

and discretions granted in this Agreement, including the power to sign checks and other instruments for the payment of money, the power to give orders for the purchase and sale of securities, and the power to have custody of all or any part of the assets of the Trust; any delegations shall be revocable at any time by the trustee making it; no discretion to distribute the net income or principal of any trust may be delegated to any trustee who is a beneficiary of that trust or who is under a legal obligation to support a beneficiary of that trust.

17. Self Dealing. To act or refrain from acting in all respects as if financially uninvolved, regardless of the existence of any conflict of interest between any trustee and the Trust, regardless of any connection or involvement which that trustee may have with a business or other asset.

18. Death Benefits. To collect all life insurance policy proceeds and other death benefits due to the Trust in a lump sum, or to elect to leave all or any part of those assets with the insurer or other payor under any available settlement options or as an annuity; to give receipts for all assets to the insurer or other payor, fully and completely discharging that payor from all further liability under the policy or other death benefit; but if any policy or other death benefit is collaterally assigned or is subject to any other indebtedness, the rights of the assignee or other creditor shall be superior to the rights of the Trust, and neither the Trust nor any beneficiary shall have any right of reimbursement, subrogation, contribution or payment because of the discharge of any loan secured by that assignment or other indebtedness.

19. Residences. To retain any residential assets, including any interest in a house, cooperative apartment or condominium; to purchase, rent and maintain any residential assets for rental or rent-free occupancy by any beneficiary; to pay all rent, taxes, mortgage principal, assessments, repairs and other charges for maintaining those assets, including any insurance which the trustees deem advisable; to make those payments from income and principal, in accordance with applicable law.

20. Uneconomical Trust. To terminate the Trust if and when its fair market value has declined to any extent making it uneconomical, imprudent or unwise to continue to retain the principal in the Trust; but no trustee who is a beneficiary of the Trust or who is under a legal obligation to support a beneficiary of the Trust shall participate in the exercise of this power to terminate; if the trustees determine that this power should be exercised, the then remaining principal of the Trust shall be distributed to the beneficiaries of the Trust with the same discretion given to the trustees in this Agreement.

21. Tax Elections.

a. Accounting Matters. To elect any permissible accounting method and taxable year for any trust under this Agreement; to elect any allowable depreciation method for any asset and to determine the useful life of any asset; to change accounting methods, taxable years and depreciation methods.

b. Subchapter S. To continue the election by any corporation, the securities of which are in the Trust; to be taxed pursuant to Subchapter S of the Internal Revenue Code of 1986, or pursuant to any amendatory or supplemental federal legislation or any corresponding state tax law; to consent to making that election if it was not previously effective, even though doing so increases the income taxes payable by the Trust.

c. Estate Tax Matters. To post any bond or other security, to consent to any lien or to enter into any other agreement required to obtain or retain the valuation of any asset as qualified real property.

d. Pension and Profit Sharing Plans. To elect to receive death benefits and any other sums payable with respect to any pension and profit sharing plans in a lump sum, in installments or as an annuity; to waive the benefits of any special income averaging provisions and capital gains treatment available for distributions from pension and profit sharing plans; to elect a different mode of distribution with respect to each applicable pension and profit sharing plan. The term "pension and profit sharing plan" includes any pension, profit sharing, thrift, stock purchase or bonus plan, as well as any so-called "Keogh" plan and any Individual Retirement Account of any type.

e. No Adjustments. To exercise any available elections and options under any tax law to obtain, to the extent practicable, both the optimum reduction in estate taxes and in the income taxes estimated to be payable by any trust, beneficiary or other person, and in the optimum deferral of those taxes, without making any adjustments between income and principal, between any beneficiaries or between two or more trusts created under this Agreement.

22. General Powers. To make any payment, to take any action, to receive any assets, and to make, execute, deliver and receive any contract, deed, instrument or other document which the trustees deem advisable to

exercise any rights and discretions, or to carry into effect any provision of this Agreement; in making any payment or distribution, or in otherwise acting under this Agreement, to rely upon any notice, certificate, affidavit, letter, telegram, cable, fax, electronic mail or other information which the trustees believe to be genuine.

Exhibit IV

Provisions to Protect the Beneficiary

Special Needs Trust Provisions

If any portion of Trust Property is set out for Jane Doe, the same shall be held in further trust by the trustee under the following terms and conditions:

a. The trustee shall pay to or expend to or for the benefit of Jane during her life so much of the annual net income from the trust and so much of the principal thereof as the trustee, in its discretion, shall deem advisable for Jane's most comfortable care and support. Any unexpended income may be accumulated and added to principal.

   In making such payments of principal or income to or for the benefit of Jane, the trustee, in its sole discretion, shall consider Jane's special needs. As used in this trust, "Special Needs" refers to the requisites for maintaining Jane's comfortable health, care, maintenance, support and education when, in the discretion of the trustee, such requisites are not being provided by any public agency, office or department of any state or of the United States. Special Needs shall include, therefor, clothing and equipment, travel, entertainment, programs of training, education and treatment and essential dietary needs.

   (i) The provisions in this trust for Jane are included expressly for Jane's extra and supplemental health, care, maintenance, support and education in addition to and over and above the benefits she may otherwise receive as a result of any handicap or disability from any local, state or federal government, or from any other private agencies, any of which provides services or benefits to handicapped persons. It is the settlor's express purpose that payments from this trust be used only to supplement other benefits received by Jane.

   (ii) It is the settlor's intent as expressed herein, that because Jane is or may be handicapped or disabled and unable to maintain or support herself independently, the trustee shall ask that Jane's guardian or conservator, as appropriate, seek support and maintenance for Jane from all available public resources, including (but not limited to) the Supplemental Security Income Program, any state supplemental income program, the Old Age Survivors and Disability Insurance Program, the Medicaid Program, and any additional similar or successor programs. The trustee shall take into consideration the applicable resource and income limitations of any public assistance programs for which Jane may be eligible when determining whether to make any discretionary distributions. In carrying out the provisions of this Article, the trustee is relieved of any necessity to consider the probable future needs of remainder beneficiaries of this trust.

   (iii) The settlor's further intent that no part of the corpus of the trust created herein shall be used to supplant or to replace public assistance benefits of any county, state, federal or governmental agency that serves persons with impairments that are the same or similar to the impairments of Jane. For purposes of determining Jane's eligibility for such benefits, no part of the principal or income of the trust estate shall be considered available to her. In the event that the trustee is requested by any department or agency to release principal or income of the trust to or on behalf of Jane to pay for equipment, medication, or services that other organizations or agencies are authorized to provide, or in the event the trustee is requested by any department or agency administering such benefits to petition the court or any other administrative agency for the release of trust principal or income for this purpose, the trustee shall deny such request and is directed to defend, at the expense of the trust estate, any contest of this Article or other attack of any nature.

Spendthrift Trust Provisions

Section (x) Provisions Applicable to Jane's Trust. As to the share of the Remainder set out for the benefit of Jane, if she is living on the Division Date, the trustee shall hold the same in trust, administer and distribute such share as a separate trust as follows:

a. Income. The trustee may, in its absolute discretion, distribute any part or all of the annual net income to such child. The trustee may distribute the income, which it believes advisable for such child's health, comfortable support and general welfare, considering the standard of living to which such child is then accustomed. The trustee shall consider the other income and resources which it knows are available to such child from all other sources. The trustee need not distribute any of the income, and shall accumulate any undistributed net income, adding it to the trust's principal at least annually. That undistributed income shall be commingled with the principal and held, administered and distributed as part of that principal.

b. Principal. The trustee may, at any time or times, distribute all or any part of the principal to such child which the trustee, in its absolute discretion, believes advisable for such child's health, comfortable support and general welfare or may refrain from making distributions. The trustee is granted the further absolute discretion to determine: when, how and whether to make distributions; the specific purposes for making them; and the assets and amounts to distribute. The trustee shall consider the income and resources which it knows are available to such child from all other sources, and shall consider the standard of living to which such child is then accustomed.

In distributing principal to such child, the trustee should keep in mind that it is the settlor's primary intention that such child have sufficient assets available for such child's support in reasonable comfort throughout such child's lifetime. The settlor is not concerned that there be any assets remaining in such child's trust after such child's lifetime or in preserving assets for such child's issue or for distribution to other beneficiaries. However, before distributing principal to such child the trustee should consider her life expectancy and the need for trust assets in the future.

The settlor suggests that the trustee be generous in exercising its discretion for such child's benefit, and consider distributing assets to such child in order to provide funds to assist such child in either the business or professional world or to make a down payment or the entire consideration necessary to provide a fitting and proper residence for such child in accordance with such child's then standard of living. It is the settlor's desire, however, that the trustee make such distributions only on the basis of specific projects, the full details of which have been explained by such child and only after determining that such projects have a reasonable prospect of success and/or that such residence has a fair market value reasonably approximate to the purchase price thereof.

c. Disposition. All of the assets of such child's trust which remain at such child's death (including accrued and undistributed income) are called the "Remaining Assets." The trustee shall distribute the Remaining Assets to those of such child's issue who survive such child in stirpital shares, subject to the provisions of Section (y) and (a section providing for retention of the trust until the beneficiary reaches a certain age). If such child is not survived by living issue, the trustee shall distribute the Remaining Assets in equal shares to settlor's then living issue, in stirpital shares outright or subject to the provisions of Section (the same section referred to in the preceding sentence. If none of the settlor's issue are then living, the trustees shall distribute the Remaining Assets in the manner provided in Section (a section describing who shall take the trust property in this case, such as certain relatives or a named charity).

d. Children's Power to Appoint. In the event that any child of the settlor shall die before receiving all of such portion of the trust set out in this Section __, then upon the death of such child, the trustee shall pay over and distribute all of this said portion, as then constituted, among the issue of the settlor in such proportions and amounts, whether outright or in trust, as such deceased child may by will appoint, provided that no exercise of such power of appointment shall be effective unless it shall make specific reference to this Section. If the limited power of appointment granted in the prior sentence shall be subject, after applicable exclusions and exemptions, to the Generation-Skipping Tax, such limited power of appointment shall, to the extent so subject, be expanded to include a general power of appointment which may be exercised by such child in favor of such child's estate. In disposing of this portion, the trustee shall be protected in relying upon an instrument admitted to probate in any jurisdiction as the Last Will of this child or in acting upon the assumption that this child died intestate, in case the trustee has no notice of the existence of a will of this child within three (3) months after the trustee has been notified of this child's death.

Section__ Delay of Distribution of Principal and Income. The trustee shall have the power, in such trustee's sole and absolute discretion, to delay distributions of trust income and/or principal to the individual beneficiary or beneficiaries of any trusts created hereunder and/or to delay distributions to the individual beneficiary or beneficiaries of any outright distribution hereunder. Distributions delayed by the trustee are called "Delayed Distributions." If the trustee exercises said power to delay distributions, the trustee shall have the power to continue the administration of such trust for as long a period of time as the trustee determines to be reasonably necessary under any of the following circumstances:

a. Involvement of such beneficiary as a defendant in a civil or criminal lawsuit or in any bankruptcy proceedings (whether voluntary or involuntary).
b. Involvement of such beneficiary with the use of any illegal chemical substances or with the misuse of any legal chemical substances and alcohol.
c. Involvement of such beneficiary in a marital dissolution action which is pending in a court of competent jurisdiction.
d. Residency of such beneficiary is in a country which will deprive the beneficiary of the enjoyment of the beneficiary's trust assets, or affiliation by such beneficiary with a group of individuals or an organization which will deprive such beneficiary of the enjoyment of the beneficiary's trust assets (including, but not limited to, such beneficiary's involvement in a religious or "cult" type organization).
e. Active military duty of such beneficiary in such case where the beneficiary will be unable to use a substantial portion of his or her trust assets (including, but not limited to, active military duty of such beneficiary in a war zone).

The trustee may at any and all times apply the Delayed Distributions from a beneficiary's trust for the benefit of said beneficiary in accordance with the terms of such trust created for the benefit of such beneficiary, or with respect to any assets otherwise distributable outright to a beneficiary, in such manner as the trustee in such trustee's sole and absolute discretion, considers reasonably necessary under the circumstances for the benefit of the beneficiary consistent with the trustee's reasonable perception of the settlor's intent. Settlor further authorizes and empowers the trustee to contest any action filed by said beneficiary, or a creditor of said beneficiary, which seeks to secure judicial approval or authorization for such a discretionary distribution, and the trustee shall be entitled to charge all fees and costs, including attorney's fees or fiduciaries' fees, incurred incident to such contest as an administrative expense of the trust estate of the beneficiary that is subject to such contest or action. In exercising discretion under this Article, the trustee is authorized to rely conclusively on any information or other representation of facts the trustee believes to be genuine.

Exhibit V

Forms for Documents to Protect the Trustee

Clauses in trust instruments that purport to relieve a trustee of various responsibilities should be regarded with caution. This is even more the case of assurances to the same effect from settlors, beneficiaries and other parties to the trust. A trustee should always act in a manner that is reasonable and prudent, regardless of the desires and assurances of others.

Having said this, however, we see no reason not to have the benefit of such clauses and written assurances to support actions a trustee intends to take that he considers reasonable and prudent, based upon his research and consultation with a qualified attorney. The following forms may therefore be useful in providing the kind of information a trustee should look for in such documents.

STATEMENT OF INTENTION

(The following form is useful when the settlor wants the trustee of an irrevocable trust to take action that the trustee feels is not clearly authorized in the trust.)

To:____________, Trustee of the ______________Trust and your successor as such Trustee:

As the Settlor of the irrevocable ________________ Trust, I wish to clarify my intentions with regard to the Trustee's powers as set forth in Article ___ of the Trust Agreement. You will note the absence of any specific power to mortgage or otherwise encumber any real or personal property consisting of a part of the trust property and/or the absence of such powers with respect to the pledging of the entire trust estate as security for the transactions entered into by the Trustee.

I am a businessman who has had extensive experience in acquiring, developing, and selling (type of real estate). I am aware of both the risks and the opportunities that the ownership of such real estate offers. I believe that real estate, properly acquired, can be a most attractive form of investment.

When the Trust Agreement was prepared and executed by me, I intentionally directed that the power to mortgage or otherwise encumber all or part of the trust property be omitted. This was done in order to prevent the trust property generally being subjected to mortgages, encumbrances or deeds incurred by the Trustees in the acquisition, development and management of the property forming any part of the trust estate, particularly real estate.

I did not, however, intend to limit to any degree, the broad investment powers set forth in Paragraph ___ of Article ___, which includes the power to purchase real estate. Furthermore, I did not intend to prohibit the Trustee from purchasing or otherwise acquiring real estate subject to an existing mortgage, provided any such mortgage and the indebtedness issued in relation thereto was on a "non-recourse basis". By such term, I intend that the holder or holders of any mortgage indebtedness secured on a non-recourse basis can look only to the property itself for the satisfaction of the payment of any such indebtedness, and that any such holder or holders cannot look to the trust estate for the payment of any deficiency judgment that might arise out of any secured transactions.

Dated at (city, state) this ___ day of ________, ____.

____

SETTLOR

REQUEST BY SETTLOR TO TRUSTEE TO TAKE ACTION AUTHORIZED BY TRUST AGREEMENT WITHOUT DUE DILIGENCE TRUSTEE FEELS IS NECESSARY

(This form would require that the settlor execute an indemnity agreement such as that which immediately follows.)

To: _____________, Trustee of the ______________Trust

Dear _____________:

I have reviewed a proposed Purchase and Sale Agreement covering the sale of certain premises situated in the (city, state) , known as (street address) to the ________ Corporation.

I, as Settlor of the Trust, am satisfied with all the terms and conditions set forth in said Purchase and Sale Agreement and am most desirous that you both execute said Agreement as Seller, and ultimately execute any and all such further documents as shall be necessary to consummate the transfer of title to the _______ Corporation pursuant to the terms of the Agreement.

I am aware of your reluctance to summarily execute said Agreement without further investigation concerning the advisability of the transaction, and most particularly certain representations and warranties to be made by you in said Agreement. However, I am most anxious that this transaction be forthwith contracted for and concluded.

Accordingly, I hereby request that you immediately execute said Purchase and Sale Agreement, and in turn, I herewith agree to indemnify you and save you harmless from any and all loss or damage arising from or resulting from your execution of said Agreement and the consummation of the transaction therein contemplated; and such obligation to indemnify and save harmless shall extend to any and all costs of defense, including counsel fees incurred by you as a result of claims or demands asserted against you.

I herein further agree that my obligation herein undertaken will also be the obligation of my estate, heirs and legal representatives.

Very truly yours,

____
SETTLOR

INDEMNITY AGREEMENT

WHEREAS, ____________, of (city, state) (the "Settlor") established an irrevocable Trust, namely "The ____________Trust" dated _______, __, ____ (the "Trust") of which ____________ is the Trustee (the "Trustee"); and

WHEREAS, the Settlor retained no investment power or authority over the Trust or the Trustee under the terms of said Agreement; and

WHEREAS, the Settlor may, from time to time, wish to offer suggestions to the Trustee with respect to appropriate investment vehicles for the Trust;

NOW THEREFORE, the Settlor agrees with the Trustee as follows:

The Settlor, on behalf of himself, his estate, his heirs, his assigns, his administrators or executors, agrees with the Trustee that he will hold the Trustee and its successor, both individually and in their fiduciary capacity, harmless against any and all damages, claims and expenses, including attorney fees and court costs, which may be asserted against them or either of them for consulting with the Settlor on investment matters and acting in accordance with the Settlor's investment advice as it may be ascertained by such consultations and as shall be contained in a form of Notice from the Donor to the Trustee, which shall be substantially in the form attached hereto, marked Exhibit A.

Dated at (city, state), this day of ___, _______, ____.

____
SETTLOR

Receipt of the foregoing Indemnity Agreement is acknowledged by the Trustee this ___ day of _____, ____.

____
TRUSTEE

RELEASE AND HOLD HARMLESS AGREEMENT

This Agreement is executed by ___________ of (city, state) in favor of _________, Trustee of the __________________________ Trust dated ________ (the "Trustee").

Statement of Facts

A. Trustee is the Trustee of the __________________________ Trust dated ________, ____ (the "Trust").

B. The Trust holds as an asset a life insurance policy on the life of (the insured) as issued by ___________ Life Insurance Company, Policy # _________ (the "Life Insurance Policy").

C. The beneficiaries under the Life Insurance Policy are the issue of (the insured).

D. The undersigned is the only child of (the insured).

E. The undersigned has two issue, being (names of the undersigned's two children).

F. The undersigned has requested the Trustee to effect a loan against the Life Insurance Policy in the amount of $ ________ and in turn lend the proceeds to ABC, LLC a limited liability company with an office at (city, state) ("ABC") for necessary working capital (the "ABC Loan"). The ABC Loan shall be guaranteed by DEF, INC,, a (state) corporation with an office at (street address, city, state) ("DEF") and secured, inter alia, by a mortgage on real property owned by DEF known as (street address, city, state) ("Mortgaged Property").

G. ABC is the tenant of DEF at the Mortgaged Property.

H. The undersigned is a shareholder of DEF.

I. The undersigned will receive material direct and indirect benefit as a result of the ABC Loan.

J. Trustee will make the ABC Loan only if the undersigned executes this Agreement in favor of him.

NOW THEREFORE, in consideration of the foregoing, the undersigned, on his own behalf, and for his heirs and assigns, and as guardian of (the undersigned's two children).

Releases and discharges Trustee from any and all manner of action and actions, cause and causes of action, suits, debts, dues, sums of money, accounts, reckonings, bonds, bills, specialties, covenants, contracts, controversies, agreements, promises, variances, trespasses, damages, judgments, extents, executions, claims and demands whatsoever made by any party in law, in admiralty, or in equity which against Trustee the undersigned, on his own behalf and as guardian for (the undersigned's two children) ever had, now has or which he or his heirs and assigns hereafter can, shall or may have for, upon or by reason of granting the ABCV Loan to ABC as guaranteed by DEF and secured, inter alia, by a mortgage on the Mortgaged Property; and

Agrees to indemnify, defend and hold Trustee harmless from and against any and all manner of action and actions, cause and causes of action, suits, debts, dues, sums of money, accounts, reckonings, bonds, bills, specialties, covenants, contracts, controversies, agreements, promises, variances, trespasses, damages, judgments, extents, executions, claims and demands, losses and costs including attorney fees and court costs, whatsoever made by any party in law, in admiralty, or in equity arising out of or in any way connected with Trustee making the ABC Loan to ABC as guaranteed by DEF and secured, inter alia, by a mortgage on the Mortgaged Property.

Signed this ___ day of ________, ____.

Witnessed by

____

____
(the undersigned) Individually and as
Guardian for (the undersigned's two children)

STATE OF ___________)
) SS
COUNTY OF ___________)

The foregoing instrument was acknowledged before me this ___ day of ________, by (the undersigned) both individually and as Guardian for (the undersigned's two children).

____
Notary Public
My commission expires:

Exhibit VI

Promissory Note

$ __________ ___________, (state)

Date ________

On demand after date for value received, I, (Trustee), in my capacity as Trustee of an Inter Vivos Trust Agreement dated _____, ____ between (Settlor) as Settlor and me as Trustee, captioned (name of Trust), hereinafter referred to as "the Trust", promise to pay (name of Payee) the principal sum of (amount) DOLLARS with no interest, together with all costs of collection including reasonable attorney's fees incurred in any action brought to collect this note.

In the event of default this note shall bear interest of (amount) percent from the date of default.

THIS NOTE IS DELIVERED ON THE FOLLOWING EXPRESS CONDITIONS:

1. Under no circumstances shall this loan be considered a personal undertaking by me, but rather an undertaking by me as Trustee of the afore described Trust.

2. This Note is a NO RECOURSE obligation: the holder hereof shall have no recourse to the assets of the Trust in the event of default hereunder; holder's sole recourse shall be to the collateral security given herewith and described in Exhibit A hereto, which shall be the sole security herefor.

______________ ________________

Witness (Name), Trustee

____

Exhibit VII

Forms for

Appointment of Trustee, Receipt of Trust Property

Acceptance of Trusteeship

Appointment of Trustee

Receipt of Trust Property

To: ____________________

(Address) ____________________
____
____

In accordance with Article ___ of that certain Trust Agreement dated _________, ___, between _____________ as Settlor and _____________ as Trustee, the undersigned ____________ hereby appoints you as Trustee under said Trust Agreement effective upon your acceptance hereof and the transfer to you of the property held by ________________.

Dated at (city, state) this ___ day of ________, _____.

________________________ (L. S.)
SETTLOR

The above Trust is accepted in accordance with the appointment by _______________, Settlor, on this ___ day of ________, ___.

____
Trustee

DATE ___________, ___

THE UNDERSIGNED HEREBY ACCEPTS AND ACKNOWLEDGES THE RECEIPT OF THE PROPERTY LISTED ON SCHEDULE A ATTACHED HERETO, SUCH PROPERTY TO BE HELD BY UNDERSIGNED IN ACCORDANCE WITH THE PROVISIONS OF THE TRUST DESCRIBED ABOVE.

____
Trustee

Exhibit VIII

Acceptance of Trusteeship

Pursuant to a __________ Trust Agreement with ______________ as Settlor and Initial Trustee dated ______________, I hereby accept my appointment as Successor Trustee and acknowledge receipt of a photocopy of such original Trust Agreement.

____

Successor Trustee

Exhibit IX

Investment Direction to Trustee

To: (Trustee)

From: (Settlor, Beneficiary, Trust Advisor or Other)

SUBJECT: Purchase/Sale of Trust Property of the (Name of Trust)

I direct you to effect the transaction(s) set forth below and agree that my/the Indemnity Agreement of _______, ____ specifically applies to these transactions.

Transactions

You Buy:
(1)
(2)
(3)

You Sell:
(1)
(2)
(3)

Date: _____________ _____________________
Settlor
Beneficiary
Trust Advisor
Other

Exhibit X

Trustee's Investment Transaction

	Item	Price	Reason
Hold	____________	_____	____________________________
Buy	____________	_____	____________________________
Sell	____________	_____	____________________________

CASH TO BALANCE: $ __________

From: _______________

To: _______________

Date: _______, ____

____
Trustee

Exhibit XI
Beneficiary Profile
Date _______

Name ____

Status Primary Beneficiary ___ Successor ___ Contingent ___ Remainderman ___

Date Of Birth _____________ Citizenship U. S. ___ Other _____________

Life Expectancy Over 5 Years ____ Under 5 years ____

Required Share of Income ____% Trustee's Discretion Up To ____%

Principal Withdrawal Rights Description ____
____
____
____

Trustee's Discretion to Invade Principal ____
____
____
____

Reliance On Trust For Support Substantial ___ Moderate ___ Negligible ___

Anticipated Principal Invasions Within Five Years

	Amount	Reason
1.		
2.		
3.		
4.		
5.		

Marginal Combined Federal /State Tax Bracket _____%
Other Applicable Taxes ____

Other Pertinent Information ____

Exhibit XII

Investment Policy Questionnaire

Personal Trusts

Date ________

I. Basic Information

Name of trust:

Type:

Revocable ___ Irrevocable ___ Testamentary ___
Charitable Lead ___ Charitable Remainder ___
Life Insurance ___ Other ______________________________

Dispositive Provisions

Current Beneficiary or Beneficiaries
Identity
Income Provisions
Principal Provisions

Successor Beneficiaries
Identity
Income Provisions
Principal Provisions

Remaindermen
Identity
Distribution Provisions

Beneficiary Profiles *(See Attachments)*

Sources Of Investment Authority

Trust Instrument: Statutory ___ Unrestricted ___

Special Provisions:

State Jurisdiction: ______________________

State Law: Prudent Man Rule ___ Prudent Investor Rule ___
Other ___

Court Determination:

Description of Corpus: Present Value $____________________

Composition:
Cash (or equivalents) ______________%
Bonds __________________________%
Stocks __________________________%
Other ___________________________%
_________________________________%

Comment:

Fee and Expense Factors

Trustee Fees Statutory ___ Instrument ___ Agreement ___
Description

How Allocated to Principal and Income

Investment Management Fees
Statutory ___ Governing Instrument ___ Agreement ___

Restricted ___ Unrestricted ___

Other Fee and Expense Factors

Tax Status

	Taxable	Tax-Exempt
Federal	______	__________
State	______	__________
Local	______	__________

II. Average Annual Inflation/Deflation Rate Expectations

One year: Inflation ___% Deflation ___%
Five years: Inflation ___% Deflation ___%
Long term: Inflation ___% Deflation ___%

III. Time Horizons

Anticipated Term of Trust _____years

Anticipated Life Expectancy of Current Beneficiary _____ years

Anticipated Distributions (Mandatory or Discretionary)
Dates Amounts Reasons

Anticipated Major Changes in Investment Strategy Due to Changing Beneficiary Needs
Dates Reasons

IV. Objectives

Preliminary Required Rates of Return

Current Income ____% $___________
Principal Growth ____%
Total Return ____%
Income Growth ____%

Risk Tolerance of Portfolio

Acceptable percentage decline of portfolio in a 3 month period

Minimal:	0%	____
High	25%	____
Other	15%	____
	10%	____
	5%	____

Acceptable percentage decline of portfolio in a 12 month period

Minimal:	0%	____
High	15%	____
Other	10%	____
	7%	____
	4%	____

Acceptable percentage decline of portfolio in a 5 year period

Minimal:	0%	____
High	20%	____
Other	15%	____
	5%	____
	7%	____

Risk Tolerance of Trustee

Acceptable percentage decline of portfolio in a 3 month period

Minimal:	0%	____
High	25%	____
Other	15%	____
	10%	____
	5%	____

Acceptable percentage decline of portfolio in a 12 month period

Minimal:	0%	____
High	15%	____
Other	10%	____
	7%	____
	4%	____

Acceptable percentage decline of portfolio in a 5 year period

Minimal:	0%	____
High	20%	____
Other	15%	____
	5%	____
	7%	____

Acceptable decline of a $1,000,000 long term segment of a total portfolio of $1,300,000, where $300,000 is invested in short term U.S. treasuries to meet anticipated expenses over the next 5 years:

Over one week	____%	($____________)
Over three months	____%	($ ____________)
Over one year	____%	($_____________)
Over five years	____%	($_____________)

Securities Guidelines

Prohibited Investments And Transactions (List)

Domestic Equities

Limit on equity holdings in any one company as a percentage of the market value of the equity portfolio ___%

Limit on market value of any one economic sectors a percentage of the equity portfolio ____%

Holdings to be limited to round lots yes ___ no ___

Domestic Fixed Income

Minimum credit quality rating (Moody's, Standard & Poor's and/or Fitch _____
(Does not apply to U.S. Treasuries or U.S. government agencies)

Maximum percentage of fixed-incomes with ratings below A ____%

Limit on holdings of any one issuer as a percentage of the market value of the fixed-income portfolio____%

Holdings to be limited to round lots yes ___ no ___

International Equities

Limit on equity holdings in any one company as a percentage of the market value of the international equity portfolio ___%

Limit on market value of any one industry a percentage of the international equity portfolio ____%

Limit on investment in any one country as a percentage of international equity portfolio ____%

Foreign exchange contract limitations:

Cash/Cash Equivalents

Minimum quality rating for reserves other than Eurodollar certificates of deposit, time deposits and repurchase agreements _________

Idle cash sweep requirements:

Revised Required Rates of Return

Current Income ____% $___________
Principal Growth ____%
Total Return ____%
Income Growth ____%

V. Manager Selection *(Discussion of Following Topics)*

Nature of the Organization

Staff-owner operated or employee operated?
experience and specialization
depth
Assets under management
Types of accounts - trust accounts?
Average size of account
Trading capability
Research
Conflicts of interest

Appropriateness of Style for Fiduciary Investing

Adherence to Style

Performance Numbers

Performance Relative to Assumed Risk

Performance among Peers

Performance in Rising and Falling Markets

VI. Performance Measurement

What would be a fair way of measuring the effectiveness of the investment manager?
Comparisons to peers in various equity and fixed income categories, what quadrants, what rolling or fixed time periods?

What events would trigger your concern that the investment manager is not meeting expectations or not meeting your criteria for retention?

Quantitative factors

Performance relative to peers, risk/return scattergrams for what periods?
Negative alpha for what periods?
Fee increases within what ranges

Qualitative factors

Changes in personnel
Changes in investment style
Changes in communication
Changes in manager's legal standing (lawsuits, regulation, etc.)
Changes in manager's clientele, assets under management

How would you alert the manager to such concerns?

Scheduled meetings frequency _________

What opportunities should you give the manager to address your concerns?

Time frames
Portfolio adjustments

What developments would require you to replace the manager?

Quantitative factors

Performance relative to peers, risk/return scattergrams for what periods?
Negative alpha for what periods?
Fee increases within what ranges

Qualitative factors

Changes in personnel
Changes in investment style
Changes in communication
Changes in manager's legal standing (lawsuits, regulation, etc.)
Changes in manager's clientele, assets under management

Exhibit XIII
The Trust Protector

The concept of a "trust protector" has been around for many years in English common law and tax haven jurisdictions. It is used to add flexibility to an irrevocable trust. A trust protector may be given powers by the settlor which range from the most limited to the broadest. For instance, the trust protector may have only the power to remove and replace trustees, or have total discretion permitting the trust protector to have control over the distribution of income or principal. There is a problem, however, if the trust protector is given the power to participate in the exercise of a power or discretion for the direct or indirect benefit of the trust protector, the trust protector's estate or the creditor of either. These powers may cause the trust protector to possess a general power of appointment within the meaning of the Internal Revenue Code and result in the trust property being includable in the trust protector's estate. An example of the appointment of a trust protector with the right to remove trustees follows:

> The protector of each trust hereunder, as hereinafter designated, shall, from time to time, review the performance of the trustee of such trust and shall have the power at any time and from time to time, to remove the trustee of such trust and to appoint a successor trustee who need not be a corporate trustee, provided, however, that such power may be exercised only once during any period of five (5) consecutive years with respect to such trust, and provided further that such power may not be exercised to appoint the settlor, settlor's spouse, or descendent of the settlor as trustee. If the trustee of such trust shall cease to act, the protector shall appoint a successor trustee of such trust, who need not be a corporate trustee, but may not be the settlor, the settlor's spouse or a descendent of the settlor. Said removals and appointments shall be made by delivering an instrument, signed and acknowledged by the protector and delivered to the trustee then serving, where applicable, and to the successor trustee, who shall signify his or her acceptance of his or her appointment in writing. Notwithstanding the foregoing whenever a trust shall come into existence, the then serving trustee of the Trust from which the trust property of such new trust shall have been transferred, shall become trustee of such new trust without need for any such appointment, and the then serving protector, if any, of the trust from which the trust property of such new trust shall have been transferred, shall become protector of such new trust without need for any such appointment.

A Trust Protector may be appointed to modify or amend trust administrative provisions relating to:

- the identity, qualifications, succession, removal and appointment of the trustee
- the financial powers of the trustee
- the provisions relating to the identity of contingent beneficiaries
- the purposes for which the trustee may distribute trust income and principal
- the circumstances and factors in which the trustee may take into account in making such distribution

The protector may also pick a termination date of the trust and the identity of permissible appointees under any testamentary power of appointment granted to a beneficiary.

Exhibit XIV

FORM 1041

Form **1041** Department of the Treasury—Internal Revenue Service

U.S. Income Tax Return for Estates and Trusts **2002**

OMB No. 1545-0092

A Type of entity (see instr.): For calendar year 2002 or fiscal year beginning , 2002, and ending , 20

- ☐ Decedent's estate
- ☐ Simple trust
- ☐ Complex trust
- ☐ Qualified disability trust
- ☐ ESBT (S portion only)
- ☐ Grantor type trust
- ☐ Bankruptcy estate–Ch. 7
- ☐ Bankruptcy estate–Ch. 11
- ☐ Pooled income fund

B Number of Schedules K-1 attached (see instructions) ▶

Name of estate or trust (If a grantor type trust, see page 11 of the instructions.)

Name and title of fiduciary

Number, street, and room or suite no. (If a P.O. box, see page 11 of the instructions.)

City or town, state, and ZIP code

C Employer identification number

D Date entity created

E Nonexempt charitable and split-interest trusts, check applicable boxes (see page 12 of the instructions):

- ☐ Described in section 4947(a)(1)
- ☐ Not a private foundation
- ☐ Described in section 4947(a)(2)

F Check applicable boxes: ☐ Initial return ☐ Final return ☐ Amended return ☐ Change in fiduciary's name ☐ Change in fiduciary's address

G Pooled mortgage account (see page 13 of the instructions): ☐ Bought ☐ Sold Date:

Income	1	Interest income	1	
	2	Ordinary dividends	2	
	3	Business income or (loss) (attach Schedule C or C-EZ (Form 1040))	3	
	4	Capital gain or (loss) (attach Schedule D (Form 1041))	4	
	5	Rents, royalties, partnerships, other estates and trusts, etc. (attach Schedule E (Form 1040))	5	
	6	Farm income or (loss) (attach Schedule F (Form 1040))	6	
	7	Ordinary gain or (loss) (attach Form 4797)	7	
	8	Other income. List type and amount	8	
	9	**Total income.** Combine lines 1 through 8 ▶	9	
Deductions	10	Interest. Check if Form 4952 is attached ▶ ☐	10	
	11	Taxes	11	
	12	Fiduciary fees	12	
	13	Charitable deduction (from Schedule A, line 7)	13	
	14	Attorney, accountant, and return preparer fees	14	
	15a	Other deductions **not** subject to the 2% floor (attach schedule)	15a	
	b	Allowable miscellaneous itemized deductions subject to the 2% floor	15b	
	16	**Total.** Add lines 10 through 15b	16	
	17	Adjusted total income or (loss). Subtract line 16 from line 9. Enter here and on Schedule B, line 1 ▶	17	
	18	Income distribution deduction (from Schedule B, line 15) (attach Schedules K-1 (Form 1041))	18	
	19	Estate tax deduction (including certain generation-skipping taxes) (attach computation)	19	
	20	Exemption	20	
	21	**Total deductions.** Add lines 18 through 20 ▶	21	
Tax and Payments	22	Taxable income. Subtract line 21 from line 17. If a loss, see page 17 of the instructions	22	
	23	**Total tax** (from Schedule G, line 7)	23	
	24	**Payments: a** 2002 estimated tax payments and amount applied from 2001 return	24a	
	b	Estimated tax payments allocated to beneficiaries (from Form 1041-T)	24b	
	c	Subtract line 24b from line 24a	24c	
	d	Tax paid with extension of time to file: ☐ Form 2758 ☐ Form 8736 ☐ Form 8800	24d	
	e	Federal income tax withheld. If any is from Form(s) 1099, check ▶ ☐	24e	
		Other payments: **f** Form 2439 ; **g** Form 4136 ; Total ▶	24h	
	25	**Total payments.** Add lines 24c through 24e, and 24h ▶	25	
	26	Estimated tax penalty (see page 18 of the instructions)	26	
	27	**Tax due.** If line 25 is smaller than the total of lines 23 and 26, enter amount owed	27	
	28	**Overpayment.** If line 25 is larger than the total of lines 23 and 26, enter amount overpaid	28	
	29	Amount of line 28 to be: **a Credited to 2003 estimated tax** ▶ ; **b Refunded** ▶	29	

Sign Here

Under penalties of perjury, I declare that I have examined this return, including accompanying schedules and statements, and to the best of my knowledge and belief, it is true, correct, and complete. Declaration of preparer (other than taxpayer) is based on all information of which preparer has any knowledge.

Signature of fiduciary or officer representing fiduciary | Date | EIN of fiduciary if a financial institution

May the IRS discuss this return with the preparer shown below (see instr.)? ☐ **Yes** ☐ **No**

Paid Preparer's Use Only

Preparer's signature | Date | Check if self-employed ☐ | Preparer's SSN or PTIN

Firm's name (or yours if self-employed), address, and ZIP code | EIN | Phone no. ( )

For Paperwork Reduction Act Notice, see the separate instructions. Cat. No. 11370H Form **1041** (2002)

Form 1041 (2002) Page 2

Schedule A **Charitable Deduction.** Do not complete for a simple trust or a pooled income fund.

1	Amounts paid or permanently set aside for charitable purposes from gross income (see page 19)	1	
2	Tax-exempt income allocable to charitable contributions (see page 19 of the instructions)	2	
3	Subtract line 2 from line 1	3	
4	Capital gains for the tax year allocated to corpus and paid or permanently set aside for charitable purposes	4	
5	Add lines 3 and 4	5	
6	Section 1202 exclusion allocable to capital gains paid or permanently set aside for charitable purposes (see page 19 of the instructions)	6	
7	**Charitable deduction.** Subtract line 6 from line 5. Enter here and on page 1, line 13	7	

Schedule B **Income Distribution Deduction**

1	Adjusted total income (see page 19 of the instructions)	1	
2	Adjusted tax-exempt interest	2	
3	Total net gain from Schedule D (Form 1041), line 16, column (1) (see page 20 of the instructions)	3	
4	Enter amount from Schedule A, line 4 (reduced by any allocable section 1202 exclusion)	4	
5	Capital gains for the tax year included on Schedule A, line 1 (see page 20 of the instructions)	5	
6	Enter any gain from page 1, line 4, as a negative number. If page 1, line 4, is a loss, enter the loss as a positive number	6	
7	**Distributable net income (DNI).** Combine lines 1 through 6. If zero or less, enter -0-	7	
8	If a complex trust, enter accounting income for the tax year as determined under the governing instrument and applicable local law — 8		
9	Income required to be distributed currently	9	
10	Other amounts paid, credited, or otherwise required to be distributed	10	
11	Total distributions. Add lines 9 and 10. If greater than line 8, see page 20 of the instructions	11	
12	Enter the amount of tax-exempt income included on line 11	12	
13	Tentative income distribution deduction. Subtract line 12 from line 11	13	
14	Tentative income distribution deduction. Subtract line 2 from line 7. If zero or less, enter -0-	14	
15	**Income distribution deduction.** Enter the smaller of line 13 or line 14 here and on page 1, line 18	15	

Schedule G **Tax Computation** (see page 21 of the instructions)

1	**Tax:** a ☐ Tax rate schedule or ☐ Schedule D (Form 1041) — 1a		
	b Tax on lump-sum distributions (attach Form 4972) — 1b		
	c Alternative minimum tax (from Schedule I, line 56) — 1c		
	d **Total.** Add lines 1a through 1c ▶	1d	
2a	Foreign tax credit (attach Form 1116) — 2a		
b	Other nonbusiness credits (attach schedule) — 2b		
c	General business credit. Enter here and check which forms are attached: ☐ Form 3800 ☐ Forms (specify) ▶ — 2c		
d	Credit for prior year minimum tax (attach Form 8801) — 2d		
3	**Total credits.** Add lines 2a through 2d ▶	3	
4	Subtract line 3 from line 1d. If zero or less, enter -0-	4	
5	Recapture taxes. Check if from: ☐ Form 4255 ☐ Form 8611	5	
6	Household employment taxes. Attach Schedule H (Form 1040)	6	
7	**Total tax.** Add lines 4 through 6. Enter here and on page 1, line 23 ▶	7	

	Other Information	Yes	No
1	Did the estate or trust receive tax-exempt income? If "Yes," attach a computation of the allocation of expenses		
	Enter the amount of tax-exempt interest income and exempt-interest dividends ▶ $		
2	Did the estate or trust receive all or any part of the earnings (salary, wages, and other compensation) of any individual by reason of a contract assignment or similar arrangement?		
3	At any time during calendar year 2002, did the estate or trust have an interest in or a signature or other authority over a bank, securities, or other financial account in a foreign country?		
	See page 22 of the instructions for exceptions and filing requirements for Form TD F 90-22.1. If "Yes," enter the name of the foreign country ▶		
4	During the tax year, did the estate or trust receive a distribution from, or was it the grantor of, or transferor to, a foreign trust? If "Yes," the estate or trust may have to file Form 3520. See page 22 of the instructions		
5	Did the estate or trust receive, or pay, any qualified residence interest on seller-provided financing? If "Yes," see page 22 for required attachment		
6	If this is an estate or a complex trust making the section 663(b) election, check here (see page 23) ▶ ☐		
7	To make a section 643(e)(3) election, attach Schedule D (Form 1041), and check here (see page 23) ▶ ☐		
8	If the decedent's estate has been open for more than 2 years, attach an explanation for the delay in closing the estate, and check here ▶ ☐		
9	Are any present or future trust beneficiaries skip persons? See page 23 of the instructions		

Form 1041 (2002) Page **3**

Schedule I **Alternative Minimum Tax** (see pages 23 through 29 of the instructions)

Part I—Estate's or Trust's Share of Alternative Minimum Taxable Income

1	Adjusted total income or (loss) (from page 1, line 17)	1	
2	Interest	2	
3	Taxes	3	
4	Miscellaneous itemized deductions (from page 1, line 15b)	4	
5	Refund of taxes	5	( )
6	Depletion (difference between regular tax and AMT)	6	
7	Net operating loss deduction. Enter as a positive amount	7	
8	Interest from specified private activity bonds exempt from the regular tax	8	
9	Qualified small business stock (42% of gain excluded under section 1202)	9	
10	Exercise of incentive stock options (excess of AMT income over regular tax income)	10	
11	Other estates and trusts (amount from Schedule K-1 (Form 1041), line 9)	11	
12	Electing large partnerships (amount from Schedule K-1 (Form 1065-B), box 6)	12	
13	Disposition of property (difference between AMT and regular tax gain or loss)	13	
14	Depreciation on assets placed in service after 1986 (difference between regular tax and AMT)	14	
15	Passive activities (difference between AMT and regular tax income or loss)	15	
16	Loss limitations (difference between AMT and regular tax income or loss)	16	
17	Circulation costs (difference between regular tax and AMT)	17	
18	Long-term contracts (difference between AMT and regular tax income)	18	
19	Mining costs (difference between regular tax and AMT)	19	
20	Research and experimental costs (difference between regular tax and AMT)	20	
21	Income from certain installment sales before January 1, 1987	21	( )
22	Intangible drilling costs preference	22	
23	Other adjustments, including income-based related adjustments	23	
24	Alternative tax net operating loss deduction	24	( )
25	Adjusted alternative minimum taxable income. Combine lines 1 through 24 **Note:** *Complete Part II below before going to line 26.*	25	
26	Income distribution deduction from line 44 below — 26		
27	Estate tax deduction (from page 1, line 19) — 27		
28	Add lines 26 and 27	28	
29	Estate's or trust's share of alternative minimum taxable income. Subtract line 28 from line 25	29	

If line 29 is:

- $22,500 or less, stop here and enter -0- on Schedule G, line 1c. The estate or trust is not liable for the alternative minimum tax.
- Over $22,500, but less than $165,000, go to line 45.
- $165,000 or more, enter the amount from line 29 on line 51 and go to line 52.

Part II—Income Distribution Deduction on a Minimum Tax Basis

30	Adjusted alternative minimum taxable income (see page 27 of the instructions)	30	
31	Adjusted tax-exempt interest (other than amounts included on line 8)	31	
32	Total net gain from Schedule D (Form 1041), line 16, column (1). If a loss, enter -0-	32	
33	Capital gains for the tax year allocated to corpus and paid or permanently set aside for charitable purposes (from Schedule A, line 4)	33	
34	Capital gains paid or permanently set aside for charitable purposes from gross income (see page 28 of the instructions)	34	
35	Capital gains computed on a minimum tax basis included on line 25	35	( )
36	Capital losses computed on a minimum tax basis included on line 25. Enter as a positive amount	36	
37	Distributable net alternative minimum taxable income (DNAMTI). Combine lines 30 through 36. If zero or less, enter -0-	37	
38	Income required to be distributed currently (from Schedule B, line 9)	38	
39	Other amounts paid, credited, or otherwise required to be distributed (from Schedule B, line 10)	39	
40	Total distributions. Add lines 38 and 39	40	
41	Tax-exempt income included on line 40 (other than amounts included on line 8)	41	
42	Tentative income distribution deduction on a minimum tax basis. Subtract line 41 from line 40	42	
43	Tentative income distribution deduction on a minimum tax basis. Subtract line 31 from line 37. If zero or less, enter -0-	43	
44	**Income distribution deduction on a minimum tax basis.** Enter the smaller of line 42 or line 43. Enter here and on line 26	44	

Form **1041** (2002)

Form 1041 (2002) Page **4**

Part III—Alternative Minimum Tax

Line	Description	Sub-line	Amount	Line	Amount
45	Exemption amount			45	
46	Enter the amount from line 29	46			
47	Phase-out of exemption amount	47			
48	Subtract line 47 from line 46. If zero or less, enter -0-	48			
49	Multiply line 48 by 25% (.25)			49	
50	Subtract line 49 from line 45. If zero or less, enter -0-			50	
51	Subtract line 50 from line 46			51	
52	Go to Part IV of Schedule I to figure line 52 if the estate or trust has a gain on lines 15a and 16 of column (2) of Schedule D (Form 1041) (as refigured for the AMT, if necessary). Otherwise, if line 51 is— • $175,000 or less, multiply line 51 by 26% (.26). • Over $175,000, multiply line 51 by 28% (.28) and subtract $3,500 from the result			52	
53	Alternative minimum foreign tax credit (see page 28 of the instructions)			53	
54	Tentative minimum tax. Subtract line 53 from line 52			54	
55	Enter the tax from Schedule G, line 1a (minus any foreign tax credit from Schedule G, line 2a)			55	
56	**Alternative minimum tax.** Subtract line 55 from line 54. If zero or less, enter -0-. Enter here and on Schedule G, line 1c			56	

Part IV—Line 52 Computation Using Maximum Capital Gains Rates

Caution: *If the estate or trust* ***did not*** *complete Part V of Schedule D (Form 1041), see page 29 of the instructions before completing this part.*

Line	Description	Sub-line	Amount	Line	Amount
57	Enter the amount from line 51			57	
58	Enter the amount from Schedule D (Form 1041), line 21, or line 9 of the Schedule D Tax Worksheet, whichever applies (as refigured for AMT, if necessary)	58			
59	Enter the amount from Schedule D (Form 1041), line 15d, column (2) (as refigured for AMT, if necessary)	59			
60	If you did not complete a Schedule D Tax Worksheet for the regular tax or the AMT, enter the amount from line 58. Otherwise, add lines 58 and 59 and enter the **smaller** of that result or the amount from line 4 of the Schedule D Tax Worksheet (as refigured for the AMT, if necessary).			60	
61	Subtract line 60 from line 57. If zero or less, enter -0-			61	
62	If line 61 is $175,000 or less, multiply line 61 by 26% (.26). Otherwise, multiply line 61 by 28% (.28) and subtract $3,500 from the result ▶			62	
63	Enter the amount from Schedule D (Form 1041), line 26, or line 16 of the Schedule D Tax Worksheet (as figured for the regular tax)			63	
64	Enter the **smallest** of line 57, line 58, or line 63			64	
65	Enter the estate's or trust's allocable portion of qualified 5-year gain, if any, from Schedule D (Form 1041) line 15c, column (2) (as refigured for the AMT, if necessary).	65			
66	Enter the smaller of line 64 or line 65			66	
67	Multiply line 66 by 8% (.08) ▶			67	
68	Subtract line 66 from line 64			68	
69	Multiply line 68 by 10% (.10) ▶			69	
70	Enter the **smaller** of line 57 or line 58			70	
71	Enter the amount from line 64			71	
72	Subtract line 71 from line 70. If zero or less, enter -0-			72	
73	Multiply line 72 by 20% (.20) ▶			73	
74	Enter the amount from line 57			74	
75	Add lines 61, 64, and 72			75	
76	Subtract line 75 from line 74			76	
77	Multiply line 76 by 25% (.25) ▶			77	
78	Add lines 62, 67, 69, 73, and 77			78	
79	If line 57 is $175,000 or less, multiply line 57 by 26% (.26). Otherwise, multiply line 57 by 28% (.28) and subtract $3,500 from the result			79	
80	Enter the **smaller** of line 78 or line 79 here and on line 52 ▶			80	

Exhibit XV

SCHEDULE D Capital Gains and Losses

FORM 1041

SCHEDULE D (Form 1041)
Department of the Treasury Internal Revenue Service

Capital Gains and Losses

▶ Attach to Form 1041 (or Form 5227). See the separate instructions for Form 1041 (or Form 5227).

OMB No. 1545-0092
2002

Name of estate or trust	Employer identification number

Note: *Form 5227 filers need to complete **only** Parts I and II.*

Part I Short-Term Capital Gains and Losses—Assets Held One Year or Less

(a) Description of property (Example, 100 shares 7% preferred of "Z" Co.)	(b) Date acquired (mo., day, yr.)	(c) Date sold (mo., day, yr.)	(d) Sales price	(e) Cost or other basis (see page 31)	(f) Gain or (Loss) (col. (d) less col. (e))
1					

2 Short-term capital gain or (loss) from Forms 4684, 6252, 6781, and 8824	2	
3 Net short-term gain or (loss) from partnerships, S corporations, and other estates or trusts	3	
4 Short-term capital loss carryover. Enter the amount, if any, from line 9 of the 2001 Capital Loss Carryover Worksheet	4	( )
5 **Net short-term gain or (loss).** Combine lines 1 through 4 in column (f). Enter here and on line 14 below ▶	5	

Part II Long-Term Capital Gains and Losses—Assets Held More Than One Year

(a) Description of property (Example, 100 shares 7% preferred of "Z" Co.)	(b) Date acquired (mo., day, yr.)	(c) Date sold (mo., day, yr.)	(d) Sales price	(e) Cost or other basis (see page 31)	(f) Gain or (Loss) (col. (d) less col. (e))	(g) 28% Rate Gain or (Loss) *(see instr. below)
6						

		(f)	(g)
7 Long-term capital gain or (loss) from Forms 2439, 4684, 6252, 6781, and 8824	7		
8 Net long-term gain or (loss) from partnerships, S corporations, and other estates or trusts	8		
9 Capital gain distributions	9		
10 Gain from Form 4797, Part I	10		
11 Long-term capital loss carryover. Enter in both columns (f) and (g) the amount, if any, from line 14, of the 2001 Capital Loss Carryover Worksheet	11	( )	( )
12 Combine lines 6 through 11 in column (g)	12		
13 **Net long-term gain or (loss).** Combine lines 6 through 11 in column (f). Enter here and on line 15 below ▶	13		

***28% rate gain or loss** includes **all** "collectibles gains and losses" (as defined on page 31 of the instructions) and up to 50% of the eligible gain on qualified small business stock (see page 30 of the instructions).

Part III Summary of Parts I and II

		(1) Beneficiaries' (see page 32)	(2) Estate's or trust's	(3) Total
14 **Net short-term gain or (loss)** (from line 5 above)	14			
15 **Net long-term gain or (loss):**				
a Total for year (from line 13 above)	15a			
b 28% rate gain or (loss) (from line 12 above)	15b			
c Qualified 5-year gain	15c			
d Unrecaptured section 1250 gain (see line 17 of the worksheet on page 33)	15d			
16 **Total net gain or (loss).** Combine lines 14 and 15a ▶	16			

Note: *If line 16, column (3), is a net gain, enter the gain on Form 1041, line 4. If lines 15a and 16, column (2), are net gains, goto Part V, and **do not** complete Part IV. If line 16, column (3), is a net loss, complete Part IV and the **Capital Loss Carryover Worksheet,** as necessary.*

Schedule D (Form 1041) 2002 Page **2**

Part IV Capital Loss Limitation

17	Enter here and enter as a (loss) on Form 1041, line 4, the **smaller** of:		
a	The loss on line 16, column (3) **or**		
b	$3,000	**17**	( )

If the loss on line 16, column (3), is more than $3,000, ***or*** *if Form 1041, page 1, line 22, is a loss, complete the* ***Capital Loss Carryover Worksheet*** *on page 34 of the instructions to determine your capital loss carryover.*

Part V Tax Computation Using Maximum Capital Gains Rates (Complete this part **only** if both lines 15a and 16 in column (2) are gains, and Form 1041, line 22 is more than zero.)

Note: *If line 15b, column (2) or line 15d, column (2) is more than zero, complete the worksheet on page 35 of the instructions to figure the amount to enter on lines 20 and 38 below and skip all other lines below. Otherwise, go to line 18.*

18	Enter taxable income from Form 1041, line 22			**18**			
19	Enter the **smaller** of line 15a or 16 in column (2)	**19**					
20	If the estate or trust is filing Form 4952, enter the amount from line 4e; otherwise, enter -0- ▶	**20**					
21	Subtract line 20 from line 19. If zero or less, enter -0-			**21**			
22	Subtract line 21 from line 18. If zero or less, enter -0-			**22**			
23	Figure the tax on the amount on line 22. Use the 2002 Tax Rate Schedule on page 21 of the instructions					**23**	
24	Enter the **smaller** of the amount on line 18 or $1,850			**24**			
	If line 24 is greater than line 22, go to line 25. Otherwise, skip lines 25 through 31 and go to line 32.						
25	Enter the amount from line 22			**25**			
26	Subtract line 25 from line 24. If zero or less, enter -0- and go to line 32			**26**			
27	Enter the estate's or trust's allocable portion of qualified 5-year gain, if any, from line 15c, column (2)	**27**					
28	Enter the **smaller** of line 26 or line 27			**28**			
29	Multiply line 28 by 8% (.08)					**29**	
30	Subtract line 28 from line 26			**30**			
31	Multiply line 30 by 10% (.10)					**31**	
	If the amounts on lines 21 and 26 are the same, skip lines 32 through 35 and go to line 36.						
32	Enter the **smaller** of line 18 or line 21			**32**			
33	Enter the amount, if any, from line 26			**33**			
34	Subtract line 33 from line 32			**34**			
35	Multiply line 34 by 20% (.20)					**35**	
36	Add lines 23, 29, 31, and 35					**36**	
37	Figure the tax on the amount on line 18. Use the 2002 Tax Rate Schedule on page 21 of the instructions					**37**	
38	**Tax on all taxable income (including capital gains).** Enter the **smaller** of line 36 or line 37 here and on line 1a of Schedule G, Form 1041					**38**	

Exhibit XVI

SCHEDULE J Accumulation Distribution for Certain Complex Trusts

(FORM 1041)

SCHEDULE J (Form 1041)

Department of the Treasury
Internal Revenue Service

Accumulation Distribution for Certain Complex Trusts

▶ Attach to Form 1041.

▶ See the Instructions for Form 1041.

OMB No. 1545-0092

2002

Name of trust	Employer identification number

Part I Accumulation Distribution in 2002

Note: *See the Form 4970 instructions for certain income that minors may exclude and special rules for multiple trusts.*

1 Other amounts paid, credited, or otherwise required to be distributed for 2002 (from Schedule B of Form 1041, line 10)			1	
2 Distributable net income for 2002 (from Schedule B of Form 1041, line 7)	2			
3 Income required to be distributed currently for 2002 (from Schedule B of Form 1041, line 9)	3			
4 Subtract line 3 from line 2. If zero or less, enter -0-			4	
5 Accumulation distribution for 2002. Subtract line 4 from line 1			5	

Part II Ordinary Income Accumulation Distribution (Enter the applicable throwback years below.)

Note: *If the distribution is thrown back to more than five years (starting with the earliest applicable tax year beginning after 1968), attach additional schedules. (If the trust was a simple trust, see Regulations section 1.665(e)-1A(b).)*		Throwback year ending	Throwback year ending	Throwback year ending	Throwback year ending	Throwback year ending ....
6 Distributable net income (see page 36 of the instructions)	6					
7 Distributions (see page 36 of the instructions)	7					
8 Subtract line 7 from line 6	8					
9 Enter amount from page 2, line 25 or line 31, as applicable	9					
10 Undistributed net income Subtract line 9 from line 8	10					
11 Enter amount of prior accumulation distributions thrown back to any of these years	11					
12 Subtract line 11 from line 10	12					
13 Allocate the amount on line 5 to the earliest applicable year first. Do not allocate an amount greater than line 12 for the same year (see page 36 of the instructions)	13					
14 Divide line 13 by line 10 and multiply result by amount on line 9	14					
15 Add lines 13 and 14	15					
16 Tax-exempt interest included on line 13 (see page 37 of the instructions)	16					
17 Subtract line 16 from line 15	17					

For Paperwork Reduction Act Notice, see the Instructions for Form 1041. Cat. No. 11382Z **Schedule J (Form 1041) 2002**

Schedule J (Form 1041) 2002 Page **2**

Part III **Taxes Imposed on Undistributed Net Income** (Enter the applicable throwback years below.) (See page 37 of the instructions.)

Note: *If more than five throwback years are involved, attach additional schedules. If the trust received an accumulation distribution from another trust, see Regulations section 1.665(d)-1A.*

If the trust elected the alternative tax on capital gains (repealed for tax years beginning after 1978), **skip** lines 18 through 25 and **complete** lines 26 through 31.		Throwback year ending -----------	Throwback year ending -----------	Throwback year ending -----------	Throwback year ending -----------	Throwback year ending -----------
18 Regular tax	18					
19 Trust's share of net short-term gain	19					
20 Trust's share of net long-term gain	20					
21 Add lines 19 and 20	21					
22 Taxable income	22					
23 Enter percent. Divide line 21 by line 22, but do not enter more than 100%	23	%	%	%	%	%
24 Multiply line 18 by the percentage on line 23	24					
25 Tax on undistributed net income. Subtract line 24 from line 18. Enter here and on page 1, line 9	25					
Do not complete lines 26 through 31 unless the trust elected the alternative tax on long-term capital gain.						
26 Tax on income other than long-term capital gain	26					
27 Trust's share of net short-term gain	27					
28 Trust's share of taxable income less section 1202 deduction	28					
29 Enter percent. Divide line 27 by line 28, but do not enter more than 100%	29	%	%	%	%	%
30 Multiply line 26 by the percentage on line 29	30					
31 Tax on undistributed net income. Subtract line 30 from line 26. Enter here and on page 1, line 9	31					

Part IV **Allocation to Beneficiary**

Note: *Be sure to complete* ***Form 4970,*** *Tax on Accumulation Distribution of Trusts.*

Beneficiary's name				Identifying number
Beneficiary's address (number and street including apartment number or P.O. box) City, state, and ZIP code		**(a)** This beneficiary's share of line 13	**(b)** This beneficiary's share of line 14	**(c)** This beneficiary's share of line 16
32 Throwback year -------	32			
33 Throwback year -------	33			
34 Throwback year -------	34			
35 Throwback year -------	35			
36 Throwback year -------	36			
37 Total. Add lines 32 through 36. Enter here and on the appropriate lines of Form 4970	37			

Exhibit XVII

SCHEDULE K-1 Beneficiary's Share of Income, Deductions, Credits, etc.

(Form 1041)

SCHEDULE K-1 (Form 1041)

Department of the Treasury
Internal Revenue Service

Beneficiary's Share of Income, Deductions, Credits, etc.

for the calendar year 2002, or fiscal year

beginning .... , 2002, ending .... , 20 ....

▶ Complete a separate Schedule K-1 for each beneficiary.

OMB No. 1545-0092

2002

Name of trust or decedent's estate

☐ Amended K-1
☐ Final K-1

Beneficiary's identifying number ▶

Estate's or trust's EIN ▶

Beneficiary's name, address, and ZIP code

Fiduciary's name, address, and ZIP code

(a) Allocable share item		(b) Amount	(c) Calendar year 2002 Form 1040 filers enter the amounts in column (b) on:
1 Interest	1		Schedule B, Part I, line 1
2 Ordinary dividends	2		Schedule B, Part II, line 5
3 Net short-term capital gain	3		Schedule D, line 5
4 Net long-term capital gain: a Total for year	4a		Schedule D, line 12, column (f)
b 28% rate gain	4b		Schedule D, line 12, column (g)
c Qualified 5-year gain	4c		Line 5 of the worksheet for Schedule D, line 29
d Unrecaptured section 1250 gain	4d		Line 11 of the worksheet for Schedule D, line 19
5a Annuities, royalties, and other nonpassive income before directly apportioned deductions	5a		Schedule E, Part III, column (f)
b Depreciation	5b		Include on the applicable line of the appropriate tax form
c Depletion	5c		
d Amortization	5d		
6a Trade or business, rental real estate, and other rental income before directly apportioned deductions (see instructions)	6a		Schedule E, Part III
b Depreciation	6b		Include on the applicable line of the appropriate tax form
c Depletion	6c		
d Amortization	6d		
7 Income for minimum tax purposes	7		
8 Income for regular tax purposes (add lines 1, 2, 3, 4a, 5a, and 6a)	8		
9 Adjustment for minimum tax purposes (subtract line 8 from line 7)	9		Form 6251, line 14
10 Estate tax deduction (including certain generation-skipping transfer taxes)	10		Schedule A, line 27
11 Foreign taxes	11		Form 1040, line 45 or Schedule A, line 8
12 Adjustments and tax preference items (itemize):			
a Accelerated depreciation	12a		Include on the applicable line of Form 6251
b Depletion	12b		
c Amortization	12c		
d Exclusion items	12d		2003 Form 8801
13 Deductions in the final year of trust or decedent's estate:			
a Excess deductions on termination (see instructions)	13a		Schedule A, line 22
b Short-term capital loss carryover	13b	( )	Schedule D, line 5
c Long-term capital loss carryover	13c	( )	Schedule D, line 12, columns (f) and (g)
d Net operating loss (NOL) carryover for regular tax purposes	13d	( )	Form 1040, line 21
e NOL carryover for minimum tax purposes	13e		See the instructions for Form 6251, line 27
f	13f		Include on the applicable line of the appropriate tax form
g	13g		
14 Other (itemize):			
a Payments of estimated taxes credited to you	14a		Form 1040, line 63
b Tax-exempt interest	14b		Form 1040, line 8b
c	14c		Include on the applicable line of the appropriate tax form
d	14d		
e	14e		
f	14f		
g	14g		
h	14h		

For Paperwork Reduction Act Notice, see the Instructions for Form 1041. Cat. No. 11380D **Schedule K-1 (Form 1041) 2002**

Exhibit XVIII

Notice Concerning Fiduciary Relationship

(FORM 56)

Form **56**
(Rev. August 1997)
Department of the Treasury
Internal Revenue Service

Notice Concerning Fiduciary Relationship

(Internal Revenue Code sections 6036 and 6903)

OMB No. 1545-0013

Identification

Name of person for whom you are acting (as shown on the tax return)	**Identifying number**	**Decedent's social security no.**

Address of person for whom you are acting (number, street, and room or suite no.)

City or town, state, and ZIP code (If a foreign address, see instructions.)

Fiduciary's name

Address of fiduciary (number, street, and room or suite no.)

City or town, state, and ZIP code	Telephone number (optional) ( )

Authority

1 Authority for fiduciary relationship. Check applicable box:

a(1) ☐ Will and codicils or court order appointing fiduciary. Attach certified copy . . **(2)** Date of death ....

b(1) ☐ Court order appointing fiduciary. Attach certified copy . . . . **(2)** Date (see instructions) ....

c ☐ Valid trust instrument and amendments. Attach copy

d ☐ Other. Describe ▶ ....

Tax Notices

Send to the fiduciary listed in Part I all notices and other written communications involving the following tax matters:

2 Type of tax (estate, gift, generation-skipping transfer, income, excise, etc.) ▶ ....

3 Federal tax form number (706, 1040, 1041, 1120, etc.) ▶ ....

4 Year(s) or period(s) (if estate tax, date of death) ▶

Revocation or Termination of Notice

Section A—Total Revocation or Termination

5 Check this box if you are revoking or terminating all prior notices concerning fiduciary relationships on file with the Internal Revenue Service for the same tax matters and years or periods covered by this notice concerning fiduciary relationship . ▶ ☐

Reason for termination of fiduciary relationship. Check applicable box:

a ☐ Court order revoking fiduciary authority. Attach certified copy.

b ☐ Certificate of dissolution or termination of a business entity. Attach copy.

c ☐ Other. Describe ▶

Section B—Partial Revocation

6a Check this box if you are revoking earlier notices concerning fiduciary relationships on file with the Internal Revenue Service for the same tax matters and years or periods covered by this notice concerning fiduciary relationship . . . . ▶ ☐

b Specify to whom granted, date, and address, including ZIP code, or refer to attached copies of earlier notices and authorizations ▶ ....

Section C—Substitute Fiduciary

7 Check this box if a new fiduciary or fiduciaries have been or will be substituted for the revoking or terminating fiduciary(ies) and specify the name(s) and address(es), including ZIP code(s), of the new fiduciary(ies) . . . . ▶ ☐

Court and Administrative Proceedings

Name of court (if other than a court proceeding, identify the type of proceeding and name of agency)			Date proceeding initiated
Address of court			Docket number of proceeding
City or town, state, and ZIP code	Date	Time a.m. p.m.	Place of other proceedings

Please Sign Here

I certify that I have the authority to execute this notice concerning fiduciary relationship on behalf of the taxpayer.

▶ Fiduciary's signature — Title, if applicable — Date

▶ Fiduciary's signature — Title, if applicable — Date

For Paperwork Reduction Act and Privacy Act Notice, see back page. Cat. No. 16375I Form **56** (Rev. 8-97)

General Instructions

Section references are to the Internal Revenue Code unless otherwise noted.

Purpose of Form

You may use Form 56 to notify the IRS of the creation or termination of a fiduciary relationship under section 6903 and to give notice of qualification under section 6036.

Who Should File

The fiduciary (see **Definitions** below) uses Form 56 to notify the IRS of the creation, or termination, of a fiduciary relationship under section 6903. For example, if you are acting as fiduciary for an individual, a decedent's estate, or a trust, you may file Form 56. If notification is not given to the IRS, notices sent to the last known address of the taxable entity, transferee, or other person subject to tax liability are sufficient to satisfy the requirements of the Internal Revenue Code.

Receivers and assignees for the benefit of creditors also file Form 56 to give notice of qualification under section 6036. However, a bankruptcy trustee, debtor in possession, or other like fiduciary in a bankruptcy proceeding is not required to give notice of qualification under section 6036. Trustees, etc., in bankruptcy proceedings are subject to the notice requirements under title 11 of the United States Code (Bankruptcy Rules).

Definitions

Fiduciary. A fiduciary is any person acting in a fiduciary capacity for any other person (or terminating entity), such as an administrator, conservator, designee, executor, guardian, receiver, trustee of a trust, trustee in bankruptcy, personal representative, person in possession of property of a decedent's estate, or debtor in possession of assets in any bankruptcy proceeding by order of the court.

Person. A person is any individual, trust, estate, partnership, association, company or corporation.

Decedent's estate. A decedent's estate is a taxable entity separate from the decedent that comes into existence at the time of the decedent's death. It generally continues to exist until the final distribution of the assets of the estate is made to the heirs and other beneficiaries.

Terminating entities. A terminating entity, such as a corporation, partnership, trust, etc., only has the legal capacity to establish a fiduciary relationship while it is in existence. Establishing a fiduciary relationship prior to termination of the entity allows the fiduciary to represent the entity on all tax matters after it is terminated.

When and Where To File

Notice of fiduciary relationship. Generally, you should file Form 56 when you create (or terminate) a fiduciary relationship. To receive tax notices upon creation of a fiduciary relationship, file Form 56 with the Internal Revenue Service Center where the person for whom you are acting is required to file tax returns. However, when a fiduciary relationship is first created, a fiduciary who is required to file a return can file Form 56 with the first tax return filed.

Proceedings (other than bankruptcy) and assignments for the benefit of creditors. A fiduciary who is appointed or authorized to act as:

- A receiver in a receivership proceeding or similar fiduciary (including a fiduciary in aid of foreclosure), or
- An assignee for the benefit of creditors, must file Form 56 on, or within 10 days of, the date of appointment with the Chief, Special Procedures Staff, of the district office of the IRS having jurisdiction over the person for whom you are acting.

The receiver or assignee may also file a separate Form 56 with the service center where the person for whom the fiduciary is acting is required to file tax returns to provide the notice required by section 6903.

Specific Instructions

Part I—Identification

Provide all the information called for in this part.

Identifying number. If you are acting for an individual, an individual debtor, or other person whose assets are controlled, the identifying number is the social security number (SSN). If you are acting for a person other than an individual, including an estate or trust, the identifying number is the employer identification number (EIN).

Decedent's SSN. If you are acting on behalf of a decedent, enter the decedent's SSN shown on his or her final Form 1040 in the space provided.

Address. Include the suite, room, or other unit number after the street address.

If the postal service does not deliver mail to the street address and the fiduciary (or person) has a P.O. box, show the box number instead of the street address.

For a foreign address, enter the information in the following order: city, province or state, and country. Follow the country's practice for entering the postal code. Please **do not** abbreviate the country name.

Part II—Authority

Line 1a. Check the box on line 1a if the decedent died **testate** (i.e., having left a valid will) and enter the decedent's date of death.

Line 1b. Check the box on line 1b if the decedent died **intestate** (i.e., without leaving a valid will). Also, enter the decedent's date of death and write "Date of Death" next to the date.

Assignment for the benefit of creditors. Enter the date the assets were assigned to you and write "Assignment Date" after the date.

Proceedings other than bankruptcy. Enter the date you were appointed or took possession of the assets of the debtor or other person whose assets are controlled.

Part III—Tax Notices

Complete this part if you want the IRS to send you tax notices regarding the person for whom you are acting.

Line 2. Specify the type of tax involved. This line should also identify a transferee tax liability under section 6901 or fiduciary tax liability under 31 U.S.C. 3713(b) when either exists.

Part IV—Revocation or Termination of Notice

Complete this part only if you are revoking or terminating a prior notice concerning a fiduciary relationship. Completing this part will relieve you of any further duty or liability as a fiduciary if used as a notice of termination.

Part V—Court and Administrative Proceedings

Complete this part only if you have been appointed a receiver, trustee, or fiduciary by a court or other governmental unit in a proceeding other than a bankruptcy proceeding.

If proceedings are scheduled for more than one date, time, or place, attach a separate schedule of the proceedings.

Assignment for the benefit of creditors.— You must attach the following information:

1. A brief description of the assets that were assigned, and
2. An explanation of the action to be taken regarding such assets, including any hearings, meetings of creditors, sale, or other scheduled action.

Signature

Sign Form 56 and enter a title describing your role as a fiduciary (e.g., assignee, executor, guardian, trustee, personal representative, receiver, or conservator).

Paperwork Reduction Act and Privacy Act Notice. We ask for the information on this form to carry out the Internal Revenue laws of the United States. Form 56 is provided for your convenience and its use is voluntary. Under section 6109 you must disclose the social security number or employer identification number of the individual or entity for which you are acting. The principal purpose of this disclosure is to secure proper identification of the taxpayer. We also need this information to gain access to the tax information in our files and properly respond to your request. If you do not disclose this information, we may suspend processing the notice of fiduciary relationship and not consider this as proper notification until you provide the information.

You are not required to provide the information requested on a form that is subject to the Paperwork Reduction Act unless the form displays a valid OMB control number. Books or records relating to a form or its instructions must be retained as long as their contents may become material in the administration of any Internal Revenue law. Generally, tax returns and return information are confidential as required by section 6103.

The time needed to complete and file this form will vary depending on individual circumstances. The estimated average time is:

Recordkeeping	8 min.
Learning about the law or the form	32 min.
Preparing the form	46 min.
Copying, assembling, and sending the form to the IRS	15 min.

If you have comments concerning the accuracy of these time estimates or suggestions for making this form simpler, we would be happy to hear from you. You can write to the Tax Forms Committee, Western Area Distribution Center, Rancho Cordova, CA 95743-0001. **DO NOT** send Form 56 to this address. Instead, see **When and Where To File** on this page.

Exhibit XIX

Application for Employer Identification Number

(FORM SS-4)

(with instructions)

Form **SS-4**

(Rev. December 2001)

Department of the Treasury
Internal Revenue Service

Application for Employer Identification Number

(For use by employers, corporations, partnerships, trusts, estates, churches, government agencies, Indian tribal entities, certain individuals, and others.)

► See separate instructions for each line. ► Keep a copy for your records.

EIN

OMB No. 1545-0003

Type or print clearly.

1 Legal name of entity (or individual) for whom the EIN is being requested

2 Trade name of business (if different from name on line 1)

3 Executor, trustee, "care of" name

4a Mailing address (room, apt., suite no. and street, or P.O. box)

5a Street address (if different) (Do not enter a P.O. box.)

4b City, state, and ZIP code

5b City, state, and ZIP code

6 County and state where principal business is located

7a Name of principal officer, general partner, grantor, owner, or trustor

7b SSN, ITIN, or EIN

8a **Type of entity** (check only one box)

- ☐ Sole proprietor (SSN) ____
- ☐ Partnership
- ☐ Corporation (enter form number to be filed) ► ____
- ☐ Personal service corp.
- ☐ Church or church-controlled organization
- ☐ Other nonprofit organization (specify) ► ____
- ☐ Other (specify) ►
- ☐ Estate (SSN of decedent) ____
- ☐ Plan administrator (SSN) ____
- ☐ Trust (SSN of grantor) ____
- ☐ National Guard ☐ State/local government
- ☐ Farmers' cooperative ☐ Federal government/military
- ☐ REMIC ☐ Indian tribal governments/enterprises

Group Exemption Number (GEN) ► ____

8b If a corporation, name the state or foreign country (if applicable) where incorporated | State | Foreign country

9 **Reason for applying** (check only one box)

- ☐ Started new business (specify type) ► ____
- ☐ Hired employees (Check the box and see line 12.)
- ☐ Compliance with IRS withholding regulations
- ☐ Other (specify) ►
- ☐ Banking purpose (specify purpose) ► ____
- ☐ Changed type of organization (specify new type) ► ____
- ☐ Purchased going business
- ☐ Created a trust (specify type) ► ____
- ☐ Created a pension plan (specify type) ► ____

10 Date business started or acquired (month, day, year)

11 Closing month of accounting year

12 First date wages or annuities were paid or will be paid (month, day, year). **Note:** *If applicant is a withholding agent, enter date income will first be paid to nonresident alien. (month, day, year)* . . . . ►

13 Highest number of employees expected in the next 12 months. **Note:** *If the applicant does not expect to have any employees during the period, enter "-0-."* . . . . ►

Agricultural	Household	Other

14 Check **one** box that best describes the principal activity of your business

- ☐ Health care & social assistance ☐ Wholesale-agent/broker
- ☐ Construction ☐ Rental & leasing ☐ Transportation & warehousing ☐ Accommodation & food service ☐ Wholesale-other ☐ Retail
- ☐ Real estate ☐ Manufacturing ☐ Finance & insurance ☐ Other (specify)

15 Indicate principal line of merchandise sold; specific construction work done; products produced; or services provided.

16a Has the applicant ever applied for an employer identification number for this or any other business? . . . . ☐ Yes ☐ No
Note: *If "Yes," please complete lines 16b and 16c.*

16b If you checked "Yes" on line 16a, give applicant's legal name and trade name shown on prior application if different from line 1 or 2 above.
Legal name ► Trade name ►

16c Approximate date when, and city and state where, the application was filed. Enter previous employer identification number if known.

Approximate date when filed (mo., day, year)	City and state where filed	Previous EIN

Third Party Designee

Complete this section **only** if you want to authorize the named individual to receive the entity's EIN and answer questions about the completion of this form.

Designee's name | Designee's telephone number (include area code) ( )

Address and ZIP code | Designee's fax number (include area code) ( )

Under penalties of perjury, I declare that I have examined this application, and to the best of my knowledge and belief, it is true, correct, and complete.

Applicant's telephone number (include area code) ( )

Name and title (type or print clearly) ►

Applicant's fax number (include area code) ( )

Signature ► Date ►

For Privacy Act and Paperwork Reduction Act Notice, see separate instructions. Cat. No. 16055N Form **SS-4** (Rev. 12-2001)

Do I Need an EIN?

File Form SS-4 if the applicant entity does not already have an EIN but is required to show an EIN on any return, statement, or other document.[1] **See also the separate instructions for each line on Form SS-4.**

IF the applicant...	AND...	THEN...
Started a new business	Does not currently have (nor expect to have) employees	Complete lines 1, 2, 4a–6, 8a, and 9–16c.
Hired (or will hire) employees, including household employees	Does not already have an EIN	Complete lines 1, 2, 4a–6, 7a–b (if applicable), 8a, 8b (if applicable), and 9–16c.
Opened a bank account	Needs an EIN for banking purposes only	Complete lines 1–5b, 7a–b (if applicable), 8a, 9, and 16a–c.
Changed type of organization	Either the legal character of the organization or its ownership changed (e.g., you incorporate a sole proprietorship or form a partnership)[2]	Complete lines 1–16c (as applicable).
Purchased a going business[3]	Does not already have an EIN	Complete lines 1–16c (as applicable).
Created a trust	The trust is other than a grantor trust or an IRA trust[4]	Complete lines 1–16c (as applicable).
Created a pension plan as a plan administrator[5]	Needs an EIN for reporting purposes	Complete lines 1, 2, 4a–6, 8a, 9, and 16a–c.
Is a foreign person needing an EIN to comply with IRS withholding regulations	Needs an EIN to complete a Form W-8 (other than Form W-8ECI), avoid withholding on portfolio assets, or claim tax treaty benefits[6]	Complete lines 1–5b, 7a–b (SSN or ITIN optional), 8a–9, and 16a–c.
Is administering an estate	Needs an EIN to report estate income on Form 1041	Complete lines 1, 3, 4a–b, 8a, 9, and 16a–c.
Is a withholding agent for taxes on non-wage income paid to an alien (i.e., individual, corporation, or partnership, etc.)	Is an agent, broker, fiduciary, manager, tenant, or spouse who is required to file **Form 1042,** Annual Withholding Tax Return for U.S. Source Income of Foreign Persons	Complete lines 1, 2, 3 (if applicable), 4a–5b, 7a–b (if applicable), 8a, 9, and 16a–c.
Is a state or local agency	Serves as a tax reporting agent for public assistance recipients under Rev. Proc. 80-4, 1980-1 C.B. 581[7]	Complete lines 1, 2, 4a–5b, 8a, 9, and 16a–c.
Is a single-member LLC	Needs an EIN to file **Form 8832,** Classification Election, for filing employment tax returns, **or** for state reporting purposes[8]	Complete lines 1–16c (as applicable).
Is an S corporation	Needs an EIN to file **Form 2553,** Election by a Small Business Corporation[9]	Complete lines 1–16c (as applicable).

[1] For example, a sole proprietorship or self-employed farmer who establishes a qualified retirement plan, or is required to file excise, employment, alcohol, tobacco, or firearms returns, must have an EIN. **A partnership, corporation, REMIC (real estate mortgage investment conduit), nonprofit organization (church, club, etc.), or farmers' cooperative must use an EIN for any tax-related purpose even if the entity does not have employees.**

[2] However, **do not** apply for a new EIN if the existing entity only **(a)** changed its business name, **(b)** elected on Form 8832 to change the way it is taxed (or is covered by the default rules), or **(c)** terminated its partnership status because at least 50% of the total interests in partnership capital and profits were sold or exchanged within a 12-month period. (The EIN of the terminated partnership should continue to be used. See Regulations section 301.6109-1(d)(2)(iii).)

[3] Do not use the EIN of the prior business unless you became the "owner" of a corporation by acquiring its stock.

[4] However, IRA trusts that are required to file **Form 990-T,** Exempt Organization Business Income Tax Return, must have an EIN.

[5] A plan administrator is the person or group of persons specified as the administrator by the instrument under which the plan is operated.

[6] Entities applying to be a Qualified Intermediary (QI) need a QI-EIN even if they already have an EIN. **See Rev. Proc. 2000-12.**

[7] See also *Household employer* on page 4. (**Note:** State or local agencies may need an EIN for other reasons, e.g., hired employees.)

[8] Most LLCs **do not** need to file Form 8832. See **Limited liability company (LLC)** on page 4 for details on completing Form SS-4 for an LLC.

[9] An existing corporation that is electing or revoking S corporation status should use its previously-assigned EIN.

Instructions for Form SS-4

Department of the Treasury
Internal Revenue Service

(Rev. December 2001)

Application for Employer Identification Number

Section references are to the Internal Revenue Code unless otherwise noted.

General Instructions

Use these instructions to complete **Form SS-4,** Application for Employer Identification Number. Also see **Do I Need an EIN?** on page 2 of Form SS-4.

Purpose of Form

Use Form SS-4 to apply for an employer identification number (EIN). An EIN is a nine-digit number (for example, 12-3456789) assigned to sole proprietors, corporations, partnerships, estates, trusts, and other entities for tax filing and reporting purposes. The information you provide on this form will establish your business tax account.

CAUTION *An EIN is for use in connection with your business activities only. Do* ***not*** *use your EIN in place of your social security number (SSN).*

File only one Form SS-4. Generally, a sole proprietor should file only one Form SS-4 and needs only one EIN, regardless of the number of businesses operated as a sole proprietorship or trade names under which a business operates. However, if the proprietorship incorporates or enters into a partnership, a new EIN is required. Also, each corporation in an affiliated group must have its own EIN.

EIN applied for, but not received. If you do not have an EIN by the time a **return** is due, write "Applied For" and the date you applied in the space shown for the number. **Do not** show your social security number (SSN) as an EIN on returns.

If you do not have an EIN by the time a **tax deposit** is due, send your payment to the Internal Revenue Service Center for your filing area as shown in the instructions for the form that you are are filing. Make your check or money order payable to the **"United States Treasury"** and show your name (as shown on Form SS-4), address, type of tax, period covered, and date you applied for an EIN.

Related Forms and Publications

The following **forms** and **instructions** may be useful to filers of Form SS-4:

- **Form 990-T,** Exempt Organization Business Income Tax Return
- **Instructions for Form 990-T**
- **Schedule C (Form 1040),** Profit or Loss From Business
- **Schedule F (Form 1040),** Profit or Loss From Farming
- **Instructions for Form 1041 and Schedules A, B, D, G, I, J, and K-1,** U.S. Income Tax Return for Estates and Trusts
- **Form 1042,** Annual Withholding Tax Return for U.S. Source Income of Foreign Persons
- **Instructions for Form 1065,** U.S. Return of Partnership Income
- **Instructions for Form 1066,** U.S. Real Estate Mortgage Investment Conduit (REMIC) Income Tax Return
- **Instructions for Forms 1120 and 1120-A**
- **Form 2553,** Election by a Small Business Corporation
- **Form 2848,** Power of Attorney and Declaration of Representative
- **Form 8821,** Tax Information Authorization
- **Form 8832,** Entity Classification Election

For more **information** about filing Form SS-4 and related issues, see:

- **Circular A,** Agricultural Employer's Tax Guide (Pub. 51)
- **Circular E,** Employer's Tax Guide (Pub. 15)
- **Pub. 538,** Accounting Periods and Methods
- **Pub. 542,** Corporations
- **Pub. 557,** Exempt Status for Your Organization
- **Pub. 583,** Starting a Business and Keeping Records
- **Pub. 966,** EFTPS: Now a Full Range of Electronic Choices to Pay All Your Federal Taxes
- **Pub. 1635,** Understanding Your EIN
- **Package 1023,** Application for Recognition of Exemption
- **Package 1024,** Application for Recognition of Exemption Under Section 501(a)

How To Get Forms and Publications

Phone. You can order forms, instructions, and publications by phone 24 hours a day, 7 days a week. Just call 1-800-TAX-FORM (1-800-829-3676). You should receive your order or notification of its status within 10 workdays.

Personal computer. With your personal computer and modem, you can get the forms and information you need using the IRS Web Site at **www.irs.gov** or File Transfer Protocol at **ftp.irs.gov.**

CD-ROM. For small businesses, return preparers, or others who may frequently need tax forms or publications, a CD-ROM containing over 2,000 tax products (including many prior year forms) can be purchased from the National Technical Information Service (NTIS).

To order **Pub. 1796,** Federal Tax Products on CD-ROM, call **1-877-CDFORMS** (1-877-233-6767) toll free or connect to **www.irs.gov/cdorders.**

Tax Help for Your Business

IRS-sponsored Small Business Workshops provide information about your Federal and state tax obligations. For information about workshops in your area, call 1-800-829-1040 and ask for your Taxpayer Education Coordinator.

How To Apply

You can apply for an EIN by telephone, fax, or mail depending on how soon you need to use the EIN.

Application by Tele-TIN. Under the Tele-TIN program, you can receive your EIN by telephone and use it immediately to file a return or make a payment. To receive an EIN by telephone, IRS suggests that you complete Form SS-4 so that you will have all relevant information available. Then call the Tele-TIN number at 1-866-816-2065. (International applicants must call 215-516-6999.) Tele-TIN hours of operation are 7:30 a.m. to 5:30 p.m. The person making the call must be authorized to sign the form or be an authorized designee. See **Signature** and **Third Party Designee** on page 6. Also see the **TIP** below.

An IRS representative will use the information from the Form SS-4 to establish your account and assign you an EIN. Write the number you are given on the upper right corner of the form and sign and date it. Keep this copy for your records.

If requested by an IRS representative, mail or fax (facsimile) the signed Form SS-4 (including any Third Party Designee authorization) **within 24 hours** to the Tele-TIN Unit at the service center address provided by the IRS representative.

TIP *Taxpayer representatives can use Tele-TIN to apply for an EIN on behalf of their client and request that the EIN be faxed to their* ***client*** *on the same day. (**Note:** By utilizing this procedure, you are authorizing the IRS to fax the EIN without a cover sheet.)*

Application by Fax-TIN. Under the Fax-TIN program, you can receive your EIN by fax within 4 business days. Complete and fax Form SS-4 to the IRS using the Fax-TIN number listed below for your state. A long-distance charge to callers outside of the local calling area will apply. Fax-TIN numbers can only be used to apply for an EIN. **The numbers may change without notice.** Fax-TIN is available 24 hours a day, 7 days a week.

Be sure to provide your fax number so that IRS can fax the EIN back to you. (**Note:** By utilizing this procedure, you are authorizing the IRS to fax the EIN without a cover sheet.)

Do not call Tele-TIN for the same entity because duplicate EINs may be issued. See **Third Party Designee** on page 6.

Application by mail. Complete Form SS-4 at least 4 to 5 weeks before you will need an EIN. Sign and date the application and mail it to the service center address for your state. You will receive your EIN in the mail in approximately 4 weeks. See also **Third Party Designee** on page 6.

Call 1-800-829-1040 to verify a number or to ask about the status of an application by mail.

If your principal business, office or agency, or legal residence in the case of an individual, is located in:	Call the Tele-TIN or Fax-TIN number shown or file with the "Internal Revenue Service Center" at:
Connecticut, Delaware, District of Columbia, Florida, Georgia, Maine, Maryland, Massachusetts, New Hampshire, New Jersey, New York, North Carolina, Ohio, Pennsylvania, Rhode Island, South Carolina, Vermont, Virginia, West Virginia	Attn: EIN Operation Holtsville, NY 00501 Tele-TIN 866-816-2065 Fax-TIN 631-447-8960
Illinois, Indiana, Kentucky, Michigan	Attn: EIN Operation Cincinnati, OH 45999 Tele-TIN 866-816-2065 Fax-TIN 859-669-5760
Alabama, Alaska, Arizona, Arkansas, California, Colorado, Hawaii, Idaho, Iowa, Kansas, Louisiana, Minnesota, Mississippi, Missouri, Montana, Nebraska, Nevada, New Mexico, North Dakota, Oklahoma, Oregon, Puerto Rico, South Dakota, Tennessee, Texas, Utah, Washington, Wisconsin, Wyoming	Attn: EIN Operation Philadelphia, PA 19255 Tele-TIN 866-816-2065 Fax-TIN 215-516-3990
If you have no legal residence, principal place of business, or principal office or agency in any state:	Attn: EIN Operation Philadelphia, PA 19255 Tele-TIN 215-516-6999 Fax-TIN 215-516-3990

Specific Instructions

Print or type all entries on Form SS-4. Follow the instructions for each line to expedite processing and to avoid unnecessary IRS requests for additional information. Enter "N/A" (nonapplicable) on the lines that do not apply.

Line 1—Legal name of entity (or individual) for whom the EIN is being requested. Enter the legal name of the entity (or individual) applying for the EIN exactly as it appears on the social security card, charter, or other applicable legal document.

Individuals. Enter your first name, middle initial, and last name. If you are a sole proprietor, enter your individual name, not your business name. Enter your business name on line 2. Do not use abbreviations or nicknames on line 1.

Trusts. Enter the name of the trust.

Estate of a decedent. Enter the name of the estate.

Partnerships. Enter the legal name of the partnership as it appears in the partnership agreement.

Corporations. Enter the corporate name as it appears in the corporation charter or other legal document creating it.

Plan administrators. Enter the name of the plan administrator. A plan administrator who already has an EIN should use that number.

Line 2—Trade name of business. Enter the trade name of the business if different from the legal name. The trade name is the "doing business as " (DBA) name.

CAUTION *Use the full legal name shown on line 1 on all tax returns filed for the entity. (However, if you enter a trade name on line 2 and choose to use the trade name instead of the legal name, enter the trade name on **all returns** you file.) To prevent processing delays and errors, **always** use the legal name only (or the trade name only) on **all** tax returns.*

Line 3—Executor, trustee, "care of" name. Trusts enter the name of the trustee. Estates enter the name of the executor, administrator, or other fiduciary. If the entity applying has a designated person to receive tax information, enter that person's name as the "care of" person. Enter the individual's first name, middle initial, and last name.

Lines 4a-b—Mailing address. Enter the mailing address for the entity's correspondence. If line 3 is completed, enter the address for the executor, trustee or "care of" person. Generally, this address will be used on all tax returns.

TIP *File **Form 8822**, Change of Address, to report any subsequent changes to the entity's mailing address.*

Lines 5a-b—Street address. Provide the entity's physical address **only** if different from its mailing address shown in lines 4a-b. **Do not** enter a P.O. box number here.

Line 6—County and state where principal business is located. Enter the entity's primary **physical** location.

Lines 7a-b—Name of principal officer, general partner, grantor, owner, or trustor. Enter the first name, middle initial, last name, and SSN of **(a)** the principal officer if the business is a corporation, **(b)** a general partner if a partnership, **(c)** the owner of an entity that is disregarded as separate from its owner (disregarded entities owned by a corporation enter the corporation's name and EIN), or **(d)** a grantor, owner, or trustor if a trust.

If the person in question is an **alien individual** with a previously assigned individual taxpayer identification number (ITIN), enter the ITIN in the space provided and submit a copy of an official identifying document. If necessary, complete **Form W-7,** Application for IRS Individual Taxpayer Identification Number, to obtain an ITIN.

You are **required** to enter an SSN, ITIN, or EIN unless the only reason you are applying for an EIN is to make an entity classification election (see Regulations section 301.7701-1 through 301.7701-3) and you are a nonresident alien with no effectively connected income from sources within the United States.

Line 8a—Type of entity. Check the box that best describes the type of entity applying for the EIN. If you are an alien individual with an ITIN previously assigned to you, enter the ITIN in place of a requested SSN.

CAUTION *This is not an election for a tax classification of an entity. See **"Limited liability company (LLC)"** on page 4.*

Other. If not specifically mentioned, check the "Other" box, enter the type of entity and the type of return, if any, that will be filed (for example, "Common Trust Fund, Form 1065" or "Created a Pension Plan"). Do not enter "N/A." If you are an alien individual applying for an EIN, see the **Lines 7a-b** instructions above.

- **Household employer.** If you are an individual, check the "Other" box and enter "Household Employer" and your SSN. If you are a state or local agency serving as a tax reporting agent for public assistance recipients who become household employers, check the "Other" box and enter "Household Employer Agent." If you are a trust that qualifies as a household employer, you do not need a separate EIN for reporting tax information relating to household employees; use the EIN of the trust.
- **QSub.** For a qualified subchapter S subsidiary (QSub) check the "Other" box and specify "QSub."
- **Withholding agent.** If you are a withholding agent required to file Form 1042, check the "Other" box and enter "Withholding Agent."

Sole proprietor. Check this box if you file Schedule C, C-EZ, or F (Form 1040) and have a qualified plan, or are required to file excise, employment, or alcohol, tobacco, or firearms returns, or are a payer of gambling winnings. Enter your SSN (or ITIN) in the space provided. If you are a nonresident alien with no effectively connected income from sources within the United States, you do not need to enter an SSN or ITIN.

Corporation. This box is for any corporation **other than a personal service corporation.** If you check this box, enter the income tax form number to be filed by the entity in the space provided.

CAUTION *If you entered **"1120S"** after the "Corporation" checkbox, the corporation **must** file Form 2553 **no later than the 15th day of the 3rd month of the tax year the election is to take effect.** Until Form 2553 has been received and approved, you will be considered a Form 1120 filer. See the Instructions for Form 2553.*

Personal service corp. Check this box if the entity is a personal service corporation. An entity is a personal service corporation for a tax year only if:

- The principal activity of the entity during the testing period (prior tax year) for the tax year is the performance of personal services substantially by employee-owners, and
- The employee-owners own at least 10% of the fair market value of the outstanding stock in the entity on the last day of the testing period.

Personal services include performance of services in such fields as health, law, accounting, or consulting. For more information about personal service corporations, see the Instructions for Forms 1120 and 1120-A and Pub. 542.

Other nonprofit organization. Check this box if the nonprofit organization is other than a church or church-controlled organization and specify the type of nonprofit organization (for example, an educational organization).

CAUTION *If the organization also seeks tax-exempt status, you **must** file either Package 1023 or Package 1024. See Pub. 557 for more information.*

If the organization is covered by a group exemption letter, enter the four-digit **group exemption number (GEN).** (Do not confuse the GEN with the nine-digit EIN.) If you do not know the GEN, contact the parent organization. Get Pub. 557 for more information about group exemption numbers.

Plan administrator. If the plan administrator is an individual, enter the plan administrator's SSN in the space provided.

REMIC. Check this box if the entity has elected to be treated as a real estate mortgage investment conduit (REMIC). See the Instructions for Form 1066 for more information.

Limited liability company (LLC). An LLC is an entity organized under the laws of a state or foreign country as a limited liability company. For Federal tax purposes, an LLC may be treated as a partnership or corporation or be disregarded as an entity separate from its owner.

By **default,** a domestic LLC with only one member is **disregarded** as an entity separate from its owner and must include all of its income and expenses on the owner's tax return (e.g., **Schedule C (Form 1040)**). Also by default, a domestic LLC with two or more members is treated as a partnership. A domestic LLC may file Form 8832 to avoid either default classification and elect to be classified as an association taxable as a corporation. For more information on entity classifications (including the rules for foreign entities), see the instructions for Form 8832.

CAUTION ***Do not*** *file Form 8832 if the LLC accepts the default classifications above.* ***However, if the LLC will be electing S Corporation status, it must timely file both Form 8832 and Form 2553.***

Complete Form SS-4 for LLCs as follows:

- A single-member, domestic LLC that accepts the default classification (above) does not need an EIN and generally should not file Form SS-4. Generally, the LLC should use the name and EIN of its **owner** for all Federal tax purposes. However, the reporting and payment of employment taxes for employees of the LLC may be made using the name and EIN of **either** the owner or the LLC as explained in Notice 99-6, 1999-1 C.B. 321. You can find Notice 99-6 on page 12 of Internal Revenue Bulletin 1999-3 at **www.irs.gov.** (**Note:** If the LLC-applicant indicates in box 13 that it has employees or expects to have employees, the owner (whether an individual or other entity) of a single-member domestic LLC will also be assigned its own EIN (if it does not already have one) even if the LLC will be filing the employment tax returns.)
- A single-member, domestic LLC that accepts the default classification (above) and wants an EIN for filing employment tax returns (see above) or non-Federal purposes, such as a state requirement, must check the "Other" box and write "Disregarded Entity" or, when applicable, "Disregarded Entity—Sole Proprietorship" in the space provided.
- A multi-member, domestic LLC that accepts the default classification (above) must check the "Partnership" box.
- A domestic LLC that will be filing Form 8832 to elect corporate status must check the "Corporation" box and write in "Single-Member" or "Multi-Member" immediately below the "form number" entry line.

Line 9—Reason for applying. Check only **one** box. Do not enter "N/A."

Started new business. Check this box if you are starting a new business that requires an EIN. If you check this box, enter the type of business being started. **Do not** apply if you already have an EIN and are only adding another place of business.

Hired employees. Check this box if the existing business is requesting an EIN because it has hired or is hiring employees and is therefore required to file employment tax returns. **Do not** apply if you already have an EIN and are only hiring employees. For information on employment taxes (e.g., for family members), see Circular E.

CAUTION *You may be required to make electronic deposits of all depository taxes (such as employment tax, excise tax, and corporate income tax) using the Electronic Federal Tax Payment System (EFTPS). See section 11, Depositing Taxes, of Circular E and Pub. 966.*

Created a pension plan. Check this box if you have created a pension plan and need an EIN for reporting purposes. Also, enter the type of plan in the space provided.

TIP *Check this box if you are applying for a trust EIN when a new pension plan is established. In addition, check the "Other" box in line 8a and write "Created a Pension Plan" in the space provided.*

Banking purpose. Check this box if you are requesting an EIN for banking purposes only, and enter the banking purpose (for example, a bowling league for depositing dues or an investment club for dividend and interest reporting).

Changed type of organization. Check this box if the business is changing its type of organization. For example, the business was a sole proprietorship and has been incorporated or has become a partnership. If you check this box, specify in the space provided (including available space immediately below) the type of change made. For example, "From Sole Proprietorship to Partnership."

Purchased going business. Check this box if you purchased an existing business. **Do not** use the former owner's EIN unless you became the "owner" of a corporation by acquiring its stock.

Created a trust. Check this box if you created a trust, and enter the type of trust created. For example, indicate if the trust is a nonexempt charitable trust or a split-interest trust.

Exception. Do **not** file this form for certain grantor-type trusts. The trustee does not need an EIN for the trust if the trustee furnishes the name and TIN of the grantor/owner and the address of the trust to all payors. See the Instructions for Form 1041 for more information.

TIP *Do **not** check this box if you are applying for a trust EIN when a new pension plan is established. Check "Created a pension plan."*

Other. Check this box if you are requesting an EIN for any other reason; and enter the reason. For example, a newly-formed state government entity should enter "Newly-Formed State Government Entity" in the space provided.

Line 10—Date business started or acquired. If you are starting a new business, enter the starting date of the business. If the business you acquired is already operating, enter the date you acquired the business. Trusts should enter the date the trust was legally created. Estates should enter the date of death of the decedent whose name appears on line 1 or the date when the estate was legally funded.

Line 11—Closing month of accounting year. Enter the last month of your accounting year or tax year. An accounting or tax year is usually 12 consecutive months, either a calendar year or a fiscal year (including a period of 52 or 53 weeks). A calendar year is 12 consecutive months ending on December 31. A fiscal year is either 12 consecutive months ending on the last day of any month other than December or a 52-53 week year. For more information on accounting periods, see Pub. 538.

Individuals. Your tax year generally will be a calendar year.

Partnerships. Partnerships must adopt one of the following tax years:

- The tax year of the majority of its partners,
- The tax year common to all of its principal partners,
- The tax year that results in the least aggregate deferral of income, or
- In certain cases, some other tax year.

See the Instructions for Form 1065 for more information.

REMICs. REMICs must have a calendar year as their tax year.

Personal service corporations. A personal service corporation generally must adopt a calendar year unless:

- It can establish a business purpose for having a different tax year, or
- It elects under section 444 to have a tax year other than a calendar year.

Trusts. Generally, a trust must adopt a calendar year except for the following:

- Tax-exempt trusts,
- Charitable trusts, and
- Grantor-owned trusts.

Line 12—First date wages or annuities were paid or will be paid. If the business has or will have employees, enter the date on which the business began or will begin to pay wages. If the business does not plan to have employees, enter "N/A."

Withholding agent. Enter the date you began or will begin to pay income (including annuities) to a nonresident alien. This also applies to individuals who are required to file Form 1042 to report alimony paid to a nonresident alien.

Line 13—Highest number of employees expected in the next 12 months. Complete each box by entering the number (including zero ("-0-")) of "Agricultural," "Household," or "Other" employees expected by the applicant in the next 12 months. For a definition of agricultural labor (farmwork), see Circular A.

Lines 14 and 15. Check the **one** box in line 14 that best describes the principal activity of the applicant's business. Check the "Other" box (and specify the applicant's principal activity) if none of the listed boxes applies.

Use line 15 to describe the applicant's principal line of business in more detail. For example, if you checked the "Construction" box in line 14, enter additional detail such as "General contractor for residential buildings" in line 15.

TIP *Do not complete lines 14 and 15 if you entered zero "(-0-)" in line 13.*

Construction. Check this box if the applicant is engaged in erecting buildings or other structures, (e.g., streets, highways, bridges, tunnels). The term "Construction" also includes special trade contractors, (e.g., plumbing, HVAC, electrical, carpentry, concrete, excavation, etc. contractors).

Real estate. Check this box if the applicant is engaged in renting or leasing real estate to others; managing, selling, buying or renting real estate for others; or providing related real estate services (e.g., appraisal services).

Rental and leasing. Check this box if the applicant is engaged in providing tangible goods such as autos, computers, consumer goods, or industrial machinery and equipment to customers in return for a periodic rental or lease payment.

Manufacturing. Check this box if the applicant is engaged in the mechanical, physical, or chemical transformation of materials, substances, or components into new products. The assembling of component parts of manufactured products is also considered to be manufacturing.

Transportation & warehousing. Check this box if the applicant provides transportation of passengers or cargo; warehousing or storage of goods; scenic or sight-seeing transportation; or support activities related to these modes of transportation.

Finance & insurance. Check this box if the applicant is engaged in transactions involving the creation, liquidation, or change of ownership of financial assets and/or facilitating such financial transactions;

underwriting annuities/insurance policies; facilitating such underwriting by selling insurance policies; or by providing other insurance or employee-benefit related services.

Health care and social assistance. Check this box if the applicant is engaged in providing physical, medical, or psychiatric care using licensed health care professionals or providing social assistance activities such as youth centers, adoption agencies, individual/ family services, temporary shelters, etc.

Accommodation & food services. Check this box if the applicant is engaged in providing customers with lodging, meal preparation, snacks, or beverages for immediate consumption.

Wholesale–agent/broker. Check this box if the applicant is engaged in arranging for the purchase or sale of goods owned by others or purchasing goods on a commission basis for goods traded in the wholesale market, usually between businesses.

Wholesale–other. Check this box if the applicant is engaged in selling goods in the wholesale market generally to other businesses for resale on their own account.

Retail. Check this box if the applicant is engaged in selling merchandise to the general public from a fixed store; by direct, mail-order, or electronic sales; or by using vending machines.

Other. Check this box if the applicant is engaged in an activity not described above. Describe the applicant's principal business activity in the space provided.

Lines 16a-c. Check the applicable box in line 16a to indicate whether or not the entity (or individual) applying for an EIN was issued one previously. Complete lines 16b and 16c **only** if the "Yes" box in line 16a is checked. If the applicant previously applied for **more than one** EIN, write "See Attached" in the empty space in line 16a and attach a separate sheet providing the line 16b and 16c information for each EIN previously requested.

Third Party Designee. Complete this section **only** if you want to authorize the named individual to receive the entity's EIN and answer questions about the completion of Form SS-4. The designee's authority terminates at the time the EIN is assigned and released to the designee. **You must complete the signature area for the authorization to be valid.**

Signature. When required, the application must be signed by **(a)** the individual, if the applicant is an individual, **(b)** the president, vice president, or other principal officer, if the applicant is a corporation, **(c)** a responsible and duly authorized member or officer having knowledge of its affairs, if the applicant is a partnership, government entity, or other unincorporated organization, or **(d)** the fiduciary, if the applicant is a trust or an estate. Foreign applicants may have any duly-authorized person, (e.g., division manager), sign Form SS-4.

Privacy Act and Paperwork Reduction Act Notice. We ask for the information on this form to carry out the Internal Revenue laws of the United States. We need it to comply with section 6109 and the regulations thereunder which generally require the inclusion of an employer identification number (EIN) on certain returns, statements, or other documents filed with the Internal Revenue Service. If your entity is required to obtain an EIN, you are required to provide all of the information requested on this form. Information on this form may be used to determine which Federal tax returns you are required to file and to provide you with related forms and publications.

We disclose this form to the Social Security Administration for their use in determining compliance with applicable laws. We may give this information to the Department of Justice for use in civil and criminal litigation, and to the cities, states, and the District of Columbia for use in administering their tax laws. We may also disclose this information to Federal, state, or local agencies that investigate or respond to acts or threats of terrorism or participate in intelligence or counterintelligence activities concerning terrorism.

We will be unable to issue an EIN to you unless you provide all of the requested information which applies to your entity. Providing false information could subject you to penalties.

You are not required to provide the information requested on a form that is subject to the Paperwork Reduction Act unless the form displays a valid OMB control number. Books or records relating to a form or its instructions must be retained as long as their contents may become material in the administration of any Internal Revenue law. Generally, tax returns and return information are confidential, as required by section 6103.

The time needed to complete and file this form will vary depending on individual circumstances. The estimated average time is:

Recordkeeping	6 min.
Learning about the law or the form	22 min.
Preparing the form	46 min.
Copying, assembling, and sending the form to the IRS	20 min.

If you have comments concerning the accuracy of these time estimates or suggestions for making this form simpler, we would be happy to hear from you. You can write to the Tax Forms Committee, Western Area Distribution Center, Rancho Cordova, CA 95743-0001. **Do not** send the form to this address. Instead, see **How To Apply** on page 2.

GLOSSARY

Glossary

The following terms are defined only with respect to their application to trusts and trust investments.

Acceleration: The passing of property to a remainderman due to the failure (death, remarriage, *etc.*) of the preceding beneficiary.

Accounting: A comprehensive financial statement that presents an historical record of administration by a trustee of a trust or by an executor of an estate. It covers the period of time from the beginning of the trustee's control, or from the last accounting.

Active Trust: A trust that requires activity by the trustee, such as investment management.

Adjudication: Approval by a court of an accounting and proposed distribution by a trust or an estate.

Amendment: In trust terms, a formally executed document that amends the terms of a previously executed trust agreement.

Asset Allocation: Investing in different types of assets in such a way as to obtain the optimum performance within the limits of a particular investment policy.

Basis Point: One one-hundredth of one percent.

Beneficiary: One for whose benefit a trust is established. Can be either a present beneficiary or a future one (remainderman). Can have a primary or contingent interest in the trust.

Bequest: A gift of tangible or intangible property under a will. A bequest can be general, demonstrative or specific. A general bequest is a gift not limited to payment or fulfillment from specifically identifiable property. A demonstrative bequest is a bequest of a certain amount of money to be paid from a particular fund. (These distinctions also apply to a devise (*see below*).)

Bond: An Insurance arrangement pledging funds to replace trust assets misappropriated by the trustee.

Book Value: For an asset, it is the value at which the asset is carried on a balance sheet. For a company, it is the sum of the company's book value assets minus intangible assets and liabilities. For a share of common stock, it is the company's book value minus the par value of any preferred stock, divided by the number of outstanding shares of the common stock.

Breach of Trust: The violation of any fiduciary duty by the trustee, for which the beneficiaries may hold the trustee personally liable. *See* Part One, Chapter II.

Carrying Value: Normally the market value of assets at the time they become property of the trust. Assets received from a decedent's estate generally are carried at their value as of the decedent's date of death, but assets received in kind to satisfy a pecuniary gift would be carried at their value when distributed to the trustee. In an accounting, carrying values are used to determine what a trustee has received, what he has left, and what he has done to create any differences.

Case Law: Law according to rulings made by judges in a court of law.

Codicil: An amendment or supplement to a will, made with the same formalities as the will.

Common Law: A body of law not codified or written in statutes that grew in England mainly from judicial decisions based upon customs and precedents. All American states, with the exception of Louisiana, use it as the basis for their legal system.

Contingent Interest: An interest in property that may never come into existence unless a stated event occurs or fails to occur. A child who will receive an interest in a trust only if he or she survives his or her parent attaining the age of thirty years has a contingent interest in the trust.

Corpus: The core assets of a trust from which any income is generated. *See* Principal.

Covariance: Positive covariance is the tendency of returns on different types of investments to behave in similar ways. Negative covariance is their tendency to behave in opposite ways.

Devise: A gift of real property under a will (*see* Bequest above for sub-classifications).

Direction: In a trust instrument, a provision stated as a command to the trustee rather than as a request, wish or hope.

Dynastic Trust: A trust intended to provide for several generations of family members, typically involving such features as provisions to minimize the generation skipping transfer tax and the selection of a situs intended to circumvent the rule against perpetuities.

Exculpatory Provision: A provision in a trust instrument that is intended to release a trustee or other party to the trust from liability.

Fiduciary: An individual or organization who is in a position of trust with respect to property held for or actually owned by others. A fiduciary is accountable for any action that is a breach of trust. A trustee is a fiduciary, but it is also possible for an agent to occupy this position, depending upon the degree of control possessed with respect to the property of his employer.

Formal Accounting: An accounting prepared for review by a court. Also called a judicial accounting.

Funding: The act of placing assets in a trust.

Grantor Trust: For federal tax purposes, a trust where the settlor or his or her spouse has retained a reversionary interest, direct or indirect income benefits, or holds certain powers such as the power to control beneficial enjoyment, administrative powers that favor him or her or the settlor's spouse, or a power to revoke the trust. Grantor trust income is taxed to the grantor or to another with power to vest the income or principal in him or herself.

Income: The earnings or yield from the corpus of a trust, or any assets derived from the corpus that the trust instrument defines as income.

***Inter-Vivos* Trust:** Any trust created by an individual under a trust agreement prior to his or her death.

Inventory Value: *See* Carrying Value.

Investment Advisor: One who acts primarily in an advisory capacity regarding investments for a client but who may sometimes be given discretion to make investment decisions for that client.

Investment Consultant: One who makes recommendations concerning investments and their management to a client but who has no discretion over the investments.

Investment Manager: One who manages investments with complete discretion for a client. Also Money Manager.

Irrevocable Trust: A trust that can not be revoked by the individual who created it without the consent of others who would be affected adversely by its revocation.

Issue: All of the descendents of an individual.

Legal List: A list set forth in a statute of permissible investments for a trust.

Legacy: A gift of tangible or intangible personal property under a will. *See* Bequest above.

Living Trust: An *inter-vivos* (generally funded) trust created by the settlor for him or herself, and often also for his or her spouse, for the primary purpose of financial management of the assets with which it is funded and protection for the settlor if he or she should become incapacitated. Another purpose is to avoid the cost and procedures of probate at his or her death by having the trust continue or distribute directly to his or her survivors.

Money Manager: One who manages investments with complete discretion for a client.

Modern Portfolio Theory: An approach to investing that balances the types and amounts of risk among different classes of investments to obtain a total performance result for a portfolio.

Nominee: In general usage, one who has been nominated, but in the investment world a registration in the name of a fictitious company in place of the real owner for convenience in transferring marketable securities.

Passive Trust: A trust requiring no activity by the trustee, other than possible custody of assets.

***Per Capita*:** "By the head." Distribution is made equally. If three children are living and one is dead at the time of distribution, the living children would share one-third to each, whether or not the deceased child had surviving issue.

***Per Stirpes*:** "By the root." Distribution follows descent. In the previous example, if the deceased child had one living son and one grandchild by a deceased daughter, the three living children would receive one-fourth, one-eighth would pass to the son of the deceased child, and one-eighth would pass to the grandchild.

Personal Trust: A trust crated by an individual for the benefit of him or herself, a family member or some other individual.

Power of Appointment: The power (and document creating one) to distribute the property of another. A trust agreement that gives an income beneficiary the right to determine how the remaining trust assets are to be distributed at his or her death, without any restrictions, confers a general power of appointment upon the beneficiary. If it restricted him or her, such as limiting the possible distributees to his or her own descendants, the power would be a limited or special power.

Power of Attorney: The power (and the document creating one) to act on behalf of the grantor of the power, such as investing, opening and closing bank accounts and executing permissible legal documents. A power may be limited to certain acts, such as selling a piece of real estate. A power of attorney becomes invalid if the grantor becomes incapacitated unless is a "durable" power which provides that it shall remain in effect if the grantor becomes incapacitated. A "springing" power of attorney becomes valid only upon the occurrence of a particular event, such as the grantor becoming incapacitated. Death of the grantor invalidates any power of attorney - except a power coupled with an interest, which is generally a power created for the benefit of the agent to protect some title or right of the agent, or to secure performance to him or her.

Principal: The underlying assets of a trust that are held or reinvested to produce income. The corpus of a trust. Also an employer of an agent. A controlling entity.

Private Trust: A trust created by an individual for other individuals, or by a corporation for its employees, as opposed to a trust which is for charitable purposes benefiting the public or some sector of it.

Probate: Technically the process of proving that the will of a decedent is valid. More broadly, the term is applied to the entire process of settling an estate under court supervision.

Prudent Investor Rule: A reformation set forth in *Restatement, Third, Trusts*, of the Prudent Man Rule that incorporates Modern Portfolio Theory. It has been adopted in some form by most states.

Prudent Man Rule: An influential rule concerning the investment of trust funds arising from an 1830 decision by the Supreme Judicial Court of Massachusetts. Also called the Massachusetts Rule.

Negligence: The failure to exercise the care of a reasonably prudent or ordinarily careful person, so as to avoid harm and loss directly or indirectly to others.

Receipt and Release: A document in which a beneficiary acknowledges receipt of trust property and releases the trustee from any further liability. It should be accompanied with an informal accounting.

Remainderman: A beneficiary who receives trust property when the trust terminates with respect to a prior beneficiary's interest.

***Restatement of the Law, Trusts*:** A compilation of standards for the administration of trusts based upon common law and periodically revised to reflect case law and uniform statutes. Adapted and promulgated by the American Law Institute, the original publication and its revisions are the work of a reporter, assisted by a panel of advisors, all of whom have been prominent legal scholars.

Rule against Perpetuities: A common law rule that limits how long property may be held in trust. In many states the original version, which limited a trust to the term measured by designated lives in being at the creation of the trust, plus twenty-one years, has become statutory.

Settlor: One who creates a trust under a trust agreement or deed of trust. Also called a creator, donor, grantor or trustor.

***Situs*:** The location of the trust for purposes of determining its legal jurisdiction.

Sprinkle Provision: A provision in a trust instrument that allows the trustee to distribute income among beneficiaries in unequal shares. Also called a "spray" provision.

Standard & Poor's 500 Composite Stock Index: An index widely used to measure the performance of stock portfolios. It consists of stocks of 400 industrial companies, forty utilities, forty financial companies and twenty transportation companies, but is dominated by a few large companies.

Statute: A law passed by a legislative body, as opposed to common law or a law established by a judicial directive.

Style: The philosophy that drives the actions of an investment manager. For example, a manager who holds a fairly unchanging group of stocks of very large companies, around which he or she holds other large company stocks that he or she trades more frequently, is said to have a large cap, core equity style.

Surcharge: An amount that a trustee is required by a court to pay to the trust to restore a loss caused by a breach of trust.

Surety: A formal pledge given for the fulfillment of an undertaking.

Testator: One who makes a will. One who makes a codicil to a will.

Tort: A breach of a non-contractual duty that results in loss or injury to others.

Total Return: The combination of an asset's income yield and capital appreciation or depreciation over a period of time (usually a twelve-month period).

Trustee: An individual, bank or trust company having responsibility for the administration of a trust, owning and managing property for the benefit of others according to the terms of a trust instrument; the legal owner of property administered for others having equitable rights in it.

Trust Agreement: A legal document that creates a trust while its creator is living, although its activation can be deferred to a time subsequent to its execution.

Trust Instrument: A legal document creating a trust, such as a will or trust agreement.

Uniform Code (or Act): A code or act drafted and approved by the National Conference of Commissioners on Uniform State Laws that can be adopted by states as their own law or serve as a model of what the law should be when such a model is needed.

Vested Interest: A right to property, even though the possession and enjoyment of it may be deferred.

Will: A legal document executed by an individual that disposes of his or her personal estate at his or her death. As such, it can be the governing instrument for a trust, but the trust comes into existence only after the death of the testator. Also a "Last Will and Testament."

BIBLIOGRAPHY

Bibliography

This is a short list of books that we think that a trustee should have on his or her shelf. Accordingly we have altered the usual form of a bibliography by including information on where the books can be obtained and what they cost, together with our comments.

Accounting

Fiduciary Accounting and Trust Administration Guide
Robert Whitman and David M. English
American Law Institute
4025 Chestnut Street
Philadelphia, PA 19104-3099

A comprehensive guide for professionals, this book is an excellent source on all aspects of fiduciary accounting. This is the 2002 Edition, which sells for $87.00 plus $5.00 shipping.

Uniform Principal and Income Act of 1997
Drafted by the National Conference of Commissioners on Uniform State Laws. This can be downloaded from http://www.nccusl.org. 66 pages, including considerable helpful commentary.

Investing

The Management of Investment Decisions
Donald B. Trone, William R. Allbright, Philip R. Taylor
Irwin Professional Publishing
Available from bookstores, usually by special order

A superior book for any investor, much of it is especially relevant for trustees of personal trusts. It covers the role and responsibility of trustees, portfolio design, investment policy, the Prudent Investor Rule, and relationships with investment management consultants and money managers, among other important subjects. The cost is $65. It was published in 1996.

Taxation

PPC's 1041 Deskbook
Hugh H. Sprunt, James F. Reeves, Dan W. Youse, Blake T. Smith
Practitioners Publishing Company
PO Box 996
Fort Worth, TX 76101-0996

This is a loose leaf, ring binder book in two volumes, updated annually. The authors, all CPAs, go into great depth in explaining all federal tax matters pertaining to estates and trusts, and many examples of completed Form 1041s are included. The cost is $135.

United States Master Tax Guide
CCH Incorporated
4025 W. Peterson Ave.
Chicago, IL 60646-6085
http://www.cch.com
Major cities have CCH sales offices

This is a general tax guide, updated annually. A non-specialist might find it helpful to cross-reference this guide with the *PPC 1041 Deskbook*. It is more abbreviated in its treatment of trust taxation, but it covers all areas of federal income tax. The cost is $42.95 in the paperback edition.

Federal Tax Forms
Internal Revenue Service
Telephone: 1 (800) 829-3676

We recommend that you order the following basic forms for reference, whether or not you intend to file returns for the trust yourself: Form 1041, Schedule D–Capital Gains and Losses (Form 1041), Schedule J–Accumulation Distribution for a Complex Trust (Form 1041), Schedule K-1–Beneficiary's Share of Income, Deductions, Credits, etc. (Form 1041). These forms are not available from the IRS by fax or by the order form in the Form 1040 package.

Trust Law

Restatement of the Law Second, Trusts
American Law Institute (see *above*)

Restatement of the Law, Trusts, published in 1935, is now out of print. *Restatement of the Law, Second* was first published in 1959. It consists of 5 volumes, the last three of which are appendices that are not recommended for the layman. The cost is $63.50 for each hardbound volume. A student paperback version, just as useful, may still be available for approximately half the cost.

Prudent Investor Rule

Restatement of the Law, Third is in progress. Its revision of the Prudent Investor portions of *Second Restatement of Trusts* was completed an published in 1992 in a separate volume and is available for $63.50

Uniform Trust Code

Drafted by the National Conference of Commissioners on Uniform State Laws. This can be downloaded from http://www.nccusl.org. 154 pages. This is the first national codification of laws pertaining to trusts. While it has already been introduced in bills in a few states, it is too new to have been adopted by any states yet, but it "will provide states with precise, comprehensive, and easily accessible guidance on trust law questions," according to the Commissioners.

Trusts–General

The Family Trust–A Financial Counselor's Guide to Trust Funds
Charles M. Aulino
CCH Incorporated (see *above*)

This is a well-written guide that explains the reasons for specific types of trusts and how they are used. It is hardbound and costs $50.00. The author is a financial planner who has practiced law and has administered trusts for both a bank and a broker-affiliated trust company.

Trustee Liability

These two articles, while not easily accessible, are important resources for the individual trustee, and they are available for reading at most law libraries.

How Individual Trustees Can Avoid Liability and Breaches of Trust
Attorney G. Michael Richwine
Estate Planning Magazine
December 1997 Vol. 24 No. 10 PP 481-487
Published by RIA Group
31 St. James Avenue
Boston, MA 02116-4112

The author, an Executive Director of Riggs & Company, is a respected authority, and his article is concise and well written.

The Co-Trustee Relationship–Rights and Duties

Real Property, Probate and Trust Journal
Spring 1973 Vol. 8.9 Pages 9 to 32
Published by the ABA Section of Real Property,
Probate and Trust Law
American Bar Association
750 North Lake Shore Drive
Chicago, IL 60611-4497

We consider this to be the best and most complete discussion of a complex and potentially perilous relationship.

INDEX

Topic **Page**

Topic **Page**